Equine Multilingual Abridged Dictionary

Dictionnaire abrégé multilingue du cheval

**Autres ouvrages disponibles / Also available:**

- Dictionnaire multilingue du cheval
(anglais-français-allemand-espagnol-latin)
Equine Multilingual Dictionary
(English-French-German-Spanish-Latin)

- Dictionnaire anglais-français du cheval
Equine French-English Dictionary

- Dictionnaire anglais-français du cheval (éd. de poche)
Equine French-English Pocket Dictionary

- Spanish-English Pocket Dictionary of the Horse
Diccionario de bolsillo español-inglés del caballo

# Equine Multilingual Abridged Dictionary

# Dictionnaire abrégé multilingue du cheval

Jean-Claude Boulet

Édition : Jean-Claude Boulet


ISBN 978-2-9804600-9-8

Auparavant publié sous le titre / Formerly published as :
"Vocabulaire multilingue du cheval / Multilingual Vocabulary of the Horse"
ISBN 978-2-9804600-3-6 (2nd ed. / 2ième édition)

# ABRÉVIATIONS ET SYMBOLES    ABBREVIATIONS & SYMBOLS

| | | |
|---|---|---|
| abréviation | abr / abbr | abbreviation |
| équitation académique | acad | academic riding |
| adjectif | adj | adjective |
| allemand | all. | German |
| américanisme | amér / amer | americanism |
| anatomie | anat | anatomy |
| ancien / vieilli | anc | old |
| anglais | ang. | English |
| attelage | att | harness driving (hd) |
| Belgique / belge | Bel | Belgium / Belgian |
| Grande-Bretagne / britannique | Brit | Britain / British |
| courses | c | races / racing (r) |
| courses attelées | ca | harness racing (hr) |
| Canada / canadianisme | Can. | Canada / Canadian |
| concours complet | cc | horse trials (ht) |
| équitation à l'anglaise | class. | classical, English style riding |
| chasseurs-sauteurs | cs | hunters and jumpers (hj) |
| courses de thoroughbred | ct | Thouroughbred racing (tr) |
| Europe / européen | Eur | Europe / European |
| féminin | f | feminine |
| France | Fr | France |
| attelage (att) | hd | harness driving |
| chasseurs-sauteurs (cs) | hj | hunters / jumpers |
| courses attelées (ca) | hr | harness racing |
| concours complet (cc) | ht | horse trials |
| invariable | inv | invariable |
| latin | lat | Latin |
| masculin | m | masculine |
| médecine / médical | méd / med | medicine / medical |
| substantif / nom | n | noun / substantive |
| neutre | ne | neuter |
| Nomina anatomica veterinaria | NAV | Nomina anatomica veterinaria |
| vieilli (anc) | old | old / dated |
| pluriel | pl | plural |
| courses (c) | r | races / racing |
| voir aussi (v.a.) | s.a. | see also |
| singulier | sg | singular |
| courses de thoroughbred (ct) | tr | Thouroughbred racing |
| États-Unis d'Amérique (E.U.) | US | United States of America |
| verbe | v | verb |
| voir aussi | v.a. | see also (s.a.) |
| équitation western | west. | western style riding |
| | | |
| variantes | / | alternatives |
| termes s'excluent mutuellement | // | terms excluding one the other |
| | | |
| renvoi | => | cross-reference |

À qui s'intéresse au cheval,

par le cheval, l'entente amicale.

# ENGLISH

## FRANÇAIS - DEUTSCH - ESPAÑOL

**abattoir** => slaughterhouse

**abdomen**
abdomen
Bauch *m* ; Abdomen
abdomen
Portion of the horse's body between the diaphragm and the pelvis.
Sa partie avant (ou crâniale) correspond à la région du passage des sangles. Il comprend aussi le rein, le ventre, le flanc et la région prépubienne (base du prépuce ou des mamelles).

**abdominal cavity**
cavité abdominale
Bauchhöhle *f* ; Bauchraum *m*
cavidad abdominal

**abduction**
abduction
Abduktion *f* ; Abspreizung *f* ; Auswärtsbewegung *f* ; Abziehen *ne*
abducción

**abductor** *n*
abducteur *adj & n*
Abduktor *m* ; Abzieher *m* ; abziehend *adj* ; Auswärtszieher *m* ; Abduktionsmuskel
abductor *adj & n m*

**above the bit** ; over the bit
au-dessus de la main
über dem Zügel ; über der Hand
delante de la mano ; sobre la brida / el freno

**abscess (in a hoof)** ; pus pocket ; gravel
abcès (dans un pied)
Hufgeschwür *ne* ; Hufabszeß *m*
absceso en el casco ; arenilla
We may think of an abscess formed by a (single grain of) gravel entering the hoof and causing a pus pocket.

**accessory carpal bone** ; pisiform bone
os accessoire du carpe ; os pisiforme ; os sus-carpien *anc*
Erbsenbein *ne* ; Erbsbein ; Anhangsbein des Karpus *(das ~)*
hueso pisiforme

**accessory cephalic vein**
veine céphalique accessoire
Vena cephalica accessoria ; Accessoria
vena cefálica accesoria

**acepromazin** ; acetylpromazine
acépromazine
Acepromazin
promazin

**acetabulum** ; hip socket
acétabulum ; cavité cotyloïde *anc*
Hüftpfanne *f* ; Gelenkpfanne des Hüftgelenks *(die ~)* ; Azetabulum *ne* ; Beckenpfanne *f*
acetábulo

**acetylpromazine** => acepromazin

**Achilles' tendon** => common calcanean / calcaneal tendon

**action**
action
Aktion *f* ; Bewegung *f*
acción
Descriptive of the movement of the horse's leg. *s.a. knee action*
Effet de la force qui préside aux mouvements du cheval, par extension, façon dont se manifeste cette force. Le mot est parfois utilisé pour ne désigner que les mouvements des membres.

**action of the seat** ; weight aid
aide du poids du corps
Gewichtshilfe *f* ; Gewichtseinwirkung *m*
ayuda de peso del cuerpo

**action of the seat**
action de l'assiette
Druckwirkung des Beckens *(die ~)*
acción del asiento

**active leg**
jambe active
aktiver / treibender Schenkel
pierna activa

**adduction**
adduction
Adduktion *f* ; Gliedheranführung *f* ; Anziehung *f*
aducción

**adductor**
adducteur *n & adj*
Anzieher *m* ; Einwärtszieher *m*
aductor

**adjust the reins** *v*
ajuster les rênes
Zügel verpassen / anpassen
ajustar las riendas

**adrenal gland**
glande surrénale
Nebenniere *f pl: Nebennieren*
cápsula suprarrenal

**ad-lib** => free choice

**aerophagia** ; air swallowing
aérophagie ; déglutition d'air
Luftschlucken *ne* ; Luftschnappen *ne*
aerofagia

**afraid** => frightened

**African horse sickness** ; equine plague
peste équine africaine
afrikanische Pferdesterbe / Pferdepest *(die ~)* ;
 Pferdepest *f*
peste equina africana ; enfermedad equina africana

**aid** ; riding aid
aide
Hilfe *f*
ayuda

**aids** ; riding aids
aides
Hilfen *f*
ayudas
 Moyens employés pour communiquer / imposer la volonté de l'homme au cheval.

**aid of the legs**
action des jambes
Schenkelhilfen *pl* ; Andruck der Schenkel *(der ~)*
acción de piernas ; ayuda de piernas

**airs above the ground**
airs relevés
Schulen über der Erde
aires sobre el piso ; aires arriba de la tierra

**air swallowing**  => aerophagia

**albino** ; white (true ~)
albinos *adj & n*
Rosenschimmel *m* ; Albino *m*
albino
 True white, with no pigmentation of the skin (which is
pink) or hairs. Eyes are also devoid of pigment and pink
or bluish.
 Très blanc dès sa naissance, sa peau est plutôt rose et
dépourvue de pigmentation, elle est très sensible à la
lumière solaire. Ses yeux sont bleu pâle, presque
translucide, ou roses, et présentent souvent une
défectuosité de la vue.

**albumin**
albumine
Eiweißstoff *m*
albúmina

**alfalfa** ; lucerne
luzerne
Luzerne *f* ; Schneckenklee *m*
alfalfa

**alfalfa pellets / cubes**
luzerne en comprimés / cubes ; comprimés / cubes de luzerne
Luzerne-Pellets
cubos de alfalfa ; bolitas de alfalfa

**allele**
allèle
Genpaar *ne*
alelo

**allotriophagia**  => pica

**aluminium shoe / plate**
fer en aluminium
Aluminium-Hufeisen *ne*
herradura de aluminio

**amateur**
amateur
Amateur *m*
aficionado

**amble** *n* ; pace *n br*
amble
Paß *m* ; Paßgang / Passgang *m*
portante ; andadura (paso de ~) ; ambladura
 (paso de ~)
 Gait in which the horse moves both legs of one side together, then the legs of the other side.
 Allure du cheval qui déplace, en alternance, ses deux
membres de gauche puis ses deux de droite. En course,
en Amérique du Nord surtout, l'amble devient une
allure à quatre temps (appelée parfois amble volant),
autrement c'est une allure rapide et confortable pour le
cavalier qui doit parcourir de longues distances. En
Angleterre et en Europe continentale, on dressa donc
des ambleurs pour les dames, pour les médecins et les
voyageurs, aussi bien pour la selle que pour la voiture.
Le dressage à l'amble se pratique aussi dans le nord de
l'Afrique et au Pérou.

**amble** *v* ; pace *v br*
ambler
Paß gehen (den ~)
marcher de andadura ; amblar

**ambler** ; pacer *br*
ambleur
Paßgänger / Passgänger *m*
amblador ; caballo de ambladura

**American Saddlebred** ; Kentucky Saddler /
 Saddlebred
cheval de selle américain
American Saddlebred Horse
caballo de silla americano
 Breed originating from USA.
 Race originaire des E.U., les chevaux sont souvent
présentés en position campée, la queue artificiellement
relevée.

**American trotter**  => Standardbred

**amnion**
amnios
Amnion *ne* ; Schafhaut *f* ; Wasserhaut *f* ;
 Embryonalhülle *f* ; Fruchthülle *f*
amnios

**anaemia** *Brit* ; anemia *US*
anémie
Blutarmut *f* ; Anämie *f*
anemia

**analgesic**
analgésique
schmerzstillendes Mittel *(das ~)* ; Analgetikum *ne* ;
 Schmerzausschaltung *f*
analgésico

**anasarca** ; generalized edema / oedema
anasarque
Anasarka *f* ; Unterhautödem *ne* ;
 Hautwassersucht *f* ; Hautödem *ne*
anasarca
 Affection vasculaire non contagieuse, caractérisée par
l'apparition d'oedèmes.

**ancestry**
ascendance
Vorfahren *m pl* ; Ahnen *f*
ascendencia
*s.a. pedigree*

**anconeus muscle**
muscle anconé
Ellbogenhöckermuskel
músculo ancóneo

## Andalusian
andalou ; cheval ibérique
Andalusier
andaluz
Spanish horse breed.
Race issue de chevaux orientaux introduits en Espagne
durant l'occupation maure.

**anemia** => anaemia

**anesthetic ; anaesthetic**
anesthésique
unempfindlich machendes Mittel *(das ~)*
anestésico

**anestrus ; anoestrus**
anoestrus ; absence de chaleurs
Brunstlosigkeit *f* ; Anöstrus *m* ; Zyklusstillstand *m*
anestro

**angle of the approach**
angle de l'approche
Annäherungswinkel *m*
ángulo del aproche ; enfoque

## Anglo-Arab(ian) (horse)
anglo-arabe
Anglo-Araber
anglo-árabe
Croisement de thoroughbred et d'arabe. La taille varie
de 1,45 à 1,60 mètres. Un livre généalogique a été établi
en France en 1942.

## Anglo-Norman => French Saddle (horse)

**animal unit** *abbr: A.U.*
unité animale *abr: U.A.*
Vieheinheit *f*
unidad animal / ganadera

**ankle**
cheville
Knöchel *m* ; Fußknöchel *m* ; Fußgelenk *ne* ;
Fessel *f*
tobillo

**ankle boot** => paddock boot

**announcer (house / track ~)**
annonceur (officiel)
Ansager *m*
anunciador ; locutor

**annulment**
rédhibition
Wandlung (beim Kauf) *f* ; Annullierung ;
Aufhebung *f* ; Nichtigkeitserklärung *f* ;
Ungültigkeitserklärung *f*
redhibición
Résiliation d'une vente par l'acheteur quand l'objet de
la transaction présente un vice dit rédhibitoire.

**anterior digital extensor muscle** =>
common digital extensor muscle

**anthelmintic (drug)** ; wormer ; dewormer ;
vermicide
vermifuge ; anthelmintique ; vermicide
Wurmmittel *ne* ; Wurmkur *f* ; Anthelminthikum *ne* ;
wurmtötendes Mittel *(das ~)*
antihelmíntico ; vermífugo
Drug used to eliminate parasites from the host.
Qualifie ou désigne un médicament destiné à lutter
contre les parasites. Dans le cas du cheval, on désigne
habituellement les parasites sous le nom de vers.

**anthrax**
charbon
Milzbrand *m* ; Anthrax *m*
ántrax
Maladie infectieuse.

**antibiotic**
antibiotique
Antibiotikum *ne*
antibiótico

**antitetanus serum** ; tetanus immune serum
sérum antitétanique
Tetanusserum *ne*
suero antitetánico

**antivenene ; antivenin**
sérum antivenimeux
Schlangengiftserum *ne*
suero antivenenoso

**anti-inflammatory** *n & adj*
anti-inflammatoire *n & adj*
entzündungshemmend ; antiphlogistisch
antiinflamatorio *adj*

**anus**
anus
After *m* ; Anus *m*
ano

**anvil**
enclume
Amboß *m*
yunque

**anvil (of the ear)**
enclume (de l'oreille) ; incus
Amboß *m*
yunque

**anvil (portable ~)**
bigorne
Sperrhorn *ne*
bigornia ; yunque de esplga / cola
Enclume portative.

**apex of the nose** => muzzle

**aponeurose**
aponévrose
Aponeurosis *f* ; Sehnenhaut *f*
aponeurosis
A sheet of connective tissue covering a muscle and at-
taching it to the bones.
Membrane conjonctive qui enveloppe un muscle et
dont les prolongements forment les tendons qui le fixent
aux os.

**Appaloosa** *breed*
appaloosa *race*
Appaloosa
appaloosa

The Appaloosa Horse Club (US established in 1938) recognizes six varieties of patterns: frost, leopard, varnish roan (marble), snowflake, spotted blanket and white blanket.

L'Appaloosa Horse Club (formé en 1938 aux E.U.) reconnaît six types de robes: givrée, léopard, marbrée, neigée (flocon de neige), croupe tachetée et croupe blanche.

**appeal committee**
commission d'appel
Schiedsgericht *ne* ; Berufungsgericht *ne* ; Renngericht *ne* ; Berufungskommission *f*
comité de apelación

**apple**
pomme
Apfel *m*
manzana

**apprentice**
apprenti
Lehrling ; Auszubildender *m*
aprendiz

**approach an obstacle** *v*
aborder un obstacle
Hindernis anreiten (ein ~) ; Sprung anreiten (einen ~)
abordar un obstáculo ; aproximarse un obstáculo ; acercarse un obstáculo

**apron (shoeing / farrier's ~)**
tablier (de maréchal-ferrant)
Hufbeschlagschürze
chaparreras

Leather horseshoeing aprons are sometimes called shoeing chaps.

**Arab ; Arabian** *breed*
arabe *race*
Araber *m* ; arabisches Vollblut
árabe

Sa taille varie de 1,40 à 1,55 mètres. Race très ancienne dont les origines se perdent dans le temps.

**arch** *n*
arcade
Zwiesel *m*
puente

The front arch of the saddle tree is usually formed by a gullet plate and a head plate riveted together. *see pommel and cantle*

Rigide et correspondant à chacune des parties relevées de la selle: le pommeau et le troussequin.

**arched neck** ; peacock-neck ; swan neck *(1)* ; turned-over neck
encolure de cygne
Schwanenhals *m*
cuello de cisne

1) This type of shape is sometimes described as tending to become ewe-necked at its lower end, sometimes as looking thin and underdeveloped below the throat, and sometimes as having a downward arch on both the lower and upper sides.

Encolure concave à la base et rouée (convexe) dans sa partie supérieure.

**arch-back** ; roach-back ; hog-back
dos convexe ; dos de carpe ; dos de mulet
gewölbter Rücken ; Karpfenrücken *m*
dorso de carpa ; espalda corvada

Convex spinal column.

**Ardennais ; Ardennes (horse)** *breed*
ardennais *race*
Ardenner
ardenés ; ardenas

**arm (upper / true ~)**
bras
Oberarm *(der ~)*
brazo

Correspondant à la région de l'humérus, entre la pointe de l'épaule, l'avant-bras, le poitrail et les côtes.

**art**
art
Kunst *f*
arte

**artery**
artère
Arterie / Arteria *f* ; Schlagader *f*
arteria

**arthritis of the knee** => carpitis

**articular cartilage**
cartilage articulaire
Gelenkknorpel *m* ; Beugefläche eines Gelenks *die ~*
cartílago articular

Couvre une surface qui fait face aux os voisins dans les articulations synoviales.

**artificial aid**
aide artificielle
künstliche Hilfe
ayuda artificial

Une des suivantes: la cravache, la chambrière, les éperons, les innombrables mors, les diverses martingales et les divers enrênements.

**artificial insemination** *abbr: A.I.*
insémination artificielle *abr: I.A.*
künstliche Besamung *(die ~) abr: KB*
inseminación artificial *abr: I.A.*

**art of equestrian riding**
art équestre *équitation*
Reitkunst *f*
arte ecuestre

**ascarid**
ascaride ; ascaris
Spulwurm *m Familie Ascarididae* ; Askaride *m* ; Ascaris *m*
ascáride

**ascending oxer**
oxer ascendant
aufsteigende Oxer *(der ~)*
oxer de barras desiguales

Dont la deuxième partie est plus haute que la première.

**ass** => donkey

**assistant judge**
juge auxiliaire
Hilfszielrichter *m*
juez auxiliar

**ass's foal** => donkey foal

**asternal ribs**
côtes asternales ; fausses côtes
falsche Rippen
costillas asternales
  Dont les cartilages n'atteignent pas directement le sternum.

**asthma** ; chronic obstructive pulmonary disease
  *abbr:* COPD
asthme ; maladie obstructive respiratoire chronique
chronische obstruktive Bronchiolitis *(die ~)*
asma ; enfermedad pulmonar obstructiva crónica ; bronquitis obstructiva crónica
  Contraction of bronchi and bronchioles, trapping air in alveoli that eventually rupture and fuse (this being irreversible, s.a. emphysema). This is often accompanied by bronchitis. Breathing problems are the most evident signs. *s.a. broken wind*
  Rétrécissement du calibre des voies respiratoires.

**astragalus** => talus

**ataxia**
ataxie
Ataxie *f*
ataxia
  Problème de coordination.

**atlanto-axial articulation**
articulation atlanto-axiale
Atlas-Axis-Gelenk *ne* ; zweites Kopfgelenk ; Atlantoaxialgelenk
articulación atlantoaxial

**atlas** ; first (cervical) vertebra
atlas
Atlas *m* ; erster Halswirbel
atlas ; primera vértebra cervical
  La première vertèbre cervicale, sa face articulaire avec la tête ne permet que des mouvements d'extension et de flexion.

**auction** *v*
vendre à l'encan ; vendre aux enchères
versteigern ; meistbietend verkaufen
vender en pública subasta

**auction (sale)**
encan ; vente aux enchères
Auktion *f*
remate ; subasta

**auditory tube**
trompe auditive ; trompe d'Eustache *anc*
Ohrtrompete *f* ; Eustachische Röhre *f*
trompa de Eustaquio ; tubo auditivo

**automatic timing device** ; teletimer
chronomètre électronique ; système de chronométrage électronique ; chronomètre à déclenchement automatique
elektrische Zeitmeßanlage *(die ~)*
cronómetro (de detención) automático

**automatic waterer (floater ~)**
abreuvoir automatique
Selbsttränke *f*
abrevadero automático

**autonomic nervous system** ; visceral nervous system
système nerveux autonome / végétatif *abr:* SNA
autonomes Nervensystem *(das ~)* ; vegetatives Nervensystem
sistema nervioso vegetativo / autónomo
  Comprend le sympathique et le parasympathique. Règle les fonctions qui se déroulent normalement de façon automatique et inconsciente.

**avulsion**
avulsion ; arrachement
Absprengung *f* ; Ausreißung *f* ; Abriß *m*
avulsión

**axilla** *pl: axillae*
aisselle
Achselhöhle *f* ; Armhöhle *f*
axila
  The equivalent to the armpit, the area between shoulder and chest through which nerves and arteries travel.

**axillary vein**
veine axillaire
Achselblutader *f* ; Achselvene *f*
vena axilar

**axis**
axis
zweiter Halswirbel *m*
axis
  Second cervical vertebra.
  Deuxième vertèbre cervicale, sa face articulaire avec l'atlas permet les mouvements de la tête perpendiculairement à l'encolure.

**azoturia** ; Monday morning sickness / disease ; myoglobinuria (paralytic ~) ; exertional myopathy / rhabdomyolisis *abbr: ER for (chronic) exertional rhabdo...* ; tying-up (syndrome) *(1)*
myoglobinurie ; eau noire *pl: eaux noires* ; maladie du lundi ; rhabdomyolyse d'effort / induite à l'exercice ; hémoglobinurie
Feiertagskrankheit *f* ; Kreuzverschlag *m* ; schwarze Harnwinde *(die ~)* ; Azoturie *f* ; Nierenverschlag / Nierenschlag *m*
azoturia ; mioglobinuria ; envardura *(1)*
  Disease characterized by red-brown urine and muscle weakness. It occurs after exercise following one or several days of inaction while still being fed a high-energy ration. Also known as setfast, myositis, cording up, weed and weedy leg. 1) Tying-up is a milder form affecting the muscles, in which the urine may not be dark-coloured.
  Douleurs dans les masses musculaires (donc une myopathie) du dos et de la croupe et couleur foncée de l'urine, à la reprise du travail après un ou quelques jour(s) de repos, alors que le cheval a été maintenu à une ration très riche. Aussi parfois appelée coup de sang.

**babesiasis ; babesiosis** ; biliary fever ; tick fever ; piroplasmosis ; redwater fever
babésiose ; piroplasmose
Piroplasmose des Pferdes *(die ~)* ; Babesiose *f* ; Tierpiroplasmose durch Babesia *(die ~)*
babesiosis ; piroplasmosis
  Due to a parasite (Babesia spp.), transmitted by blood-sucking ticks.
  Affection due au babésia et transmise par des tiques.

**back**
dos
Rücken *m*
espalda
*s.a. loin(s) for the lower back*

**back** *v* ; rein-back *v* ; step back *v*
reculer *v*
zurücktreten
recular ; retroceder

**backside** => back stretch ; backstretch

**back straight** => back stretch ; backstretch

**back stretch ; backstretch** ; back straight ;
backside *US*
autre droit (l'~) ; ligne d'en face
Gegengerade *f* ; Gegenseite *f*
estero de atrás

The straightaway opposite to the finishing line on the racetrack.
Ligne arrière de la piste de course, la plus éloignée de l'estrade principale.

**bald face** => white face

**ballotade**
ballotade ; ballottade
Ballotade *f*
balotada

Un des airs relevés.

**bandage** ; wrap
bandage ; bande
Bandage *f training and racing* ; Binde *f* ; Binde *m*
*surgical dressing*
venda ; vendaje

Morceau de matériel beaucoup plus long que large que l'on entoure autour des membres du cheval.

**bandy-legged (in the forelimb)** =>
knee-wide

**bandy-legged (in the hindlimb)** ; out at the
hocks ; bowlegged / bow-legged (in the
hindlimb)
cambré des jarrets
hinten faßbeinig
estevado

L'adjectif « cambré » qualifie habituellement plutôt les jarrets que le cheval.

**bank**
banquette ; talus
Wall *m* ; Erdwall
banqueta ; talud

**bar** => swingle-tree

**bar** => rail

**barb** *breed*
barbe *race*
Berber *m*
beréber

**bardot** => hinny

**barley**
orge
Gerste *f*
cebada

**barn** ; stable
écurie
Stall *m* ; Pferdestall
cuadra ; caballeriza

**barn cleaner (automatic ~)**
nettoyeur (d'étable, automatique) ; écureur (auto-matique)
automatische Stallreiniger *der ~*
evacuador transportador de estiércol

**barrel-mouth bit** => egg-butt / eggbutt snaffle

**barrel (of the horse)** => trunk

**barrel (of the horse)**
milieu (du cheval)
Mittelhand *f* ; Mittelleib *m* ; Mittelstück *ne* ;
Mittelhand *f*
tercio medio

The middle of the body, between the forehand and the rear end.
On dira par exemple, dans ce sens-ci, que le cheval pivote sur son milieu.

**barren**
bréhaigne ; stérile
Hakenstute *n f (1)* ; unfruchtbar *adj (2)* ; güsste
(Stute) *(die ~)* ; güst *niederdeutsch* ; nichttragend
machorra *n* ; infecunda

A mare that is incapable of conceiving and producing a foal.
La jument bréhaigne est parfois présentée comme ayant des crochets dentaires (1) et étant supposée stérile, et parfois comme étant simplement stérile (2). Cette dernière définition correspond au mot anglais « barren » qui apparaît avoir la même origine que le mot bréhaigne.

**barrier boot** ; easy-boot
hipposandale
Hufschuh *m*
zapatilla para casco

Sorte de sandale ou de botte dans laquelle on glisse le sabot et qui a son propre système d'attache.

**bar shoe**
fer à planche *(1)* ; fer à traverse *(2)*
Stegeisen *ne* ; geschlossen Hufeisen ; Ringeisen *ne*
herradura de barra

A shoe with a bar connecting the heels.
La distinction n'est pas toujours faite entre ces deux termes. 1) Dont les éponges sont prolongées et soudées ensemble. 2) Avec une lame (appelée le plus souvent traverse mais aussi barre) rivée ou soudée pour relier les éponges.

**bar (of the mouth)**
barre (de la bouche)
Lade *f* ; Zahnlücke *f*
barra

The space on the jaw, between the incisors, or the canine, and the molars.
Espace édenté et sensible, entre les molaires et le crochet, ou les incisives, sur lequel repose le canon du mors.

## base narrow

serré (du devant // du derrière) *(1)* ; cagneux des membres *(2)*
bodeneng
cerrado de abajo ; cerrado de brazos / adelante *anteriores* ; cerrado de atrás *posteriores*

The entire limbs (forelimbs or hindlimbs) are sloping inwards, toward each other. There is a greater distance between the horse's legs at the top than at the bottom, usually caused by an improper angulation at the elbow or stifle, the horse being pigeon-toed.

1) Quand les membres, bipède antérieur ou postérieur, se rapprochent davantage à leur base que ne l'est leur articulation supérieure (i.e. leur point d'origine). Ceci est habituellement dû à une mauvaise angularité du coude ou du grasset qui fait que 2) les membres restent tournés en dedans, convergent l'un vers l'autre lorsque vus de face.

## base of the tail => dock

## base wide

ouvert (du devant // du derrière)
bodenweit
abierto de abajo ; abierto de brazos / adelante *anteriores*

When there is a greater distance between the horse's legs at the bottom than at the top, the entire limb being deviated, usually caused by an improper angulation at the elbow or hip, the feet being toed out.

Quand les pieds, bipède antérieur ou postérieur, s'écartent davantage que ne l'est le point d'origine du membre.

## basic dressage test

épreuve de dressage élémentaire
Anfänger-Dressurprüfung *f*
prueba de adiestramiento para principiantes

## bay

bai *adj & n*
Braune *m* ; Brauner *m* ; Braun *ne* ; braun *adj*
bayo

Even with a large variety for this coat; mane and tail are always black and lower legs almost always are. In the darker coats, reddish or brown hairs are present on the muzzle and on other parts of the body.

Sur une peau à pigmentation foncée, la robe baie présente une grande variété de nuances, les crins sont cependant toujours noirs, et le bas des membres l'est presque toujours. Dans les teintes foncées, il y a présence de poils rougeâtres ou bruns sur le bout du nez et en d'autres endroits du corps.

## bay-brown => brown

## bay roan ; red roan

rouan
Rotschimmel
roano

Bay roan and red roan are often presented as equivalent. They do not present necessarily a bay pattern as do the French word « rouan ».

Mélange de poils blancs, alezans (rouges), et noirs. Les noirs prédominent aux extrémités.

## bay (to be / stand at ~) *hunting*

accul (être à l'~) *c. à courre*
gestellt sein ; zum Äußersten getrieben sein ; in die Enge getrieben sein ; sich verzweifelt zur Wehr setzen
tierra (a la ~)

Where the hunted turns to face and challenge the hounds.

Lorsque, acculée, la bête se défend aux extrémités d'un terrier.

## beak => horn (of an anvil)

## beat (hoof...)

battue
Hufschlag *m*
batida

Moment où le(s) sabot(s) se dépose(nt) sur le sol, et bruit que fait / font le(s) sabot(s) en se déposant sur le sol. Se posant simultanément, les pieds ne produisent qu'une battue.

## bed ; bedding => litter

## beet

betterave
Rübe *f* ; Bete *f*
remolacha

## behavior => behaviour

## behaviour *Brit* ; behavior *US*

comportement ; conduite
Verhalten *ne*
conducta

## behind the bit

en dedans de la main ; en arrière de la main
hinter dem Zügel ; hinter der Hand
detrás de la mano

A horse is behind the bit when avoiding the contact with the mouthpiece.

Cheval en dedans ou en arrière de la main, qui ne prend pas contact avec le mors.

## behind the motion

retarder sur le mouvement (du cheval)
hinter der Bewegung sitzen
sentarse detrás del movimiento

To be or to get left ~ of the horse.

## beige breeches

culottes de chasse
Jagdhose *f*
pantalón de caza

## Belgian (draft / heavy draught horse)

*breed* ; Brabancon (horse)
belge (trait lourd ~) *race* ; brabançon ; brabant
Belgisches Kaltblut ; Brabanter
caballo de tiro belga ; brabanzón

## bell

cloche
Glocke *f*
campana ; timbre

**belly**
ventre
Bauch *m*
vientre ; barriga
  1st: The softer, ventral part of the abdomen. 2nd: The
fleshy, contractile part of a muscle.
  1° Partie ventrale de l'abdomen du cheval, située en
arrière des côtes, sous les flancs et dans leur partie
basse. 2° Partie contractile d'un muscle.

**belly band** *bd (1)* ; shaft girth / strap *br*
sangle sous-ventrière *att* ; sangle de brancards *ca*
kleine Bauchgurt *(der ~)*
barriguera (cincha ~) ; zambarco
  1) A strap, attached from one shaft or trace to the
other, under the belly of the horse.

**bell boot** ; overreach boot
cloche *protège-couronne*
Glocke *f* ; Springglocke ; Gummiglocke ;
  Sprungglocke *f*
campana de hule ; bota de goma cubrecasco ; al-
canzadora
  A circular boot pulled up over the front foot and resting loosely on it, usually to protect coronet against
injury.
  Le mot désigne habituellement une forme particulière
de protecteur au niveau de la couronne: un bracelet qui
passe autour du paturon et descend comme une jupe
autour du pied.

**bend** => flexion

**bend at the poll** *n*
flexion de la nuque
Genickwölbung *f* ; seitwärtige Biegung im Genick
flexión en la nuca

**benzimidazole**
benzimidazole
Benzimidazol *ne*
benzimidazole

**bet** *v* ; wager *v* ; place a bet *v* ; stake *v*
parier ; miser ; gager *Can.*
wetten ; setzen ; spielen ; zocken
apostar

**bet** *n* ; wager *n* ; stake *n*
pari ; mise ; gageure *Can.*
Wette *f* ; Rennwette *f*
apuesta

**bettor** ; punter ; wagerer
parieur
Wetter *m*
apostante

**between legs and hands** => on the aids

**biceps brachii muscle** ; biceps m. of arm ;
  flexor brachii m. *old*
muscle biceps brachial
zweiköpfiger Armmuskel ; Zweikopfmuskel
músculo bíceps del brazo

**biceps femoris muscle** ; biceps (muscle) of
  (the) thigh
muscle biceps fémoral ; m. glutéobiceps *(1)* ; m.
  long vaste *anc*
zweiköpfig Oberschenkel-Muskel *(der ~)*
músculo bíceps femoral
  1) Dénomination qui suggère une partie crâniale (m.
glutéofémoral) et une partie caudale (m. biceps fémoral).

intimement liées pour constituer le muscle dont il est
question ici.

**biceps muscle of arm** => biceps brachii
  muscle

**biceps (muscle) of (the) thigh** => biceps
  femoris muscle

**bick** => horn (of an anvil)

**bicorne**
bicorne
Zweispitz ; Zweimaster
bicorne *adj* ; sombrero de dos picos
  A two-cornered hat.

**bid**
enchère ; mise
Gebot *ne ; auf einer Auktion*
puja

**bike** => sulky

**biliary fever** => babesiasis ; babesiosis

**billet (of a buckle)** ; tongue
ardillon *m*
Dorn *m* ; Schnallendorn
hebijón

**biotin**
biotine
Biotin *ne* ; Biotinum *ne* ; Vitamin H
biotina

**birth coat**
pelage à la naissance
Haarkleid bei der Geburt *(das ~)*
pelaje de nacimiento

**bit**
mors
Gebiss / Gebiß *ne*
freno
  Part of the bridle which includes the mouthpiece, the
rings and the cheeks.
  Partie de la bride qui comprend l'embouchure / le(s)
canon(s), les anneaux, les aiguilles et les branches. Le
mors et l'embouchure étaient autrefois appelés « frein ».

**bite** *v*
mordre
beißen
morder

**black** *adj & n*
noir *adj & n*
Rappe *m* ; schwarz *adj*
negro
  Black colour is general except may be for a few white
hairs in the coat and markings.
  Poils et crins noirs, il peut y avoir quelques poils
blancs et des marques.

**blacksmith**
forgeron
Schmied *m*
herrero ; forgador *amer*
  Personne qui forge le métal.

**black-faced**
cap de maure / more *adj*
scharzgesichtig
carinegro

**black fly**
mouche noire
Kriebelmücke *f Familie Simuliidae*
mosca negra
  May be applied to a number of different flies.

**bladder (urinary ~)**
vessie
Harnblase
vejiga de la orina
  Sa capacité oscille généralement autour de 1,5 litres chez le cheval.

**blanket (horse ~)** ; horse cloth ; rug
couverture
Decke *f*
manta (para caballos) ; camisa *Mexico*

**blaze** => broad stripe

**bleeder**
sujet à des hémorragies
Nasenbluter *m*
caballo sangrante

**bleeding** => epistaxis

**blemish** => defect

**blindgut** => cecum / caecum

**blind spavin** => occult spavin

**blind ; blinder** => blinker

**blinker** ; winker ; blind ; blinder
oeillère ; cache-oeil
Scheuklappe *(die ~)* ; Blendkappe *(die ~)* ; Scheuleder
anteojera
  Destinée principalement à empêcher le cheval de voir en arrière et sur le côté, mais aussi à protéger l'oeil contre les coups possibles dans un attelage.

**blinkers** => blinker hood

**blinker hood** ; blinkers *r*
bonnet avec oeillères ; cagoule avec oeillères
Blinkers
mascarilla

**blister**
ampoule ; bulle ; vésicule
Blase *f*; Bläschen *ne*
ampolla
  Lesion of the skin: a vesicle, especially a bulla.

**blister beetle / fly** ; Spanish fly
cantharide ; mouche d'Espagne / de Milan
Kantharide
cantárida

**blister ; blistering** ; vesicant
vésicatoire *n* ; feu liquide
Zugpflaster *ne* ; Blister *m*
vejigatorio ; vesicatorio ; blistera *amer* ; revulsivo (agente ~)
  Containing an irritant for the skin and used to increase circulation. This might encourage healing of another irritation like a strained tendon or ligament.
  Produit vésicant, c'est-à-dire irritant et provocant l'apparition de bulles ou de vésicules remplies de liquide sur la peau.

**block (horse ~)** => mounting step

**blood**
sang
Blut
sangre

**bloodline** => lineage

**blood-letting** ; phlebotomy
saignée *n*
Blutentnahme *f*; Blutentziehung *f*; Aderlaß *m*
sangría

**blood examination**
analyse de sang
Blutuntersuchung *f*
análisis sanguíneo

**blood test**
test sanguin
Blutprobe *(die ~)*
test sanguíneo

**blowfly strike** => cutaneous blowfly myiasis

**blue-dun** => mouse-dun ; mouse-coloured

**blue roan** *(1)* ; iron grey *(2)*
gris (de) fer ; gris-bleu ; pinchard *Fr adj & n (1)*
Rappschimmel *Stichelhaar*
tordo
  1) Coat having a blue tinge, usually resulting from a mixture of black and white hairs. Lower limbs, mane and tail are mainly black (or of the dark colour) and the colour is permanent. 2) Grey coat having a blue tinge, the colour is not permanent.
  Robe grise à reflets bleuâtres. 1) Qualifie ou désigne le cheval ou la robe de cette couleur.

**bob tailed** => docked tail(ed) ; docked

**bob the head** *v* ; toss the head *v* ; throw the head *v* ; shake the head (up and down) *v*
battre à la main ; encenser *(1)* ; bégayer
Kopf schlagen (mit dem ~)
cabecear ; subir y bajar la cabeza
  Moving the head up and down to fight against the contact of the bit.
  Lorsque le cheval donne des coups de tête en haut et en bas, notamment en guise de défense contre la main du cavalier. 1) Terme appliqué plus particulièrement au cheval qui donne de tels coups de tête lorsqu'il n'a pas de bride.

**body-brush** => brush

**body length**
longueur du corps
Körperlänge
longitud corporal

**bog spavin**
éparvin mou ; vessigon articulaire tarsien / du jarret
Kreuzgalle *f*; weiche Spat ; Weichteilspat *(der ~)*
esparaván falso
  Distension of the talocrural synovial sac of the hock.
  Distension de la synoviale tibio-talienne du jarret. Il peut prendre trois formes qui communiquent largement entre elles: vessigon du pli du jarret et vessigon médial // latéral du creux du jarret.

**bolt** *v* ; run away *v*
emballer (s'~)
durchgehen ; durchbrennen
desbocarse ; embalarse ; escaparse ; huir

**bolting horse ; bolter** ; runaway horse
cheval emballé
stätiges Pferd *(das ~)*
caballo desbocado

A bolter may be a horse having a tendency to bolt (i.e. to be bolting) quite easily.

**bone**
os
Knochen *m, pl: Knochen*
hueso

**bone fracture**
fracture d'un os
Knochenbruch *m*
fractura

**bone marrow**
moelle osseuse
Knochenmark
médula ósea

**bone spavin**
éparvin (calleux)
Spat *m* ; Knochen-Spat / Knochenspat
esparaván óseo

Osteitis or osteo-arthritis of upper end of canon and inner side of hock. A large spavin is called a jack, and a small is a blind or occult spavin. The latter may present no palpable or radiographic sign.

Ostéite ou ostéo-arthrite au sommet interne du canon et à la face inférieure interne du jarret.

**bonus point**
point de bonification
Gutschrift
punto de bonificación

**bony withers**
garrot maigre / décharné
magerer Widerrist
cruz delgada

**bootjack**
tire-botte
Stiefelknecht
sacabotas

Comportant une encavure dans laquelle on cale le talon de la botte pour l'enlever.

**bootmaker**
bottier
Stiefelmacher
zapatero (a la medida) ; botero

**boots**
bottes
Stiefel
botas

**boot hook**
tire-botte (crochet ~)
Stiefelhaken ; Stiefelanzieher
tirabotas ; gancho para botas

**boot (for horses)**
guêtre *f (1)* ; protecteur ; protège-~ ; botte
  *protection des membres (2)*
Streichkappe *f* ; Streichkappen *m* ;
  Sehnenschoner *m* ; Gamasche *f*
protector ; bota ; zapatilla

To protect legs against self-injuries, and for foot and/or leg therapy, which is sometimes called slip-on boot or (rubber) poultice boot. *s.a. barrier boot*

Servent de protection des membres du cheval contre les blessures. On utilise souvent ces termes en précisant la partie des membres qu'ils protègent. 1) Le terme guêtre s'utilise habituellement plus spécifiquement pour désigner une protection à la hauteur des canons (et incluant habituellement le boulet), et plus haut. v.a. cloche 2) Peut aussi désigner une véritable botte dans laquelle on met le pied ou même une partie de la jambe du cheval pour les soigner. Pour désigner une guêtre, ce mot semble être une traduction littérale de l'anglais.

**bore** => lean (heavily) on the hand / bit

**Borna disease** ; Near Eastern equine encephalomyelitis
maladie de Borna ; méningoencéphalomyélite enzootique ; méningoencéphalite infectieuse du cheval
Bornasche Krankheit *(die ~)* ; infektiöse Meningoenzephalitis der Pferde *(die ~)*
Borna

**boron**
bore
Bor *ne*
boro

**bosal**
bosal
Bosal
bozal

The rawhide noseband of the true hackamore.
Grosse muserolle de cuir tressée faisant partie du hackamore. Ce mot sert aussi parfois à désigner le véritable hackamore.

**both legs coming out of one hole (having ~)**
=> narrow at the chest

**bottom of a stirrup**
grille (d'un étrier)
Bügeltritt
largo de lo estribo

**botulism**
botulisme
Botulismus *m*
botulismo

**bot fly (horse ~)** ; nose fly *(1)* ; Gasterophilus
gastrophile ; gastérophile ; oestre
Magenbremse *f* ; Dasselfliege *f* ; Pferdebremse ; Pferdemagenbremse ; Magenfliege
gastrophilus ; gastrófilo ; estro

A genus of six flies, the larvae of which develop in the gastro-intestinal tract. 1) Two of the bot flies lay their eggs around the mouth and on the cheeks.

Mouches (il y en a six espèces) qui pondent leurs oeufs (pour la plupart d'entre elles) sur les poils des chevaux et dont les larves se développent à l'intérieur du tube digestif.

**Boulonnais (horse)** *breed*
boulonnais
Boulonnais ; boulonnaiser Kaltblut
bullones
    Race de chevaux de trait lourd d'origine française.

**bowed tendon**
tendon claqué
Bogen *m*
tendón arqueado
*s.a. tendon bow*

**bowel movement** => droppings

**bowlegged / bow-legged (in the forelimb)**
  => knee-wide

**bowlegged / bow-legged (in the hindlimb)** => bandy-legged (in the hindlimb)

**bowler (hat)** ; derby (hunt ~) *US*
melon (chapeau ~)
Melone *f*
bombín ; hongo (sombrero ~)

**box (stall)** ; loose box
box
Box ; Pferdebox
box ; cubículo
    Loge d'écurie, individuelle et fermée.

**Brabancon (horse)** => Belgian (draft / heavy draught horse)

**brace** => liniment

**brachialis muscle**
muscle brachial
innerer Armmuskel
músculo braquial

**brachygnathia ; brachygnathism** ; parrot mouth / jaw ; overshot jaw
brachygnathie (mandibulaire) ; bec de perroquet
Karpfengebiss *ne* ; Überbiß *m* ; verkürzter Unterkiefer *m*
boca de loro
    Abnormal shortness of the mandible (lower jaw) and protrusion of the maxilla.
    Lorsque la mâchoire inférieure est plus courte que la mâchoire supérieure. Les défauts de jonction entre les incisives des deux mâchoires se définissent normalement en fonction de la mâchoire inférieure: (brachygna...) plus courte, (progna...) plus longue que la mâchoire supérieure.

**bradoon** => bridoon

**braid** => plait

**braided mane** => plaited mane

**brain**
cerveau ; encéphale
Gehirn
encéfalo
    Pèse environ 420 g chez le cheval.

**bran**
son
Weizenkleie *(die ~)*
salvado ; afrecho

**branch (of a bit)** *(1)* ; shank *west. (1)* ; cheek *(2)*
branche (d'un mors)
Baum *m* ; Anzug *m*
cama
    1) Any of the lateral shanks or legs of varying length, fixed or sliding, including 2) cheeks of the snaffle bits, e.g. dee and eggbutt cheeks. The French term « branches » does not include the cheeks of the snaffle bits.
    Chacune des barres latérales du mors. Celles-ci demeurent donc à l'extérieur de la bouche du cheval et c'est sur elles que s'attachent les autres accessoires (rênes, gourmette etc.), au moyen d'anneaux ou de crochets. Cette désignation ne comprend pas, contrairement à la désignation anglophone « branch », les aiguilles et les autres tiges des filets, comme celles du filet Verdun par exemple.

**branch (of a shoe)**
branche (d'un fer)
Schenkel *m*
rama
    Chacune des moitiés du fer, il y a donc une branche interne et une externe.

**branding iron**
fer à marquer
Brandeisen *ne* ; Brenneisen *ne*
hierro de marcar

**branding (hot ~)**
marquage au fer (rouge / chaud)
Brandmarken *ne*
marcación a fuego

**branding (hot ~ mark)** ; brand-mark (hot ~) ; brand (hot ~) *n*
marque (au fer rouge / au feu)
Gestütsbrand ; Brandzeichen *ne*
marca de / a fuego ; marca (a hierro) candente ; hierro

**brand-mark (hot ~)** => branding (hot ~ mark)

**brand (hot ~)** => branding (hot ~ mark)

**bray** *v*
braire
Esel schreien (wie ein ~) ; i-ahen
rebuznar

**breadth of the forehead**
largeur du front
Stirnbreite
anchura de la frente

**break into** *v* ; proceed *v*
rompre ; partir
anreiten
partir
    Changer d'allure, de mouvement; ex.: rompre au pas à partir de l'arrêt.

**break (a horse)** *v*
débourrer (un cheval) ; dompter ; casser
anreiten ; zureiten ; einfahren *att / bd*
domar (un caballo) ; amansar (un caballo) ; aparejar (un caballo)

**breast** ; presternal region
poitrail ; région présternale
Vorderbrust *f* ; Vorderbrustgegend *f*
pecho (parte delantera del ~)

Area just in front of the sternum, part of the chest and of the thorax.  *s.a. chest*

Région située entre l'encolure et les épaules du cheval, soit entre les deux pointes des épaules. Cette région fait partie de la poitrine et du thorax.

**breast collar** *bd*
bricole *att*
Brustblatt *ne*
petral

**breast collar / plate**
bricole ; collier de poitrine
Vorderzeug *ne*
petral (pecho-~) ; pechera

**breeches**
pantalons d'équitation ; culottes
Reithose *f* ; Breeches *f*
pantalón de montar

**breeches-maker**
culottier
Reithosenschneider
pantalonero

**breeching**
avaloire ; acculoire *Can.* ; harnais de recul ; recul-ement *(1)*
Hintergeschirr *ne*
ataharre ; retranca

Courroie autour de l'arrière-train du cheval qui se termine par des chaînes à fixer aux brancards, elle permet de reculer. 1) Parfois présenté comme étant l'ensemble qui permet au cheval de reculer et retenir ce à quoi il est attelé lors des arrêts et des descentes. Il comprend dans ce sens l'avaloire, la barre et les crampons de reculement.

**breeching strap**
courroie de reculement
Scherenriemen *(der ~)*
correa de retranca

**breed**
race
Rasse *f*
raza

Les noms de races sont assez souvent écrits avec la première lettre en majuscule. Toutefois, lorsqu'utilisé comme adjectif, le mot ne devrait jamais comporter cette majuscule.

**breeder**
éleveur (-naisseur)
Züchter *m*
seleccionador y criador

Mating horses and getting the mares to foal.

**breeder's association**
association d'éleveurs
Züchterverband *m* ; Züchtervereinigung *f* ; Verband
asociación de ganaderos / criadores

**breeder's premium**
prime à l'éleveur ; prime d'élevage
Züchterprämie
premio al criador

**breeder (up)** ; rearer
éleveur
Aufzüchter *m*
criador

Raising and caring for horses.

**breeding** ; coupling ; mating
accouplement
Paarung *f* ; Begattung *f*
apareamiento

**breeding**
élevage
Zucht *f*
cría

**breeding farm (horse-~)**  => stud farm

**breeding herd**
troupeau d'élevage
Zuchtherde
yeguada de cría

**breeding hopples / hobbles** ; service / serving hobbles
entraves d'accouplement
Spanngeschirr
maneas ; trabas

**breeding selection**
sélection (pour l'élevage)
Zuchtwahl ; Auslese
selección

**breeding stock**
reproducteurs (sujets ~) ; cheptel reproducteur
Zuchtmaterial *ne* ; Zuchttiere *ne pl* ; Zuchtbestand *m*
reproductores (animales ~)

**breed association**  => breed society

**breed society** ; breed association
société d'élevage
Zuchtverband *m* ; Zuchtverein *m*
sociedad de cría

**breed type**
type de (la) race
Rassetyp *m*
tipo racial

**brewer's draff / grains**
drêche (de brasserie)
Biertreber *m* ; Schlempe *f* ; Trockentreber
bagazo de cervecería

**bridge of the nose** ; nose (bridge of the ~)
chanfrein ; dos du nez ; nez (dos du ~)
Nasenrücken *m* ; Untergesicht *ne*
testuz ; puente de la nariz

Corresponding to the flat anterior surface of the nasal bones.

Correspondant aux deux os nasaux.

**bridle** ; headstall *west. (1)*
bride
Zaum *m* ; Zaumzeug *ne*
brida
*1) s.a. halter*

**bridle (a horse)** *v*
brider (un cheval)
aufzäumen ; zäumen
embridar

**bridoon** ; bradoon
filet (mince / de bride)
Unterlegtrense
bridón
A small snaffle bit, like the one usual in double bridles.

**bright bay** => cherry bay

**bringing in hand**
mise en main
An-die-Hand-Stellen *(das ~)*
puesta en mano
Placer du cheval en état de soumission et d'attention à la main du cavalier, la bouche étant plus décontractée et le cheval étant plus léger en main à mesure que le degré de dressage s'élève. On peut dire que c'est l'étape finale de la mise en impulsion et du rassembler du cheval et qu'elle peut conduire à une bonne position du ramener avec un cheval léger en main.

**brisket**
bréchet ; région sternale
Unterbrust *f* ; Brustkern
costillar
Area of body covering the sternum.

**brittle foot / hoof**
pied dérobé
Bröckelhuf ; bröckeliger Huf *(der ~)*
casco quebradizo
The hoof wall chips off, separates from the sole and/or readily splits when nails are driven into it.
Dont le bord inférieur de la muraille est brisé, éclaté en certains endroits.

**broad jump** => spread jump

**broad stripe** ; blaze *(1)*
liste large
breite Blesse *(die ~)*
lucero ; cordón corrido
1) Extensive white covering most of the forehead between the eyes, but not including them, and the entire width of the nasal bones, usually down to muzzle. The full blaze reaches down to the upper lip.

**broken** => jointed

**broken canter** => disunited canter

**broken wind** => heaves
souffle ; pousse
Dämpfigkeit *f* ; Dampf *m*
huélfago
A chronic cough and other difficulties in breathing, characterized by a double expiratory effort, related to asthma and pulmonary emphysema.
Difficultés respiratoires, caractérisées par une expiration en deux temps (appelée soubresaut), qui sont reliées à l'asthme et à l'emphysème pulmonaire.

**broken winded** ; short winded
poussif
dämpfig
asmático ; corto de resuello

**bronchial tube** => bronchus

**bronchiole**
bronchiole
Bronchiole *f* ; Bronchiolus *m*
bronquiolo

**bronchitis**
bronchite
Bronchitis *f*
bronquitis
Inflammation of the bronchi.
Inflammation des bronches.

**bronchus** *pl: bronchi* ; bronchial tube
bronche
Bronchus ; Hauptast der Luftröhre
bronquio
Airway connecting the trachea with the smaller airways in the lungs.
Conduit cartilagineux faisant suite à la trachée, deux bronches-souches se dirigent chacune vers un poumon et s'y subdivisent davantage.

**broodmare station**
jumenterie
Stuterei *f* ; Stutendepot ; Stutenstation
depósito de yeguas

**broodmare** ; brood mare
poulinière ; jument poulinière
Fohlenstute *f* ; Mutterstute ; Zuchtstute *Stute mit Zuchttyp*
madre ; yegua madre ; yegua de cría ; yegua de vientre

**brook** => water jump (open ~)

**browband**
frontal ; frontière *Can. ca*
Stirnband *ne* ; Stirnriemen *m*
frontalera

**brown** *(1)* ; bay-brown *(2)*
bai-brun
Schwarzbraune *m* ; Dunkelbrauner
bayo obscuro / oscuro ; marrón *(1)*
Hairs are brown, almost black. 1) With no true bay cast in any part of the coat and lacking the red shade and brilliance of bay. Brown and « marrón » horses will often be called « bai-brun » in French. 2) With some true bay cast in parts of the coat, and black mane, tail and lower limbs.
Robe dont les poils bruns sont presque noirs. Les ouvrages francophones ne présentent habituellement pas de robe brune qui ne soit pas baie. Cette robe est cependant reconnue dans les ouvrages anglophones et semble l'être dans les ouvrages hispanophones. Le terme s'emploierait donc ainsi souvent pour décrire des chevaux qualifiés « brown » en anglais et « marrón » en espagnol.

**brucellosis**
brucellose
Brucellose *f*
brucelosis

**bruise** ; contusion
contusion
Prellung *f* ; Quetschung *f*
contusión

**bruise (of the sole)** ; contusion of the sole ; sole ulcer ; stone bruise
contusion de la sole
Steingalle *f*
contusión de la suela / de piedra
A blood-soaked fleck, resulting from trauma to the underlying dermis. A corn is often presented as being a

bruise specifically occurring within the angles of the sole, also called seat of corn.

Un corps étranger (roche ou autre) a blessé la sole et peut même y être resté incrusté. De petites hémorragies sont produites dans le tissu velouté. On identifie parfois la bleime comme étant spécifiquement située en talon.

## brush *v*

atteindre (s'~) ; attraper (s'~) ; couper (se ~) ; entrecouper (s'~) ; tailler (se ~) ; entretailler (s'~) ; toucher (se ~) ; raser (se ~)
streichen (sich ~) ; streifen (sich ~)
rozar

Definitions found for brushing can be classified in two groups: 1st: a general term for light striking between limbs, this would not include translations like « se couper, s'entrecouper, se tailler, s'entretailler »; 2nd: the striking of a hoof against the inside of the opposite leg, which might be the most common case of light striking.

Se dit du cheval dont un membre en heurte ou en blesse un autre lorsqu'il se déplace. Bien qu'il n'y ait pas toujours de distinctions de faites entre tous ces termes, la logique donne à penser qu'un cheval qui se touche, s'attrape ou s'atteint, ne se coupe ou se taille pas nécessairement. On dit parfois spécifiquement qu'un cheval s'entretaille lorsque deux de ses membres se coupent mutuellement.

## brush *n hunting* ; fox tail
queue de renard *c. à courre*
Fuchslunte *f*
cola de zorro

## brush *n* ; body-brush
brosse (à panser)
Kardätsche *(die ~)*
cepillo de cuerpo

Spécifiquement destinée aux soins des chevaux, habituellement de forme ovale et avec une poignée dans laquelle on glisse la main.

## brush and rails
haie barrée
schräge Hecke
valla con barras

## brush (jump) => hedge

## buccal cavity
cavité buccale
Maulhöhle ; Mundhöhle
cavidad bucal

## buckle
boucle
Schnalle *f*
bucle ; hebilla

## buckskin *(1)* ; zebra-dun *(2)*
isabelle
Falbe *m*
isabela ; perla isabela

A very light bay coat with yellow shades (tanned deerhide) on the body. Lower limbs, mane and tail are black. 1) Without primitive marks. 2) With primitive marks: dorsal, withers and zebra stripes.

Robe baie très claire dont les poils sont jaunes ou jaunâtres, et les crins et extrémités sont noirs. Elle peut comporter une raie de mulet et des zébrures.

## buckwheat
sarrasin
Buchweizen
alforfón ; trigo sarraceno

## buck-kneed => over at / in the knees

## buck off => throw the rider

## bulb (of a heel)
glome *m*
Ballen *m* ; Hufballen
punta del talón

## bullfight
corrida
Stierkampf *m*
corrida

## bull-finch / bullfinch
bull-finch
Bullfinch *(der ~)*
bull-finch

## bull neck ; heavy neck
cou de taureau ; encolure épaisse
Speckhals *m* ; dicker Hals ; schwerer Hals
cuello grueso / de toro

Lourde, souvent chargée de graisse.

## bursitis of the hock => capped hock

## bursitis of the point of elbow => capped elbow

## buttock
fesse
Hinterbacke *f*
nalga

Fleshy prominence formed by the gluteal muscles on either side of the tail.

Région située de chaque côté de la queue et correspondant aux muscles fessiers. Attention cependant puisqu'on y inclut souvent une partie que certains considéreront comme appartenant à la cuisse (région fémorale caudale ou Regio femoris caudalis (NAV)) et qui s'étend entre deux points dont les noms sont révélateurs: de la pointe de la fesse au pli de la fesse.

## buyer
acheteur
Käufer
comprador

## Caballo de Paso Peruano => Peruvian paso / ambler

## calcaneal tuberosity => calcanean tuber

## calcanean tuber ; calcaneal tuberosity ; tuber calcis
tubérosité du calcanéus ; sommet du calcanéum *anc*
Fersenhöcker *m*
tuberosidad calcánea

Point d'attache de la corde du jarret.

## calcaneus ; fibular tarsal bone *old* ; os calcis *old*
calcaneus ; calcanéus ; calcanéum *anc*
Fersenbein *ne* ; Calcaneus *m*
calcáneo

Sert de bras de levier aux muscles extenseurs du pied et forme la pointe du jarret.

## calcium
calcium
Kalzium *m*
calcio

**calf-knee / calf knee** ; sheep knee
genou creux *pl: genoux creux* ; genou renvoyé ; genou de mouton ; genou effacé
Kalbsknie *ne* ; rückbiegig *adj* ; kalbsbeinig *adj*
rodilla de carnero ; rodilla hueca
　Posterior deviation of the carpal joint.
　Déviation de l'articulation du genou vers l'arrière; quand, vu de côté, le genou est trop en arrière par rapport à l'axe du membre.

**calf face**  => white face

**calico**  => pinto ; pintado

**calk (screw-in ~)** ; stud (horseshoe / screw-in ~)
crampon à vis / vissé
Schraubstollen *m*
remache atornillado

**calk ; caulk ; calkin ; caulkin**
crampon
Stollen *m*
ramplón (de herradura)
　Part of the horseshoe being turned down or added for raising, or for traction to prevent slipping.
　Crampon formé directement avec le matériel du fer, ou soudé sur celui-ci.

**calliphorine myiasis**  => cutaneous blowfly
　myiasis

**camel neck**  => dip in front of the withers

**camel withers**
garrot coupé
kurzer Widerrist
cruz corta
　Withers that are high, and dropping quite abruptly to the rear.
　Garrot bien sorti mais insuffisamment prolongé vers l'arrière.

**camped (out)** ; standing stretched
campé
gestreckt
plantado adelante // de atrás
　Front limbs sloping toward the front (camped in front) of the horse or hind feet standing too far back, the entire limb deviating back behind the plumb line ©. behind).
　Quand, vus de côté, les membres sont déportés à l'extérieur, les antérieurs étant trop en avant (campé du devant), ou les postérieurs trop en arrière (c. du derrière), par rapport à leurs articulations supérieures.

**canine teeth** ; tushes
canines ; crochets
Hakenzähne ; Kaninus ; Fangzähne
caninos (dientes ~)
　Au nombre de deux par mâchoire, petites dents habituelles chez le mâle et rares chez la jument.

**canine (tooth)** ; tush
canine ; crochet
Hakenzahn *m*
canino

**canker** ; hoof cancer
crapaud
Strahlkrebs *m* ; Hufkrebs
galápago
　Severe disease similar to thrush.

**cannon**
canon
Röhre *f*
caña

**cannon's circumference** ; circumference of cannon bone
tour du canon
Röhrbeinumfang *m*
perímetro de la caña ; circunferencia de la caña

**cannon bone** ; shin bone *rare*
os du canon
Röhrbein *ne*
caña (hueso)
　Leg bone above the fetlock (the large metacarpal // metatarsal bone). Specifically, shin is the dorsal surface (front part) of the cannon bone.

**cannon bone (fore...)**  => metacarpal bone
　(large / third ~)

**cannon bone (hind-~)**  => metatarsal bone
　(large / third ~)

**canter** *n* ; lope *west.*
galop (petit ~)
Kanter *m* ; Galopp (kurzer ~) *m*
galope (corto)
　An easy, rather collected, gallop. Canter is a contraction of « cantering gallop » or « Canterbury pace »; supposedly used by the medieval pilgrims on their way to the shrine at Canterbury.

**canter** *v*
galoper (au petit galop)
kantern ; kurzen Galopp gehen (in ~)
galopar (corto)

**canter counter-lead** *n* ; counter-canter
galop à faux ; contre-galop
Außengalopp *(der ~)* ; Kontergalopp
galope (en) falso ; galope en trocado ; contra galope
　Canter on the outside lead, performed purposely.
　Galop sur le pied extérieur, demandé par le cavalier.

**canter on / at the wrong lead** *n* ; false canter
galop à faux
falscher Galopp
galope falso
　Canter on the outside lead, performed unpurposely.
　Galop sur le pied extérieur, se produisant par erreur.

**canter (on the) left (lead)** *n*
galop à gauche ; galop sur le pied gauche
Linksgalopp *m*
galope a la izquierda

**canter (on the) right (lead)** *n*
galop à droite ; galop sur le pied droit
Rechtsgalopp *m*
galope a la derecha

**canter / gallop at / on the true lead** *n* ; true canter / gallop
galop juste ; galop sur le bon pied
Innengalopp ; richtiger Galopp
galope en firme

**cantle**
trousséquin
Hinterzwiesel *m* ; Sattelkranz
borrén trasero ; cantileja

**caparison** => trappings (horse's ~)

**capillary (vessel)**
capillaire (vaisseau ~)
Kapillare ; Haargefäß
capilar (vaso ~)
  Tiny blood vessel.
  Minuscule vaisseau sanguin à parois minces.

**capped elbow** ; shoe boil ; elbow hygroma ;
  bursitis of the point of elbow
éponge ; hygroma du coude
Stollbeule ; Stollenbeule *f* ; Ellbogenbeule
codillera ; bursitis del codo ; higroma del codo

**capped hock** ; hock hygroma ; bursitis of the
  hock
capelet ; hygroma du tarse ; bursite du tarse
Piephacke *f*
talón de pollo ; bursitis del corvejón ; alifafe ; higroma del corvejón
  Swelling over the point of the hock.
  Hygroma situé à la pointe du jarret.

**capped knee** => carpal hygroma

**capriole**
cabriole ; capriole
Kapriole *(die ~)*
cabriola
  Saut d'école, après s'être élevé au-dessus du sol, le
  cheval dégage une ruade au moment où il est à
  l'horizontale.

**cap (hunting / skull / jockey's ~)** ; helmet *r*
  *& class.: (safety ~), class.: (riding ~)* ; hard hat
  *class.*
casque protecteur ; bombe (de chasse) *class.* ;
  toque *c & class.*
Reitkappe *f* ; Sturzkappe ; Springkappe
casco protector ; gorra (de montar)

**carbon dioxide**
gaz carbonique
Kohlensäure *f*
gas carbónico

**carcinoma**
carcinome ; épithélioma malin
Karzinom *ne* ; Krebs *m*
carcinoma
  A malignant new growth of epithelial cells, a form of
  cancer.

**cardia**
cardia *m*
Kardia *f* ; Mageneingang *m*
cardias
  Part of the stomach.
  Partie de l'estomac.

**cardiac muscle** ; heart muscle ; myocardium
muscle cardiaque ; myocarde
Herzmuskel ; Myokard
músculo cardiaco ; miocardio
  Muscle à contraction involontaire, d'un type qui lui est
  propre.

**care of hooves** ; hoofcare ; hoof care
soin(s) aux / des sabots
Hufpflege *f*
cuidado(s) de los cascos

**carpal bones** ; knee bones
os du carpe (les ~) ; os du genou (les ~)
Karpalknochen ; Vorderfußwurzelknochen
huesos carpianos ; huesos del carpo
  Au nombre de sept ou huit, entre le radius et les métacarpiens.

**carpal hygroma** ; popped knee ; capped knee
hygroma du genou
Knieschwamm *m* ; Kniebeule *f*
higroma carpiano
  Tuméfaction fluctuante située sur la face antérieure du
  genou et provenant généralement d'un coup.

**carpal joint(s)**
articulation(s) du carpe
Karpalgelenk(e) *ne* ; Vorderfußwurzelgelenk(e)
articulación(/ones) del carpo

**carpitis** ; arthritis of the knee ; knee spavin
carpite
Carpitis *f* ; Handwurzelgelenkentzündung *f*
carpitis
  Inflammation du carpe, impliquant les os, et/ou la capsule articulaire, et/ou les ligaments.

**carpus** => knee

**carpus varus** => knock-knees

**carriage horse** => cart-horse

**carrier's horse** => dray horse

**carrot**
carotte
Mohrrübe ; Karotte
zanahoria

**cartilage**
cartilage
Knorpel *m*
cartílago

**cartilage of prolongation** => scapula(r)
  cartilage

**cartilage of the third phalanx (flat ~)** =>
  fibrocartilage of the third phalanx

**cart-horse** ; carriage horse ; coach horse
cheval d'attelage
Wagenpferd ; Kutschpferd ; Schrittpferd
caballo de carro / coche ; caballo de tiro
  The size and type of these horses must vary to fit the
  work required.
  Il s'agit plutôt ici d'une utilisation d'un cheval que
  d'un type, lequel pourra naturellement varier en
  fonction du travail demandé (lourd, rapide, élégant ...),
  ce pourra être un cheval d'attelage léger, moyen ou
  lourd, un postier, un carrossier etc.

**castor oil**
huile de ricin
Rizinusöl
aceite de ricino

**castrate** => geld

**castrated horse** => gelding

**castration**
castration
Kastration *f*
castración ; capadura

**catheter**
cathéter ; sonde
Einführungssonde *f*
catéter

**caudal vertebrae** ; coccygeal vertebrae ; tail vertebrae
vertèbres caudales / coccygiennes
Schwanzwirbel *m* ; Steißwirbel
vértebras coccígeas ; vértebras de la cola
Le cheval peut en avoir de 12 à 21, elles forment le squelette de la queue. Leur nombre normal se situe entre 17 et 20, l'interprétation de ce nombre varie aussi du fait que seule la première, ou les deux premières, est/sont complète(s).

**cautery** => firing

**cavaletti** *sg & pl*
cavaletti *sg & pl*
Cavaletti *ne* ; Bodenrick *ne*
caballete
Low, moveable jump(s), the supporting arms are not crossed at right angles and the bar is attached in one of the closer angles between the two arms, thus offering two possibilities of height as an obstacle.
Petit obstacle dans lequel les supports ne sont pas fixés ensemble à angle droit, la barre est fixée entre ces supports, dans un des petits angles. La construction ainsi obtenue présente deux possibilités de hauteur comme obstacle.

**cavalry**
cavalerie
Reiterei *f* ; Truppen (berittene ~) *f pl* ; Kavallerie *f*
caballería

**cavalry horse**
cheval de cavalerie
Kavalleriepferd
caballo de ejército

**cavesson (lungeing / longeing / breaking ~)**
caveçon
Kappzaum
cabezón (de trabajo a cuerda)
Licol renforcé à l'avant, sur le dessus duquel on attache la longe.

**cecum / caecum** ; blindgut
caecum
Blinddarm *m* ; Zäkum / Zaekum *ne*
ciego (intestino ~)
Premier compartiment du gros intestin, il renferme habituellement une grande quantité de liquide.

**cement (of a tooth)**
cément (d'une dent)
Zahnzement
cemento

**central incisor** ; pincer
pince *dent*
Mittelzahn *m*
pinza ; incisivo (central)

**central incisors** ; pincers
pinces
Zangen
pinzas ; palas
They are two on each jaw.
Les plus centrales des incisives, elles sont au nombre de deux par mâchoire.

**central nervous system**
système nerveux central *abr: SNC* ; système nerveux cérébro-spinal
zentrales Nervensystem *(das ~) abr/abbr: ZNS*
sistema nervioso cerebroespinal / central *abr: SNC*
Comprend, entre autres, le cerveau, le cervelet, le bulbe et la moelle épinière, il commande les actes volontaires.

**centre of gravity**
centre de gravité
Schwerpunkt *m*
centro de gravedad

**cephalic vein**
veine céphalique
Vena cephalica
vena cefálica

**cerebellum**
cervelet
Kleinhirn *ne* ; Zerebellum *ne*
cerebelo
Coordonne l'activité des muscles et le maintien de l'équilibre.

**cervical vertebrae**
vertèbres cervicales
Halswirbel
vértebras cervicales
Le cheval en a sept.

**cervix of uterus** ; neck of uterus
col utérin
Gebärmutterhals *m* ; Cervix *f* ; Zervix
cuello uterino

**cestodes**
cestodes
Zestoden *m Klasse Cestoda*
cestodos
Group of parasites that includes tapeworms.
Groupe de parasites qui inclut les vers plats.

**chaff**
chaff *(1)* ; balle *(2)*
Häcksel *ne* ; Spreu *f* ; Kaff *ne*
cascabillo
Chopped hay or straw that is used to add bulk to food and encourage the horse to chew.
1) Mélange de grains et de paille ou de foin, hachés. 2) Mélange de fourrage et de paille hachée.

**chafing**
irritation
Entzündung *f*
irritación

**chain**
chaîne
Kette
cadena

**chalk** => favourite / favorite

## chambons
chambon
Chambon *ne*
chambón

## champ (the bit) *v* ; chew (the bit) *v*
mâcher le mors
am Gebiss kauen ; abkauen (am Gebiss)
masticar la embocadura

## change of direction
changement de direction
Richtungsänderung ; Richtungswechsel
cambio de dirección

In a ring the expression will often be used as an equivalent to the change of rein.

Dans un manège sera souvent confondu avec le changement de main.

## change of gait / pace
changement d'allure
Wechsel der Gangart
cambio de aire

## change of hand in / through the circle
changer (de main) dans le cercle
durch den Zirkel wechseln
cambio de rienda dentro del círculo

acad: Changement de main par deux demi-cercles dans le diamètre du cercle, c'est-à-dire la largeur, ou la demie de la longueur du manège.

## change of lead / leg
changement de pied
Galoppwechsel
cambio de pie

Action effectué par le cheval, cette notion n'a vraiment de sens qu'au galop.

## change of leg *v*
changer de pied
Galopp / Fuß wechseln
cambiar de pie

## change of leg in the air => flying change of lead / leg

## change of rein
changement de main
Handwechsel
cambio de mano

Changement de sens de déplacement dans un manège.

## change rein *v*
changer de main
Hand wechseln
cambiar de mano

## change (of lead) in the air *v*
changer de pied en l'air
Fuß fliegend wechseln *(den ~)*
cambiar de pie en el aire

## changing of coat => shedding

## chaps
jambières ; pantalon de cuir
Chaps *(die ~)*
chaparreras ; zahones *España*

## character
caractère
Charakter *m* ; Merkmal *ne Genetik*
carácter

## charger
cheval de troupe ; troupier
Truppenpferd
corcel

## Charolais *breed*
charolais
Charollais-Pferd
charollais

Race originaire du centre de la France.

## chart maker ; sheetwriter
statisticien
Statistiker(in) *m(f)*
estadista ; estadístico

The sheetwriter is the person who notes the results of a race on US racetracks.

## cheat *v*
tricher
mogeln ; schummeln
trampear

## cheating
tricherie
Schummelei *f* ; Mogelei *f*
trampa ; fullería

## cheek => branch (of a bit)

## cheek
joue
Backe *f* ; Wange *f*
carrillo ; mejilla

Spécifiquement, la joue s'étend de la commissure des lèvres, au chanfrein, à l'oeil, à la région parotidienne et à la ganache. Elle comprend donc la poche de la joue et le plat de la joue.

## cheekbone => zygomatic bone

## cheekpiece
montant (de bride // muserolle)
Backenriemen *m* ; Backenstück *ne*
carrillera ; quijera ; mejillera ; pieza para mejilla

## Chef d'équipe
chef d'équipe
Equipenchef *m* ; Chef d'Equipe
jefe de equipo

## cherry bay ; bright bay
bai cerise ; bai acajou
Kirschbrauner
bayo cereza

Bright reddish coat.
D'un rouge vif.

## chest
poitrine
Brust *f*
pecho

The words chest and thorax are often used as synonyms. Specifically, the thorax includes the withers and the upper back. The chest usually designates only the ventral border (around the sternum) and part of the sides of the thorax.

On utilise souvent indistinctement les désignations poitrine et thorax. Le thorax a pour base osseuse la cage thoracique, laquelle est formée des vertèbres thoraciques, des côtes et, ventralement, du sternum. Le thorax inclut donc le garrot et la partie supérieure du dos. Le mot poitrine désigne plutôt le bord ventral et une partie des côtés du thorax.

**chestnut** *(1)* ; sorrel *(2)*
alezan *adj & n*
Fuchs *m* ; fuchsfarbig ; Isabelle *f (2)*
alazán

  Coat ranging from a yellowish / reddish to a brownish shade. 1) Medium and darker shades: lower limbs, mane and tail are usually the same or darker than the body. 2) Lighter shades: lower limbs, mane and tail are usually the same or lighter than the body.

  Robe allant du jaune au roux et comportant des tons fauves, rougeâtres, cuivrés, dorés etc., les crins et les extrémités sont de la même couleur mais peuvent être plus ou moins foncés.

**chestnut**
châtaigne ; torus carpien // tarsien
Kastanie *f* ; Karpalballen
espejuelo

  Corne irrégulière présente sur la face interne des jambes du cheval.

**chest cavity**  => thoracic cavity

**cheval de frise**
cheval de frise
spanischer Reiter *(der ~)*
caballo de frisa

**chew (the bit)**  => champ (the bit)

**chin groove** ; curb groove
barbe ; passage de la gourmette
Kinngrube *(die ~)* ; Kinnkettengrube *f*
barba

  Région située en arrière du menton.

**chin (swelling)**
menton (houppe du ~)
Kinn
mentón ; barba ; barbilla

  Région comprise entre la lèvre inférieure et la barbe.

**chivalry** ; knighthood
chevalerie
Rittertum *ne*
caballería

**chlorine**
chlore
Chlor *ne*
cloro

**chopped straw**
paille hachée
Häcksel
paja picada / cortada

**chromosome**
chromosome
Chromosom *ne*
cromosoma

**chronic laminitis**  => founder

**chronic obstructive pulmonary disease**
  => asthma

**cinch**  => girth

**cinch cover**  => girth cover

**circle** *acad*
grande volte ; cercle *acad*
Zirkel
círculo

  Cercle de plus de six mètres de diamètre, habituellement dans toute la largeur du manège.

**circumference of cannon bone**  =>
  cannon's circumference

**circumference of chest**  => girth's
  circumference

**circus rider**
écuyer de cirque
Zirkusreiter
jinete de circo

**clear an obstacle** *v*
franchir un obstacle
Hindernis überwinden (ein ~)
franquear un obstáculo

**clear (jump ~)** *v*
sauter juste / net
sauber springen
saltar limpio

**clear (round)**
parcours sans fautes
fehlerloser Ritt *(der ~)*
recorrido sin faltas

**click (of the tongue)** ; clucking ; tongue clicking
claquement de langue ; appel de langue
Zungenschlag
chasquido (de la lengua)

**clincher(s) / clencher(s) (nail ~)** ; clinching tongs
pince(s) à river ; tenaille(s) serre-clou
Hufnietzange *(die ~)* ; Nietzange
tenaza de remachar ; apretador de clavos

  Different models are available.
  Il existe différents modèles.

**clinching tongs**  => clincher(s) / clencher(s)
  (nail ~)

**clip** *v*
tondre
scheren
esquilar ; trasquilar ; rasurar

**clip** *n*
pinçon
Aufzug eines Hufeisens *(der ~)* ; Kappe *f* ; Griff *m*
pestaña ; agarradera

  Petites languettes tirées du fer (ou soudées sur celui-ci) et appuyant sur la paroi du sabot.

**clipper**
tondeuse
Schermaschine *(die ~)*
máquina de rasurar ; esquilador

**close-coupled**  => short-coupled

**close breeding**  => inbreeding

**close to the ground**  => well let down

**clover**
trèfle
Klee
trébol

**club foot**
pinçard (cheval / pied ~) *(1)* ; pied rampin *(2)* ;
    pied bot *(3)*
Bockhuf *m* ; steiler Huf ; Stelzhuf *m (1)*
pie zopo
  Ranging from cases where a slight contracture of the
tendons causes too much weight bearing on the toe,
sometimes bearing only on the toe (« pied pinçard »), to
cases where the horse walks on the front of the hoof
wall (« pied bot »). *s.a. knuckling*
  1) Lorsque le pied appuie seulement sur la pince. 2)
Lorsque la pince est renversée. 3) Lorsque, dans un cas
encore plus exagéré, le cheval marche sur le devant de
sa muraille.

**clucking**  => click (of the tongue)

**Clydesdale (horse)** *breed*
clydesdale
Clydesdale
clydesdale
  Race de trait, d'origine écossaise.

**coach**  => trainer

**coach**
carrosse
Kutsche
coche

**coachman**
cocher
Kutscher *m*
cochero

**coach horse**  => cart-horse

**coat**  => jacket

**coat**
pelage (le ~) ; poil (le ~) ; poils (les ~)
Haarkleid *ne* ; Haardecke *f*
pelaje ; pelo(s) ; capa

**coat (colour)** ; robe ; color *US* ; colour *Brit*
robe
Farbe *f*
pelaje ; capa
  Constituée par l'ensemble des poils et des crins du
cheval.

**cobby**  => short-coupled

**coccygeal vertebrae**  => caudal vertebrae

**cochlea**
cochlée ; limaçon (de l'oreille) *anc*
Schnecke *f*
caracol

**cockade**  => rosette

**cocked ankle**  => knuckling (over)

**coefficient of relationship**
coefficient de consanguinité
Verwandtschaftskoeffizient
coeficiente de parentesco

**coffin bone**  => distal phalanx

**coffin joint** ; pedal joint ; distal interphalangeal
    joint
articulation du pied ; deuxième art. interphalan-
    gienne ; art. interphalangienne distale
Hufgelenk ; drittes Zehengelenk
segunda articulación interfalangiana ; articulación
    interfalangiana distal
  Implique la deuxième phalange, la troisième et le petit
sésamoïde.

**coldblood ; cold-blooded (horse)**
cheval à sang froid
Kaltblüter *m* ; Kaltblut *ne unzählbar* ; kaltblütige
    Schlag *(der ~)*
caballo linfático ; caballo de raza de tempera-
    mento frío
  Rather heavy horse, strong and with a calm temperament.

**colic**
colique
Kolik *f*
cólico
  n: Douleur abdominale dont l'origine est le plus souvent le tractus digestif. adj: Qui se rapporte au côlon.

**collar** *hd*
collier *att*
Kumt ; Kummt ; Kummet
collera ; collerón ; collar

**collect** *v*
placer
stellen (an die Hilfen / Zügel ~)
colocar el caballo en la rienda
  To collect the horse up to the bit.
  Placer le cheval au moyen des aides, bien rassemblé,
sur la main et entre les jambes.

**collected**
rassemblé
beigezäumt
reunido

**collected canter / gallop**
galop rassemblé
versammelter Galopp
galope reunido

**collected trot**
trot rassemblé
versammelter Trab
trote reunido

**collected trot sitting**
trot rassemblé assis
versammelter Trab ausgesessen
trote reunido sentado

**collected walk**
pas rassemblé
versammelte Schritt *(der ~)*
paso reunido

**collection (of a horse)**
rassembler (d'un cheval) *n*
Versammlung *(die ~)*
reunión ; colección

**collect (a horse)** *v*
rassembler (un cheval) *v*
versammeln
reunir

**colon**
côlon
Kolon *ne* ; Grimmdarm *m*
colon
Portion of the large intestine, includes ascending, transverse and descending parts.
Partie du gros intestin, entre le caecum et le rectum.

**color** => coat (colour)

**colostrum**
colostrum
Kolostralmilch *f* ; Kolostrum *ne*
colostro ; calostro
The first milk, secreted at the end of pregnancy.
Premier lait de la jument, il est laxatif et très nutritif, et a une fonction immunitaire pour le poulain.

**colour** => coat (colour)

**colt**
poulain (mâle entier)
Hengstfohlen ; Junghengst
potro macho / entero
An entire male horse, from birth till he is considered as an adult, which depends on breeds and disciplines (usually from three to five years old).
De la naissance jusqu'à ce qu'il soit considéré comme un adulte, ce qui dépend des races et des disciplines (en général de trois à cinq ans).

**comb**
peigne
Kamm *m*
peine ; peineta

**combination (of obstacles)**
combinaison (d'obstacles)
Kombination *f*
combinación (de obstáculos)

**common calcanean / calcaneal tendon** ; Achilles' tendon
tendon calcanéen commun ; tendon d'Achille ; corde du jarret
Fersensehnenstrang *m* ; Achillessehne *f*
tendón de Aquiles
The term common calcaneal tendon is convenient to designate the aggregated tendons (including the Achille or calcaneal tendon) which are attached to the calcaneal tuber.
Plus précisément, le tendon d'Achille ou calcanéen fait partie du tendon calcanéen commun ou corde du jarret chez le cheval.

**common digital extensor muscle** ; long digital extensor m. ; anterior digital extensor m. *old* ; extensor pedis m. *old*
muscle extenseur dorsal du doigt ; m. extenseur commun des doigts ; m. extenseur antérieur des phalanges *anc*
gemeinsamer Zehenstrecker
músculo extensor común digital / de las falanges
This muscle includes a major head (the specific French term « m. ext. dorsal du doigt ») and two vestiges of the proper extensors of the digits, sometimes called « m. of Phillips » and « m. of Thiernesse ».
Le cheval n'ayant qu'un doigt complet, le terme m. ext. commun des doigts (s'appliquant de façon générale aux ongulés) implique quelques subtilités. Ce muscle comporte une partie principale (m. ext. dorsal du doigt); une branche accessoire située latéralement que l'on appelle parfois « m. de Philips » correspond au véritable muscle extenseur commun des doigts des ruminants. Une autre branche mineure peut exister, elle est appelée « m. de Thiernesse », et est un vestige d'un autre extenseur de doigts disparus.

**common (digital) extensor tendon** ; extensor pedis t. *old* ; t. of common digital extensor ; dorsal digital extensor t.
tendon de l'extenseur dorsal du doigt ; t. extenseur des phalanges ; t. de l'extenseur antérieur des phalanges / du doigt *anc*
Strecksehne
tendón extensor digital
S'attache au sommet de la troisième phalange.

**compact** => short-coupled

**competition against the clock** => scurry jumping (with time factor)

**competition with jump-off**
épreuve de précision *cs* ; épreuve avec barrage *cs*
Prüfung mit Stechen *(die ~)*
prueba con desempate

**complainant**
plaignant
Kläger(in) *m(f)*
demandante

**complaint**
plainte
Klage *f*
demanda

**conchofrontal sinus** => frontal sinus

**confidence**
confiance
Vertrauen
confianza

**conformation**
conformation ; morphologie
Körperbau *(der ~)*
conformación
The build of a horse.
Manière dont est organisé ou assemblé le corps du cheval.

**conformation judging** => judgment of (external) conformation

**congenital**
congénital
angeboren ; kongenital
congénito

**conjunctiva**
conjonctive
Bindehaut
conjuntiva
Membrane conjonctive de l'oeil.

**conjunctivitis**
conjonctivite
Lidbindehautentzündung *(die ~)*
conjuntivitis

**Connemara (pony)** *breed* ; Hobbie
connemara
Connemarapony
connemara
Race d'origine irlandaise.

**consanguinity**
consanguinité
Blutgemeinschaft
consanguinidad

**consistency** => regularity

**contact**
contact
Kontakt *m*
contacto

**contact with the bit (horse moving into a ~)**
appui
Anlehnung *f*
apoyo de la boca
Action du cheval qui prend contact, par sa bouche, avec le mors.

**contagious equine metritis** *abbr: CEM*
métrite équine contagieuse
kontagiöse equine Metritis *(die ~)*
metritis contagiosa equina

**control of the horse**
contrôle du cheval
Pferd in der Gewalt haben
control del caballo

**control the hindquarters** *v*
maître de l'arrière-main (être ~)
Hinterhand beherrschen
dominar el posterior

**contusion** => bruise

**contusion of the sole** => bruise (of the sole)

**convex face** => roman nose

**cooler (horse ~)**
couverture de refroidissement
Abschwitzdecke *f*
manta para enfriar

**copper**
cuivre
Kupfer *ne*
cobre

**corium** => dermis

**corn** ; maize
maïs
Mais
maíz

**cornea**
cornée
Kornea ; Hornhaut des Auges
córnea

**corner**
coin
Ecke *f*
rincón
Corner of a riding ring.
Coin d'une piste ou d'un manège.

**corner incisor**
coin
Eckzahn ; Eckschneidezahn *m*
incisivo del borde
One of the incisors, there is two of them on each jaw.
Une des incisives, il y en a deux par mâchoire.

**corner of the lips**
commissure des lèvres
Maulwinkel
comisura de los labios

**coronary band**
bourrelet générateur de la corne ; bourrelet principal
Fleischkrone
banda coronaria
The word « bourrelet » is usually used to designate both the coronary corium and the coronary cushion at once, we might think that these two are forming the coronary band, a term that is sometimes used to include the external coronet as well.
Formation de chair dont la couche kératogène (le chorion coronaire) nourrit la corne du sabot. Le bourrelet se situe dans le sillon coronaire, au bord supérieur du sabot et se termine au niveau des glomes. Il possède une couche interne de fibres élastiques (le coussinet coronaire).

**coronet**
couronne
Krone *f*
corona (del casco)
Area where hair stops and hoof growth begins at the bottom of the pastern.
Relief aux trois-quarts circulaire où le sabot commence au bas du paturon.

**corpus luteum** => yellow body

**costal arch**
arc costal
Rippenbogen *m*
arco costal

**costal cartilage**
cartilage costal
Rippenknorpel
cartílagos de las costillas
Relie un os costal (os d'une côte vraie ou sternale) au sternum.

**cough** *v*
tousser
husten
toser

**cough** *n*
toux
Husten *m*
tos

**counter-canter** => canter counter-lead

**counter-change of hand** ; zigzag half-pass
contre-changement de main ; zigzag
Konter-Wechsel *m* ; Zick-Zack / Zickzack Traversale *(die ~)*
contracambio de mano ; zig-zag
The « Zick-Zack Traversalen », and probably other zig-zag related terms, are series of counter-changes of hand at half-pass, i.e. series of half-passes performed in zig-zag.
Quittant la piste comme dans le changement de main, arrivé au centre on prend l'autre diagonale pour revenir juste avant l'autre coin du côté que l'on vient de quitter. L'expression allemande « Zick-Zack Traversalen », ainsi que sans doute les expressions reliées à zigzag, désignent une série de contre-changements de main que

le cheval exécute sur deux pistes, c'est-à-dire en appuyer d'un côté puis de l'autre.

**coupling**  => breeding

**course**
parcours
Parcours
recorrido

**course designer**
dessinateur de parcours
Parcourschef *(der ~)*
diseñador (del curso)

**course of obstacles**
parcours d'obstacles
Sprungfolge ; Springbahn ; Hindernisparcours
recorrido de obstáculos

**covering disease**  => dourine

**covering of mare**  => service

**covering station**  => service station

**cover (a mare)** *v* ; serve *v*
saillir (une jument) ; servir ; couvrir ; monter
decken ; springen
montar ; cubrir ; saltar ; dar servicio
  For a male horse, to copulate with a mare.
  Action du cheval mâle qui s'accouple par les voies gé-nitales naturelles avec une jument.

**cowboy**
vacher ; cow-boy
Cowboy
vaquero

**cowlick**  => whorl

**cow-belly**
ventre avalé ; ventre de vache ; ventre tombant
Heubauch *m* ; Grasbauch ; Kuhbauch ;
  Hängebauch
barriga de vaca
  Ventre trop volumineux.

**coxal tuber** ; tuber coxae
tuber coxae ; angle de la hanche *ostéologie*
Hüfthöcker
tuberosidad coxal

**crack (hoof ~)**  => sandcrack / sand crack

**cranium**  => skull

**crease nail puller**
pince arrache-clous / tire-clous
Nagelziehzange *(die ~)*
pinzas para sacar los clavos de la clavera
  Used to remove driven nails from creased shoes.
  Pince pour retirer les clous dans les rainures.

**crest**
crête (de l'encolure)
Mähnenkamm *m*
pescuezo ; cresta (del cuello)

**cribbing**  => crib biting

**crib biting** ; cribbing
tic aérophagique (à l'appui) ; tic à l'appui
Krippensetzen *ne* ; Aufsetzkoppen
tiro de apoyo
  A vice, the horse presses down on something with the upper incisor teeth and swallows air.
  Tic du cheval qui avale de l'air en appuyant ses dents sur quelque chose.

**Criollo**
créole *adj & n* ; criollo
Criollo ; Crioller
criollo
  Terme générique pour les races de chevaux dévelop-pées en Amérique du Sud. Ce sont des descendants des chevaux amenés par Colomb, Cortés, Mendoza et Pizarro.

**crop** ; cutting whip ; riding whip
cravache
Reitgerte *f* ; Reitpeitsche
fusta (de montar) ; fuete

**crossbred (animal)**
métis
Mischling ; Mischblut
producto de cruza
  Rejeton de deux géniteurs de races différentes.

**crossing**  => cross-breeding ; crossbreeding

**cross-breeding ; crossbreeding** ; inter-breeding ; crossing
croisement
Kreuzung(zucht)
cruzamiento (método de crianza por ~)
  The mating of two individuals of different breeds.
  Accouplement de deux reproducteurs de races diffé-rentes.

**cross-country course**
parcours de cross
Querfeldeinstrecke *(die ~)*
recorrido a campo través

**cross-country horse**
cheval de cross-country ; cheval d'extérieur *class.*
Geländepferd
caballo campero

**cross-over noseband** ; Grackle noseband ; figure 8 noseband
muserolle en forme de 8 ; muserolle croisée
mexikanische Reithalfter *(das ~)*
muserola de ocho
  Made of two straps, one above and one below the bit, crossing at angles on the horse's nose. The original Grackle was an elaborate cross-over noseband.
  Formée de deux bandes, une passant de chaque côté du mors, et se croisant sur le nez du cheval.

**cross canter / gallop**  => disunited canter

**cross country riding**
équitation d'extérieur
Geländeritt
equitación de exterior

**croup** ; rump
croupe *f*
Kruppe *f*
grupa
   Partie limitée par la queue, le rein, la cuisse et la partie supérieure de la fesse.

**crownpiece**  => headpiece

**cruelty**
cruauté
Grausamkeit
crueldad

**crupper dock**
culeron *att*
Schweifmetze *f*
baticola

**cryptorchid** *adj* ; ridgling ; ridgeling ; risling *n* ; rig *adj*
cryptorchide *adj* ; vert *adj* ; pif *adj* & *n*
Kryptorchide *m*
criptórquido ; cryptorchidio
   Male horse with one or, rarely, both testicle(s) retained in the abdomen.
   Cheval dont l'un ou, rarement, les deux testicule(s) demeure(nt) inapparent(s).

**cryptorchidism ; cryptorchism**
cryptorchidie ; cryptorchisme
Kryptorchismus *m*
criptorquidia ; cryptorchidismo

**cubbing ; cub-hunting**
chasse au renardeau
Jungfuchsjagd
caza de cachorro / zorrillo

**cubitus**  => ulna

**cull** *v*
sélectionner (pour élimination) ; éliminer
merzen ; ausrangieren
eliminar

**cup**
cuillère ; cuiller
Auflage *f*
soporte
   As a part on an obstacle, a shaped holder for one end of a pole.
   Dans un obstacle, pièce portée par le chandelier et dont la partie plus ou moins courbe supporte une extrémité d'une barre.

**curb**
jarde
Hasenhacke *f*
corva ; corvaza
   Thickening of the plantar tarsal ligament in the hock of the horse. It is obvious a few inches below the point of the hock.
   Inflammation du ligament plantaire long du jarret au point d'attache avec l'os métatarsien principal et l'os rudimentaire externe.

**curby conformation**  => sickle hock(s)

**curb-rein**
rêne (de mors) de bride
Stangenzügel ; Kandarenzügel
rienda del bocado

**curb bit** ; Weymouth (curb bit) *class. (1)*
mors de bride ; mors à levier *west.*
Reitkandare *f* ; Kandare *f* ; Kandarenmundstück *ne*
bocado ; freno de palanca / curva
   1) May be fixed-cheek or slide-cheek, used in the double bridle.
   Dans la bride complète, le mors de bride repose devant le filet et, ayant une branche supérieure et une inférieure, agit sur les barres et sur la nuque.

**curb chain**
gourmette ; chaînette
Kinnkette *f*
barbada ; cadenilla / cadena (para la brida)

**curb groove**  => chin groove

**curry** *v*
étriller
striegeln
almohazar ; rasquetear

**currycomb**
étrille *f*
Striegel *m*
almohaza ; rasqueta

**curve**  => flexion

**cutaneous blowfly myiasis** ; calliphorine myiasis ; blowfly strike
myase / myiase cutanée
Hautmyiasis *f*
miasis del gusano barrenado
   Caused by Calliphoridae.

**cutaneus trunci muscle**
muscle cutané du tronc
Rumpfhautmuskel
músculo cutáneo abdominal

**cutting nipper**  => nipper(s) (hoof ~)

**cutting whip**  => crop

**cyst**
kyste
Zyste *f*
quiste
   1° Membrane sécrétée pour isoler un corps étranger qui s'est introduit dans un organisme. 2° Forme dans laquelle se conservent, dans le sol, les femelles de certains nématodes et leur ponte.

**cysticercosis** ; measles
ladrerie ; cysticercose
Zystizerkose *f* ; Finnenbefall *m*
cisticercosis muscular ; ladrería
   Infestation de certains muscles par des formes larvaires de certaines variétés de taenia.

**daily ration**
ration journalière
Tagesration *f*
ración diaria

**dam**
mère
Mutter *f* ; Muttertier *ne*
madre (yegua ~)
   A mother of horse(s).

30

**dapple(d) grey / gray**
gris pommelé
Äpfelschimmel *m veränderlich*
tordo / tordillo rodado
Two shades of grey resulting in darker circles or mottling on a lighter ground.
Avec des taches rondes ou zones foncées, sur un fond plus clair.

**dark chestnut** ; mahogany chestnut *US*
alezan foncé
Dunkelfuchs *m*
alazán obscuro / oscuro
Robe tirant sur le brun.

**dark grey** ; sad grey *old* ; powdered grey *old*
gris foncé
Schwarz-Schimmel ; Schwarzschimmel
*veränderlich*
tordo obscuro
A grey coat with mainly dark hairs.
Robe grise à forte prédominance des poils foncés.

**dark head**
cap de maure / more *n* ; tête de maure
Mohrenkopf
cabeza de moro
Tête très foncée et différente du reste de la robe.

**daughter**
fille
Tochter *(die ~)*
hija

**deciduous teeth** => milk teeth

**declaration** => entry

**deep digital flexor muscle** *forelimb* ; flexor perforans muscle *old*
muscle fléchisseur profond du doigt / des phalanges *membre antérieur* ; muscle perforant *anc* ; muscle fléchisseur externe / péronéal des phalanges *anc*
tiefer Zehenbeuger ; Hufbeinbeuger
músculo flexor digital profundo
Le plus puissant des deux fléchisseurs du doigt.

**deep (digital) flexor tendon**
tendon (du) fléchisseur profond (des phalanges / du doigt) ; tendon (du) perforant
tiefe Beugesehne ; Hufbeinbeugesehne
tendón flexor digital profundo ; tendón flexor profundo (de las falanges)
Descend contre la face antérieure du fléchisseur superficiel, il passe entre les deux branches de ce dernier, (il le « perfore »), et s'attache à la face inférieure de la troisième phalange.

**deer fly**
mouche du cerf / daim *Eur* ; mouche du chevreuil *Can.*
Goldaugenbremse *f*
mosca de ciervo
Blood-sucking fly of the family Tabanidae.
Taon, de la famille des tabanidés (Tabanidae).

**defect** ; blemish *(1)*
défaut ; tare *(1)*
Fehler *m*
tara ; defecto
1) Defect that does not interfere with the horse's action and function.
1) Défaut physique. On parle aussi de tare molle (d'origine synoviale) et de tare dure (d'origine osseuse).

**defence** => resistance

**deferent duct** ; ductus deferens
conduit déférent
Samenleiter
conducto deferente

**degree of training** ; training level
niveau d'entraînement
Ausbildungsgrad *m*
grado de entrenamiento

**dehydration**
déshydratation
Austrocknung *f*
deshidratación

**deltoid(eus) muscle**
muscle deltoïde
Deltamuskel
músculo deltoides

**dental table** ; grinding surface ; table surface
table dentaire
Reibfläche *f des Zahnes*
tabla dentaria ; superficie moledora
The masticatory surface of a tooth.
Extrémité externe d'une dent, sur laquelle s'exerce l'usure.

**dentine**
ivoire (d'une dent) ; dentine
Zahnbein ; Dentin
marfil

**dentition**
dentition
Zahnen
dentición

**depraved appetite** => pica

**depth of chest**
profondeur de la poitrine
Brusttiefe *f*
profundidad del pecho

**depth of flank**
profondeur des flancs / de l'abdomen
Flankentiefe *f* ; Bauchtiefe
profundidad de los flancos / del abdomen

**derby (hunt ~)** => bowler (hat)

**dermatitis**
dermatite
Dermatitis *f* ; Hautentzündung *f*
dermatitis ; dermitis
Inflammation of the skin.
Inflammation de la peau.

**dermatophytosis** => ringworm

**dermatosis**
dermatose
Hautkrankheit *f*
dermatosis

**dermis** ; corium
derme ; chorion
Lederhaut *f* ; Korium *ne*
dermis

Disposé sous l'épiderme, c'est la partie sensible qui nourrit et entretient la partie insensible de la surface. Dans le pied il s'agit du bourrelet principal, du bourrelet périoplique, des lamelles podophylleuses et du tissu velouté.

**descendants (the ~)**
descendance (la ~) ; descendants (les ~)
Nachkommenschaft
descendencia
*s.a. pedigree*

**description**
signalement
Signalement *ne*
filiación

Description of the physical characteristics of a horse.
Description permettant d'identifier un cheval, il peut inclure la robe et ses particularités ainsi que la taille du cheval.

**destroy a horse** *v* ; put a horse to sleep *v*
abattre un cheval ; euthanasier
Pferd töten (ein ~) ; Pferd schlachten ; Pferd euthanasieren
eutanasiar un caballo

**deworm** *v*
vermifuger
entwurmen
desparasitar ; quitar las lombrices

**dewormer** => anthelmintic (drug)

**dew claw** => ergot

**diagonal aid**
aide diagonale
diagonale Hilfe *(die ~)*
ayuda diagonal

Aide qui est appliquée simultanément des deux côtés du cheval, par exemple: jambe gauche en même temps que main droite.

**diagonal pair**
bipède diagonal
diagonale Beinpaar *(das ~)*
bípedo diagonal

The front foot moving or working with the hind foot from the opposite side.
aire de membres formée par l'antérieur d'un côté et le postérieur de l'autre.

**diaphragm**
diaphragme
Diaphragma *ne* ; Zwerchfell *ne*
diafragma

**diarrhea** => diarrhoea

**diarrhoea** *Brit* ; diarrhea *US* ; scour(s) ; scouring
diarrhée
Durchfall *m* ; Diarrhö(e) *f* ; Ruhr *f*
diarrea

**difficult horse** => unruly horse

**digestive system**
système digestif
Verdauungssystem
aparato digestivo

**digestive tract**
tube digestif
Verdauungskanal
tubo digestivo

Comprend la bouche, l'oesophage, l'estomac, les intestins et le rectum, il mesure environ trente-trois mètres chez le cheval.

**digital cushion** ; plantar cushion
coussinet digital / plantaire ; coussin plantaire
Strahlkissen *ne* ; Strahlpolster
cojinete digital / plantar

Doté d'une grande élasticité, il occupe une partie importante de la moitié postérieure du pied.

**dipped back** => saddle-back

**dip in front of the withers** ; camel neck
coup de hache
Axthieb *m*
golpe de hacha

Dépression en avant du garrot.

**discharge**
écoulement
Ausfluß *m* ; Auswurf *m*
secreción

**disease** ; illness
maladie
Krankheit *f*
enfermedad

**disease(s) (horse / equine ~)**
maladie(s) des chevaux
Pferdekrankheit(en)
enfermedad(es) del ganado caballar

**dish** => dished (face)

**dish** => paddle

**dished (face)** ; dish-face(d) ; stag face ; dish *n (1)*
concave *adj*
Hechtkopf *m* ; konkaver Kopf
cara cóncava

Markedly concave (depressed) lateral profile of the head, usual on Arab horses. 1) The dish being the indentation itself.
Profil du chanfrein, habituel chez le cheval arabe.

**dish-face(d)** => dished (face)

**dismount** *v*
démonter ; descendre de cheval ; mettre pied à terre
absitzen ; absteigen
desmontar ; descabalgar

**disobedience**
désobéissance
Ungehorsam *(der ~)* ; Verweigerung
desobediencia

**disqualification**
disqualification
Disqualifikation *f*
descalificación

**distal interphalangeal joint** => coffin joint

32

**distal phalanx** ; coffin bone ; os pedis *old* ; pedal bone *old* ; third phalanx
phalange distale ; troisième phalange ; os du pied ; phalange unguéale *anc*
Hufbein *ne* ; Klauenbein ; Krallenbein
tercera falange ; hueso del pie / casco ; hueso podal
Criblé(e) de petits orifices laissant passer des vaisseaux sanguins et des filaments nerveux.

**distal sesamoid bone** ; navicular bone *old* ; shuttle bone *old*
os petit sésamoïde ; os sésamoïde distal ; os naviculaire *anc*
Strahlbein *ne*
sesamoideo distal ; hueso navicular
Sa forme générale est celle d'une navette de tisserand, d'où son ancien nom (qui est officiellement réservé aujourd'hui à l'os central du tarse). Il s'articule contre la partie postérieure de la deuxième phalange, le tendon du fléchisseur profond des phalanges coulisse sur sa face inférieure.

**distance**
distance
Abstand *m* ; Distanz *f*
distancia

**distemper (equine ~)** => strangles

**disunited canter** ; cross canter / gallop ; broken canter
galop désuni
Kreuzgalopp *(der ~)*
galope desunido ; galope cruzado

**ditch**
fossé
Graben
foso ; zanja

**ditch with rail(s)**
fossé barré ; trakehnen *obstacle*
Trakehner (Graben) *(der ~)* ; Graben mit Stange / Bodenrick *(der ~)*
foso con barrera ; vertical sobre zanja

**docile**
docile
gehorsam
dócil
Se dit du cheval qui a bon caractère.

**docility**
docilité
Folgsamkeit *f* ; Gehorsam *m* ; Gelehrigkeit ; Willigkeit
docilidad

**dock** *n* ; base of the tail
base de la queue ; coire
Schweifrübe *f* ; Schwanzwurzel
maslo
The solid bony part of the horse's tail.

**dock** *v*
courtauder ; tronçonner ; écourter ; écouer
kupieren *Schweif*
truncar (la cola) ; troncar ; descolar
To cut short the tail of the horse.
Raccourcir ou couper la queue d'un cheval. Hormis les cas de nécessité, ce procédé est limité aux chevaux

d'attelage dans certains pays alors qu'il est très mal vu, voire illégal, dans d'autres.

**docked tail(ed)** ; **docked** ; bob tailed
courte queue *n & adj* ; courtaudé *adj* ; courtaud *n & adj*
Stummelschweif ; Schwanzstumpf ; Schwanzstummel
cola cortada ; rabón *adj*
A section of the tail bones has been removed.
Dont la queue a été amputée (écourtée).

**donkey** ; ass
âne (en général) ; baudet
Esel *m* ; Hausesel
asno

**donkey foal** ; ass's foal
ânon
Eselfüllen / Eselfohlen *ne*
asno joven ; buche

**donkey stallion** ; jack ; he-ass
âne (mâle) ; baudet
Eselhengst *m*
burro ; garañón

**donkey stripe** => dorsal stripe / list / band

**Don (horse)** *breed*
don ; cheval du Don
Donpferd / Don-Pferd
don
Chevaux de selle d'origine russe.

**doping**
dopage
Doping *ne*
drogado

**dorsal digital extensor tendon** => common (digital) extensor tendon

**dorsal stripe / list / band** ; donkey stripe ; eel stripe
raie de mulet
Aalstrich *m*
raya de mulo
A dark stripe down the spine, from the mane to the base of the tail, it can occur on any coat colour.
Bande plus foncée allant du garrot à la base de la queue.

**dosage**
posologie
Dosierung *f*
posología

**double bridle** ; Weymouth bridle
bride double ; bride complète
Kandarenzaum ; Stangenzaum
brida completa; brida doble
With, or designed for, a bridoon bit and a curb bit.
Munie de, ou destinée à recevoir, deux embouchures: mors de filet et mors de bride.

**double jointed mouthpiece** ; link (mouthpiece
with ~) ; spatula (mouthpiece with ~)
double brisure (embouchure à ~) ; trois pièces
(embouchure à ~)
doppelgliedrige Trense
doble articulación (embocadura con ~)
 « Link snaffle » or any mouthpiece « with (centre) link
/ spatula ».
 Dont les deux canons sont réunis par une pièce cen-
trale.

**double (obstacle)**
double (obstacle / combinaison ~)
zweifache Kombination *(die ~)*
obstáculo doble ; combinación doble

**dourine** ; covering disease
dourine ; mal du coït ; syphilis du cheval
Beschälseuche *f*
durina ; mal del coito
 Sexually transmitted disease caused by Trypanosoma
equiperdum.

**draft horse** => draught horse

**drag-hunting**
chasse sur une piste artificielle / odorante
Schleppjagd
caza de arrastre

**draught horse** *Brit* ; draft horse *US*
cheval de trait
Zugpferd *ne* ; Wirtschaftspferd
caballo de tiro
 Les chevaux de trait lourd sont conformés pour travail-
ler surtout en puissance à des allures lentes. Les
chevaux de trait léger sont destinés à tirer des charges
moins lourdes à des allures plus vives.

**draw**
tirage au sort
Losen ; Auslosen
sorteo

**drawing knife** => hoof knife

**draw rein**
rêne allemande
Schlaufzügel *m*
rienda de plancha
 Fastening usually to the girth, it passes through the bit
rings back to the rider's hands.
 Elle coulisse dans un anneau du filet et va habituellement s'attacher à la sangle.

**dray horse** ; lorry / lorrie horse ; van horse ;
carrier's horse
cheval de camionnage ; cheval de roulage
Industriepferd ; Camionnage-Pferd
caballo de tiro industrial
 The horses used for trotting work were lighter than
those used for walking.

**dress** => pare (a hoof)

**dressage** => training

**dressage competition**
concours de dressage ; compétition de dressage
Dressurprüfung
concurso de doma clásica
 *s.a. dressage test*

**dressage horse**
cheval de dressage
Dressurpferd
caballo de doma clásica

**dressage rider**
cavalier de dressage
Dressurreiter *m*
jinete de doma

**dressage ring / arena**
rectangle de dressage
Dressurviereck *ne*
cuadrilongo (de doma) ; pista de doma

**dressage saddle**
selle de dressage
Dressursattel
silla de doma

**dressage seat**
position de dressage
Dressursitz *m*
asiento de adiestramiento

**dressage test**
reprise
Dressuraufgabe *ne*
reprise
 Dans un concours de dressage, on parle en général de
reprise pour désigner le test à être exécuté. En français,
le mot reprise désigne aussi la chorégraphie exécutée
dans une épreuve ou dans le travail de manège en
dehors de la compétition.

**dressage test**
épreuve de dressage
Dressurprüfung *f*
prueba de doma (clásica)
 Dans un concours complet on parle d'épreuve de dressage, de la même façon que d'épreuve de fond et
d'épreuve de saut.

**dressage whip**
cravache de dressage
Dressurgerte *f* ; Dressurpeitsche *f*
fuete de adiestramiento / dressage ; fusta de
 dressage

**dressage (classical ~)**
dressage (classique)
Dressur *f*
doma clásica

**dressing** *for wounds*
pansement
Verband *(der ~)*
cura

**drinking trough** => water(ing) trough

**driver** => jockey

**driver** *bd*
conducteur (d'un attelage) ; meneur
Fahrer *m* ; Gespannführer *m*
conductor (de carruaje)

**driving whip**
fouet (d'attelage)
Fahrpeitsche
látigo de coche ; fuete de tiro

**droppings** ; dung ; faeces *Brit* ; feces *US* ;
  bowel movement
crottin *m sg, comptable ou non* ; crottins *pl* ; fèces ;
  selle
Pferdeäpfel *m pl* ; Stuhlgang *m*
cagajón / cagajones ; heces

**drop a foal** => foal

**drug** => medicine

**drug** *prohibited substance*
drogue
Dopingmittel *ne*
droga

**dry ditch**
fossé sec
trockene Graben *m*
zanja seca

**ductus deferens** => deferent duct

**dull coat**
robe terne ; pelage terne
glanzloses Haarkleid / Fell ; stumpfes Haarkleid /
  Fell
pelo sombrío

**dung** => droppings

**duodenum**
duodénum
Zwölffingerdarm
duodeno
  Première partie de l'intestin grêle, il est directement relié à l'estomac et sa forme empêche les aliments d'y
  retourner.

**dust**
poussière
Staub *m*
polvo

**ear**
oreille
Ohr *ne*
oreja ; oído

**ear (internal // middle // external ~)**
oreille (interne // moyenne // externe)
Ohr (inneres // mittel // äußeres ~)
oído (interno // medio // externo)

**East Prussian (horse)** => Trakehner ;
  Trakehnen horse

**easy-boot** => barrier boot

**eczema**
eczéma
Ekzem *ne*
eczema
  A general term for any inflammation of the skin,
  marked early by redness.
  Affection cutanée caractérisée par des rougeurs.

**edema** => oedema

**eel stripe** => dorsal stripe / list / band

**effect of reins**
effet de rênes
Wirkung der Zügelarbeit
efecto de las riendas

**egg-butt / eggbutt snaffle** ; barrel-mouth bit *br*
filet à olives
Olivenkopftrense *f* ; Renntrense
bridón ovalado ; filete ovalado
  The eggbutt itself is the oval hinge where the rings are
  attached.
  Avec une charnière bombée à chaque bout de l'embouchure, dans laquelle s'insère l'anneau.

**eight** => figure (of) eight

**eight (at withers)**
taille (au garrot)
Widerristhöhe *(die ~)*
altura a la cruz ; alzada a / de la cruz
  The height of a horse (unless otherwise stated) is mea-
  sured « at withers »: from the ground to the top of the
  withers.
  Mesure habituelle de la taille d'un cheval, se mesure
  en mains ou en mètres, du sol au sommet du garrot.

**elbow**
coude
Ellenbogen *m* ; Ellbogen
codo
  Il unit le bras à l'avant-bras.

**elbow hygroma** => capped elbow

**elbow inclined inwards** => turned-in elbow

**elbow inclined outwards** => turned-out
  elbow

**elbow joint**
articulation du coude ; art. huméro-antébrachiale
Ellbogengelenk *ne* ; Ellenbogengelenk
articulación cubital / del codo
  Implique l'humérus, le radius et l'ulna.

**electrolytes**
électrolytes
Elektrolyte *m pl*
electrólitos

**elimination**
élimination
Ausschluß *m*
eliminación

**embrocation**
embrocation
Einreibung *f*
embrocación

**emphysema (pulmonary ~)**
emphysème (pulmonaire)
Lungenemphysem *ne*
enfisema
  Due to destruction of the walls of alveoli, interfering
  with respiration and with the uptaking of oxygen by the
  blood. *s.a. broken wind*
  Déchirement des parois des alvéoles pulmonaires, lesquelles se confondent ainsi les unes avec les autres, ce
  qui rend la respiration et le passage de l'oxygène dans le
  sang difficiles.

**empty mare**
jument vide
güsste Stute ; leere Stute ; unträchtige Stute
yegua vacía

## enamel (of a tooth)
émail (d'une dent)
Zahnschmelz ; Zahnemail
esmalte

## encephalomyelitis (equine viral ~) ; E and W (1) ; sleeping sickness
encéphalomyélite (équine) ; maladie du sommeil
Enzephalomyelitis der Pferde (seuchenhafte ~)
encefalomielitis equina

There are three strains: eastern (EEE), western (WEE) and Venezuelan (VEE). 1) US abbr: Stands for eastern and western (strains of the) equine encephalomyelitis.
Infection virale aiguë transmise surtout par les insectes piqueurs, la maladie affecte les humains, les oiseaux et d'autres mammifères.

## endocardium
endocarde
Endokard *ne*
endocardio

Membrane interne du coeur.

## endoparasite => internal parasite

## endurance test / phase (speed and ~) *ht*
épreuve de fond *cc*
Geländeprüfung *f*
prueba de fondo ; fase de velocidad y resistencia

## engagement (of the hindquarters)
engagement (de l'arrière-main)
Engagement (der Hinterhand) *ne*
remetimiento (del tercio posterior)

## engage (the haunches) *v* ; hock *v*
engager (l'arrière-main)
heranstellen (die Hinterhand ~)
entrar / emplear el posterior ; reunir el posterior ; emplear las ancas

## English saddle
selle anglaise
Sportsattel ; englischer Sattel
silla inglesa

## entire (male horse) => stallion

## entry ; declaration (1)
inscription ; engagement (1)
Engagement *ne*
inscripción ; entrada ; apunte

1) Declaration of a horse for a given race: The naming of a particular horse to be a starter in a given race.
1) Engagement d'un cheval dans une course: L'inscription d'un cheval sur la liste des partants pour une course donnée.

## entry fee
droit d'inscription
Einsatz *m* ; Nennungsgeld *ne*
derecho de inscripción

## epidermis
épiderme
Oberhaut ; Epidermis
epidermis

## epiglottis
épiglotte
Kehldeckel ; Epiglottis
epiglotis

## epistaxis ; exercise-induced pulmonary haemorrhage (1) *abbr: EIPH* ; bleeding
épistaxis ; hémorragie pulmonaire provoquée par l'exercice (1)
Epistaxis *f*
epistaxis ; hemorragia pulmonar inducida por esfuerzo (1)

Horse's bleeding from the nose that occurs without apparent causes, usually during or after hard exercise (1).
Saignement par les voies aériennes supérieures, qui apparaît sans cause apparente, habituellement durant ou après un exercice violent (1).

## epithelium
épithélium
Epithel *ne*
epitelio

## epizooty
épizootie
Tierseuche *f*
epizootia

## equestrian => rider

## equestrian *adj*
équestre
Reit... ; Reiter...
ecuestre

## equestrian sport
sport équestre *équitation*
Reitsport *m*
deporte ecuestre

## equines (the ~) ; horse family
équidés (les ~)
Equiden *pl*
équidos ; equinos

## equine contagious pleuropneumonia
pleuropneumonie contagieuse du cheval
Brustseuche der Pferde (die ~)
pleuroneumonía contagiosa de los equinos

## equine infectious anaemia / anemia *abbr: EIA*
anémie infectieuse équine / des équidés
infektiöse Anämie der Pferde / Einhufer (die ~) ; ansteckende Blutarmut der Pferde (die ~)
anemia infecciosa equina / del caballo

Maladie due à un virus, si l'animal survit il reste quand même porteur de ce virus. Le test de Coggins vise à repérer les animaux porteurs.

## equine plague => African horse sickness

## equine recurrent uveitis *abbr: ERU* ; moonblindness ; moon blindness ; periodic ophthalmia
uvéite (récidivante)
periodische Augenentzündung *f* ; Mondblindheit
uveítis

## equine veterinarian ; horse-doctor
vétérinaire de chevaux
Pferdetierarzt *m*
veterinario especialista en caballos

## equine viral arteritis *abbr: EVA*
artérite virale du cheval
infektiöse Arteritis / Arteriitis des Pferdes (die ~)
arteritis viral equina

**equipment**
équipement ; attirail
Ausrüstung *f*
equipo

**Equisetum** => horsetail

**equitation** => horseback riding

**ergot** ; dew claw *rare*
ergot
Afterklaue *f* ; Sporn *m* ; Griffelbein *ne*
garra ; ergot
  Corne située au bas et à l'arrière du boulet.

**error in the course**
erreur de parcours
Verreiten
error de recorrido

**esophagus** => oesophagus

**estrus** => heat

**ethmoid bone**
os ethmoïde
Siebbein
hueso etmoides

**event** => horse trial

**eventer** => event rider

**event horse**
cheval de concours complet
Vielseitigkeitspferd *ne*
caballo de concurso completo ; caballo de prueba
  completa / militar

**event rider** ; eventer
cavalier de concours complet
Reiter von Vielseitigkeitsprüfungen
jinete de concurso completo ; jinete de prueba
  completa / militar

**ewe neck** ; upside-down neck
encolure renversée ; encolure de cerf
Hirschhals *m* ; verkehrter Hals
cuello de ciervo ; cuello invertido ; cuello hundido
  A conformation fault, the neck makes a concave line
  from ears to withers.
  Dont le bord supérieur est concave.

**excluded from competition**
hors concours
außer Konkurrenz
fuera de concurso ; fuera de la carrera

**exercise-induced pulmonary
  haemorrhage** => epistaxis

**exertional myopathy / rhabdomyolisis**
  => azoturia

**Exmoor** *breed*
exmoor
Exmoorpony
exmoor
  Race de poneys rustiques d'origine britannique.

**exostosis**
exostose
Überbein *ne*
exóstosis
  Bony growth projecting from the surface of a bone.
  Excroissance de la surface d'un os.

**expert** *about horses*
connaisseur *en matière de chevaux* ; expert
Pferdekenner
experto
  *s.a. horseman*

**extend** *v* ; lengthen *v*
allonger
zulegen ; verlängern
alargar

**extended canter**
galop allongé
starker Galopp
galope largo

**extended canter, half-seat**
galop allongé, demi-assiette
starker Galopp im leichten Sitz
galope largo elevado

**extended trot**
trot allongé ; trot en extension
starker Trab
trote largo ; trote extenso

**extended trot rising**
trot allongé enlevé
starker Trab leichttraben
trote largo a la inglesa ; trote largo levantado

**extended trot sitting**
trot allongé assis
starker Trab ausgesessen
trote largo sentado

**extended walk**
pas allongé
starke Schritt *(der ~)*
paso largo ; paso extendido

**extensor muscle**
muscle extenseur
Streckmuskel ; Strecker
músculo extensor
  Muscle dont la contraction ouvre une ou plusieurs articulations.

**extensor pedis muscle** => common digital
  extensor muscle

**extensor pedis tendon** => common (digital)
  extensor tendon

**extensor process**
processus extensorius ; éminence pyramidale *anc*
Hufbeinkappe ; Streckfortsatz
eminencia piramidal
  Éminence qui coiffe la face antérieure de la troisième
  phalange.

**external acoustic / auditory meatus**
méat acoustique externe ; conduit auditif externe *anc*
äußerer Gehörgang
conducto auditivo externo

**external conformation**
extérieur (du cheval)
Exterieur *ne*
exterior

**eye**
oeil *pl: yeux*
Auge *ne*
ojo

**eyeball**
oeil (globe de l'~)
Augapfel *m*
cuenca del ojo ; globo ocular / del ojo

**eyelids**
paupières
Augenlider *ne*
párpados

**eyes**
yeux
Augen *(die ~)*
ojos

**eye socket** ; orbit (eye ~)
orbite (de l'oeil)
Augenhöhle
órbita del ojo

**E and W** => encephalomyelitis (equine viral ~)

**écuyer** => riding master

**face**
face
Gesicht *ne*
cara
Région antérieure inférieure de la tête. Son squelette comprend la partie antérieure des cavités nasales et les os maxillaires.

**face (of an anvil)** ; table
table (d'une enclume)
Bahn (die gehärtete ~)
tabla ; plano
The flat top section of an anvil.

**facial vein**
veine faciale
Gesichtsblutader *f*
vena facial

**faeces** => droppings

**fall**
chute
Sturz *m*
caída

**false canter** => canter on / at the wrong lead

**false martingale**
fausse martingale
Sprungriemen *(der ~)*
media gamarra

**farrier** => horseshoer

**farriery** *(1)* ; forge *(2)* ; smithy
forge *n*
Schmiede *f* ; Hufschmiede
herrería ; fragua ; forja
1) The workshop. 2) The workshop or the furnace / hearth for heating the metal.

**fascia**
fascia
Muskelbinde ; Fascie
fascia
Fibrous membrane (aponeurose like) serving to support a muscle or group of muscles.

**fault** ; foul *(1)*
faute
Fehler *m*
falta
1) r: An unfair or invalid action.

**favourite / favorite** *n & adj* ; chalk *n (1)* ; preferred *adj*
favori *n & adj*
aussichtsreichstes Pferd *(das ~)* ; Favorit *m*
favorito
1) US r: The favourite horse, as determined by the bettors, in a given race.
c: Le cheval favori est celui sur lequel les parieurs ont misé le plus.

**fawn bay** ; tawny bay
bai fauve
Rehbrauner *m* ; rehbraun *adj*
bayo leonado

**fear**
peur
Scheu
miedo

**feather(ing)** => fetlock (tuft)

**feces** => droppings

**feed** *v*
nourrir
füttern
nutrir ; alimentar

**feeding trough / tub** => feed tub

**feed tub** ; feeding trough / tub ; manger
mangeoire ; auge
Futterkrippe *m* ; Krippe
comedero ; cubeta de comida

**feed (conversion) efficiency**
capacité de transformation des aliments ; efficience alimentaire
Futterverwertung *f*
capacidad de transformación de alimentos
The efficiency with which a horse is able to use ingested nutrients.

**Fell (pony)** *breed*
fell
Fellpony
fell poney
Race de poneys rustiques du nord de l'Angleterre.

**felt**
feutre
Filz *m*
fieltro

**female**
femelle
Weibchen ; weibliches Tier
hembra

**female descendant**
descendant femelle ; descendante
weiblicher Nachkomme
descendente femenino

**female line** ; maternal family / line ; tail-female lineage
lignée femelle ; famille maternelle
mütterliche Linie *(die ~)* ; weibliche Linie
línea femenina / materna
   Line of female ancestors of a horse (from dam to dam on a direct genealogical line from female to female only). The maternal family is usually to be traced to a single tap root mare which is the maternal line source identifying this line, e.g. the Jessie Pepper (maternal) family, Jessie Pepper being the name of the tap root mare. *s.a. pedigree*
   Lignée des ascendants femelles en ligne directe (de mère en grand-mère maternelle en arrière-grand-mère maternelle etc.) d'un individu. L'expression famille maternelle est habituellement utilisée pour désigner une lignée femelle qu'on remonte ainsi jusqu'à une jument-souche dont le nom identifie cette famille, par exemple, la famille maternelle de Jessie Pepper.

**femoral trochlea** ; trochlea of the femur
trochlée du fémur
Kniescheibenrolle
tróclea femoral
   Surface patellaire (Facies patellaris NAV) du fémur.

**femoral vein**
veine fémorale
Oberschenkelblutader *f*
vena femoral

**femur** ; thigh bone
fémur
Oberschenkelbein *ne* ; Femur
fémur
   Très gros os qui constitue l'armature de la cuisse, de l'articulation de la hanche à celle du grasset.

**fence (vertical ~)**  => gate

**fender**  => mud guard

**fender**  => flap (of a saddle)

**fetlock**
boulet ; région métacarpo-phalangienne // méta-tarso-phalangienne
Fesselkopf *m* ; Fesselgelenkgegend ; Köte
menudillo
   Région de la jambe du cheval, entre le canon et le paturon.

**fetlock joint** ; metacarpophalangeal // metatarsophalangeal joint
articulation du boulet ; art. métacarpo-phalan-gienne // métatarso-phalangienne
Kötengelenk *ne* ; Fesselgelenk *ne (1)*
articulación metacarpofalangiana // metatarsofa-langiana
   1) Sometimes used for the pastern joint (prox. interphalangeal joint).
   Implique l'os métacarpien // métatarsien principal, les grands sésamoïdes et la première phalange. 1) Parfois utilisé pour l'articulation du paturon (première art. interphalangienne).

**fetlock (tuft)** *(1)* ; feather(ing) *(2)*
fanon
Kötenbehang *m* ; Kötenhaare *ne* ; Kötenschopf *m* ; Fesselbehang ; Fesselhaare
cerneja
   1) Tuft of hair behind the fetlock joint. 2) When these hairs are long and abundant, sometimes continuing up the back of the limb almost to the knee or hock.
   Touffe de crins derrière le boulet, les crins peuvent être plus ou moins abondants et même occuper une bonne partie de la face arrière des canons.

**fever**
fièvre
Fieber *ne*
fiebre

**fibrocartilage of the third phalanx** ; carti-lage of the third phalanx (flat ~) ; lateral cartilage of the foot ; lateral cartilage of the third phalanx
fibrocartilage (complémentaire) de la troisième phalange ; cartilage ungulaire ; cartilage complé-mentaire / latéral de la troisième phalange
Hufknorpel *m*
cartílago del hueso del casco

**fibula**
fibula ; péroné *anc*
Wadenbein *ne* ; Fibula
peroné
   Os soudé au tibia, il s'étend environ sur la moitié supé-rieure de celui-ci.

**fibular tarsal bone**  => calcaneus

**field** *r* ; pack *r*
peloton *c*
Feld *ne*
grupo de los caballos en la carrera (el ~)

**field boot**  => riding boot (laced ~)

**figure 8 noseband**  => cross-over noseband

**figure (of) eight** ; eight
huit (de chiffre) ; figure de huit
Acht *f*
figura de ocho ; ocho (de cifra)
   Correspondant à deux voltes tangentes.

**file (finishing ~)**
lime (de finition)
Feile *f*
lima

**filly (foal)**
pouliche
Stutfohlen ; junge Stute
potrilla ; potranca ; potra
   Female horse, from birth till she is considered as a mare, which depends on breeds and disciplines (usually from three to five years old).
   Cheval femelle, de la naissance jusqu'à ce qu'elle soit considérée comme une jument, ce qui dépend des races et des disciplines (en général de trois à cinq ans).

**fine** *n*
amende
Geldstrafe *f*
multa

**fine mouth**  => soft mouth

**finish**
arrivée
Ziel
llegada ; final

**finish(ing) line** ; wire (finish ~)
ligne d'arrivée ; fil d'arrivée
Ziellinie
línea de llegada ; línea de final

**firing** ; cautery
feu ; cautère
Brennapparat *m* ; Brennmittel *ne* ; Ätzmittel *ne*
fuego ; cauterio
  Treatment of an injury with a hot iron.
  Traitement thérapeutique au fer rouge.

**firing iron**
thermocautère
Brennstift *m*
termocauterio

**first phalanx** => proximal phalanx

**first (cervical) vertebra** => atlas

**fistulous withers**
fistule du garrot ; bursite brucellique du garrot
Widerristfistel *(die ~)*
fístula de la cruz ; mal de cruz *Argentina*
  Results from an infection in the supraspinous bursa.

**fixed martingale** => standing martingale

**Fjord pony** *breed*
fjord ; fjoring ; fjordhest
Fjordpony ; Fjordpferd
caballo de los fiordos
  Race originaire du nord de l'Europe.

**flank**
flanc
Flanke *f*
flanco ; ijada ; ijar
  Région comprise entre les côtes, le ventre, les reins et les hanches.

**flank fold**
pli latéral ; pli du grasset / flanc
Kniefalte
pliegue de la babilla
  Pli cutané qui relie la partie inférieure de la cuisse (au-dessus et en avant du grasset) au flanc.

**flap (of a saddle)** ; fender *west.*
quartier (d'une selle)
Sattelblatt *(das ~)* ; Seitenblatt (des Sattels)
faldón (lateral) ; hoja lateral ; falda *amer*

**flash noseband**
muserolle éclair / combinée
englische Reithalfter / Halfter mit Pulleriemen / Sperriemen *(das ~)* ; kombinierte Reithalfter
muserola doble
  Ordinary cavesson with an additional band (« Sperriemen ») (or possibly two straps sewn diagonally ) fixed to it and fastening below the bit, acting as a drop noseband, this is intended to be used with a standing martingale attached to the cavesson.

**flat croup** ; horizontal croup
croupe horizontale ; croupe plate
horizontale Kruppe ; waagerechte Kruppe
grupa plana

**flat race**
course sur le plat ; course de plat
Flachrennen
carrera lisa / plana

**flax seed ; flax-seed** => linseed

**flea-bitten grey** ; nutmeg *rare*
gris moucheté
Fliegen-Schimmel ; Fliegenschimmel *veränderlich*
tordillo mosqueado
  Small flecks of coloured hairs are distributed through the coat.
  Robe parsemée de petites taches foncées sur un fond plus clair.

**fleece** => sheath

**flexion** ; bend ; curve
incurvation ; inflexion
Stellung *f*
flexión ; curva ; curvatura

**flexion test**
test de flexion
Beugeprobe *(die ~)*
prueba de la flexión

**flexor brachii muscle** => biceps brachii muscle

**flexor muscle**
muscle fléchisseur
Beugemuskel ; Beuger
músculo flexor
  Muscle dont la contraction ferme une ou plusieurs articulations. Un muscle peut être fléchisseur au niveau d'une articulation et extenseur au niveau d'une autre.

**flexor perforans muscle** => deep digital flexor muscle

**flexor tendon**
tendon fléchisseur
Beugesehne
tendón flexor

**flight**
fuite
Flucht *f*
huida

**floating rein** => hanging rein

**fluke (common liver ~)**
douve (grande ~ du foie)
großer Leberegel *m* ; Lerberegelbefall *m*
distoma hepático ; duela del hígado ; fasciola hepática

**flu (equine ~)** => influenza (equine ~)

**flying change of lead / leg** ; change of leg in the air *n*
changement de pied en l'air
fliegender Galoppwechsel / Wechsel *m*
cambio de pie / galope en el aire

**flying jump**
saut de volée ; saut d'extension
fliegender Sprung
salto volando

**fly sheet (scrim ~)**
couverture à mailles ; chemise anti-mouches
Fliegendecke
manta para proteger de moscas
  Prévue pour protéger le cheval contre les insectes.

**foal** *v* ; drop a foal *v*
pouliner ; mettre bas
abfohlen ; fohlen
parir

**foaling** ; parturition
poulinage ; mise bas ; parturition
Geburt ; Abfohlen *ne*
parto (de la yegua) ; parición ; parturición *amer*

**foal ataxia**
ataxie du poulain
Fohlenataxie *f*
ataxia

**foal (colt // filly ~)**
poulain // pouliche (de moins d'un an)
Fohlen (Hengst… // Stut...) *ne*
potrillo // potrilla
  A young horse under one year old or still with his dam
(French « non-sevré »), according to interpretations.
  Poulain ou pouliche non-sevré(e) ou de l'année.

**foam**
écume ; bave
Schaum
baba ; babaza
  Salive mousseuse du cheval, lorsqu'il mâche son mors
par exemple.

**fodder** ; forage
fourrage
Futter *ne*
forraje ; pienso

**foot**
pied
Fuß *m*
pie
  Extrémité d'un membre sur laquelle gens et chevaux
marchent, et unité de mesure équivalente à 0,3048
mètres. En anatomie la notion de pied, dans le sens
strict, ne s'applique qu'au membre postérieur.

**foot pad**  => stirrup pad / tread

**foot turned out**  => toed-out

**forage**  => fodder

**foramen magnum** ; occipital foramen *old*
foramen magnum ; trou occipital *anc*
Hinterhauptloch
cavidad occipital
  Dans le squelette de la tête, par où passe la moelle épinière.

**forearm**
avant-bras
Vorarm ; Unterarm *(der ~)*
antebrazo ; brazuelo
  Formé par le radius et l'ulna, entre le coude et le genou.

**forecannon**
canon (antérieur)
Vorderröhre *f*
caña anterior
  Partie des membres antérieurs, comprise entre le genou
et le boulet.

**forecannon bone**  => metacarpal bone (large
  / third ~)

**forehand** ; front end
avant-main ; avant-train
Vorhand ; Vorderhand *f* ; Vorderteil
tercio anterior ; antemano
  The front part of the horse: head, neck, shoulders,
breast and forelegs.
  Partie avant du cheval, comprend la tête, l'encolure,
les épaules, le poitrail et les membres antérieurs.
  Avant-main est une expression plus adéquate pour un
cheval monté et avant-train pour un cheval attelé.

**forehead**
front
Stirn *f*
frente
  Compris entre la nuque, les oreilles, les tempes, les sa-
lières, les yeux et le chanfrein.

**forelegs**
membres antérieurs ; bipède antérieur
Vorderbeine
manos (del caballo)

**forelimb ; foreleg** ; thoracic limb ; front leg
membre antérieur / de devant ; antérieur ;
  membre thoracique ; jambe avant
Vorderbein *ne* ; Vorderglied(maße) ;
  Brustgliedmaße
remo delantero ; miembro anterior

**forelock**
toupet
Schopf *m* ; Stirnschopf ; Schubrine
tupé ; mechón ; copete
  Partie de la crinière qui pousse entre les oreilles et
tombe sur le front.

**forge**  => farriery

**forge** *v*
forger
schmieden
forjar

**formalin**
formol ; aldéhyde formique
Formaldehyd *ne*
formol

**forward seat**
monte en avant ; position de saut ; position en
  avant
Springsitz ; Vorwärtssitz
posición de salto ; asiento para saltar

**foul**  => fault

**foundation mare**  => tap root / taproot mare

**founder** ; chronic laminitis
fourbure chronique
Hufrehe (chronische ~)
aguadura ; infosura ; dermatitis crónica del casco

The normal attachment of the coffin bone to the hoof wall is loosened, the bone rotates away from the wall and the space is filling with irregular horn produced by a new set of sensitive laminae that forms near the surface of the bone. *s.a. laminitis (acute ~)*

Au début il s'agit d'une inflammation du tissu sensible (laminite) à l'intérieur du sabot, dans les cas extrêmes la troisième phalange peut en venir à passer à travers la sole.

**fox-hunting**
chasse au renard
Fuchsjagd
caza de zorros

**fox tail**  => brush

    => horsetail

**Fox trotter (Missouri ~)** *breed*
fox trotteur *race*
Missouri Foxtrotter
caballo trote-zorro de Misuri

**freestyle dressage**  => kur

**freeze branding**
marquage à froid
Kaltbrand *m*
marcación en frío

**free choice** ; ad-lib
à volonté
ad-libitum ; nach Belieben
ad líbitum ; a discreción

**free flight (moment of ~)**  => suspension
  (moment of ~)

**free walk**
pas libre
freier Schritt ; langer Schritt
paso libre ; paso franco

**French Saddle (horse)** *breed* ; Anglo-Norman
selle français ; anglo-normand
Französisches Reitpferd ; Anglo-Normänner Warmblut
silla francesa

Issu du croisement de l'ancien cheval normand et du thoroughbred, ses origines se confondent avec celles du trotteur français. Il est inscrit au livre généalogique du cheval de selle français depuis 1958.

**French trotter** ; Norman trotter
trotteur français
französischer Traber
trotador francés ; caballo trotón francés

**frightened** ; afraid
effrayé
erschrocken
asustado

**frog**
fourchette ; coin du sabot *rare*
Strahl *m* ; Hufstrahl ; Hornstrahl ; Klauenstrahl
ranilla

**frontal bone**
os frontal
Stirnbein *ne*
hueso frontal

**frontal sinus** ; conchofrontal sinus
sinus frontal ; sinus concho-frontal
Stirnhöhle
seno frontal

Il comporte deux compartiments, l'un étant le sinus frontal vrai (Sinus frontalis NAV) et l'autre, le sinus conchal dorsal (Sinus conchae dorsalis NAV).

**front end** => forehand

**front leg**  => forelimb ; foreleg

**frozen semen**
sperme congelé ; semence congelée
tiefgefrorener Samen
semen congelado ; esperma congelado

**full brother**
frère propre
Vollbruder
doble hermano

**full mouth**
bouche faite ; dentition complète
Vollgebiß
dentadura completa ; boca cerrada

When all the milk teeth have been replaced by the permanent teeth.

Quand, vers l'âge de cinq ans, les coins d'adulte sont en contact et que les dents d'adultes sont toutes très visibles, y compris les crochets chez le mâle.

**full sister**
soeur propre
Vollschwester
doble hermana

**full stocking**  => white to above knee // hock

**Furioso ; Furioso-North Star (horse)**
  *breed*
furioso
Furioso-Northstar
furioso
Race d'origine hongroise.

**gag bit**
filet releveur ; gag
Durchziehtrense *f* ; Aufziehtrense ; Steiggebiss ; Zugtrense
ahogador (filete para ~)

Any bit with rounded cheekpieces passing through holes in the bit rings, or rollers, pulleys etc., its primary purpose being to raise the head.

**gait** ; pace *n*
allure
Gangart ; Gang *f; m*
aire ; marcha

N'importe laquelle parmi les façons qu'utilise le cheval pour se déplacer. Peut aussi désigner la rapidité des mouvements du cheval qui se déplace.

**gaits** ; paces
allures
Gangarten
aires

**galactia**
agalactie ; agalaxie
Agalaktie *f* ; Milchmangel *m*
agalactia

**gallop**
galop
Jagdgalopp *m*
galope
 *s.a. canter*

**gallop** *v*
galoper
Galopp reiten ; galoppieren
galopar

**ganglion**
ganglion
Nervenknoten ; Ganglion
ganglio
 Centre nerveux secondaire, ils sont pour la plupart dans le voisinage de la moelle épinière.

**gaskin** ; second thigh ; leg *(1)* ; lower thigh
jambe
Unterschenkel *(der ~)*
pierna
 1) Stricto sensu, part of the horse's hind limb, between the stifle and the hock.
 Au sens strict: partie du membre postérieur correspondant au tibia et comprise entre le grasset et le jarret du cheval.

**Gasterophilus** => bot fly (horse ~)

**gastric juice**
suc gastrique
Magensaft *m*
jugo gástrico

**gastritis**
gastrite
Magenkatarrh *m* ; Gastritis *f*
gastritis
 Inflammation of the lining of the stomach.
 Inflammation de la muqueuse de l'estomac.

**gate** ; fence (vertical ~)
barrière
Tor *ne* ; Gatter *ne* ; Barriere *f* ; Zaun *m*
barrera
 An upright jumping obstacle looking like a fence around a field, paddock or park. *s.a. other entry*
 Le mot barrière désigne ici un obstacle vertical composé de barres ou de planches disposées horizontalement ou verticalement et rappelant une clôture autour d'un champ ou d'un parc.

**gate**
barrière
Tor *ne*
puerta
 A gate that is to be opened in some western-riding competitions. *s.a. other entry*

**gauze**
gaze
Gaze *f*
gasa

**gear** => tack ; tackle

**geld** *v* ; castrate *v*
castrer ; châtrer ; hongrer
kastrieren
castrar ; capar ; émascular

**gelded horse** => gelding

**gelding** ; gelded horse ; castrated horse
hongre ; cheval castré / châtré
Wallach *m*
caballo castrado / capón
 A male horse, at any age, that has no testicles left, or whose testicles are atrophied and not functioning.
 Cheval mâle n'ayant plus de testicules, ou ayant des testicules atrophiés et non fonctionnels.

**gene**
gène
Gen *ne*
gen(e)

**genealogy**
généalogie
Genealogie *f*
genealogía
 *s.a. pedigree*

**generalized edema / oedema** => anasarca

**genet** => hinny

**genetic** *adj* ; genetics *n pl (treated as sing.)*
génétique *n & adj*
Entwicklungslehre *f* ; Genetik *f*
genético

**genetics** => genetic

**genu valgum** => knock-knees

**gestation**
gestation
Trächtigkeit
gestación

**get in the saddle** *v*
monter (en selle) ; mettre en selle (se ~)
aufsitzen
subir a la silla

**get on one's high horse** *v*
monter sur ses grands chevaux
sich aufs hohe Roß setzen
subirse a la parra
 Grande colère ou réaction similaire. Au Moyen-Âge les seigneurs passent pour avoir laissé leurs palefrois à la maison et montaient sur leurs grands chevaux quand ils partaient se battre.

**get the tongue over the bit** *v*
passer la langue sur l'embouchure ; lâcher son
 mors *Bel*
Zunge über das Gebiss nehmen (die ~)
poner la lengua sobre el freno

**Gidran** *breed* ; Hungarian Anglo-Arab horse
anglo-arabe hongrois *race* ; gidran
Gidran
gidranés

**girth** *west.* ; cinch *west.*
sangle *west.*
Westernsattelgurt *m*
cincha
 Normally attached on one side by its buckle to the off-billet (already fixed to the saddle), and on the other

side by the cinch / tie strap (already fixed to the saddle) which passes through the ring of its second buckle.

Pour la selle western, la sangle proprement dite comporte une boucle de métal à chacune de ses extrémités, c'est par ces boucles qu'elle sera attachée à deux courroies déjà attachées à la selle.

**girth** *v* ; tighten the girth *v*
sangler
gurten ; Gurte anziehen
cinchar

**girth** *n* ; cinch
sangle
Sattelgurt *m* ; Gurt *m* ; Gurtriemen *m* ; große Bauchgurt *(der ~) att/bd* ; Bauchgurt
cincha

**girth's circumference** ; circumference of chest
tour de sangle / poitrine ; périmètre thoracique
Gurtumfang *m* ; Brustumfang
perímetro torácico ; circunferencia del pecho

**girth cover** ; cinch cover *west.*
couvre-sangle ; gaine de sangle
Sattelgurtüberzug
cubierta de la cincha

**girth strap** *class.*
contre-sanglon *class.*
Strippe
latiguillo

To which the girth is buckled on the saddle.
Courroie trouée fixée à la selle et sur laquelle vient s'attacher la boucle de métal de la sangle.

**give the signal to start** *v*
donner le départ
Startzeichen geben
dar la salida

**glanders (equine ~)**
morve
Rotz ; Rotzkrankheit *;f*
muermo

Caused by Pseudomonas mallei.
Maladie d'origine microbienne très grave et très contagieuse. Des foyers de suppuration apparaissent dans la cloison médiane du nez et ailleurs sur le corps.

**glans penis**
gland du pénis
Eichel *f*
glande

**glossy coat**
robe brillante / lustrée
glänzendes Haarkleid / Fell
pelo brillante

**glove**
gant
Handschuh
guante

**gluteus maximus muscle** => superficial gluteal muscle

**gluteus superficialis muscle** => superficial gluteal muscle

**glycerin**
glycérine
Glycerin
glicerina

**goiter** => goitre

**goitre** *Brit* ; goiter *US*
goitre
Kropf *m* ; Schilddrüsenwucherung *f*
bocio

**golden bay**
bai doré
Goldbrauner *m*
bayo dorado

Golden yellowish-brown bay coat.
Robe baie avec des reflets dorés.

**golden chestnut**
alezan doré
Gold-Fuchs / Goldfuchs *m*
alazán oro / dorado

**good action**
allure énergique
viel Gang
buena acción

**good and easy seat** ; supple seat
assiette souple et élastique
geschmeidiger Sitz
asiento elástico / flexible

**good seat**
bonne assiette
guter Sitz
asiento correcto

**good seat (rider with a ~)**
bonne assiette (cavalier ayant une ~) ; bien en selle (cavalier ~)
gut sitzender Reiter
bien sentado (jinete ~)

**gooseneck trailer**
semi-remorque
Sattelanhänger *m*
acoplado de quinta rueda

**goose rump** ; jumping rump
croupe en pupitre ; croupe avalée ; croupe abattue
abschüssige Kruppe
grupa de ganso / pollo

The rump inclines sharply downwards, the slope of the pelvis being significantly greater than 30 degrees with the horizon. *s.a. sloping croup*
Trop oblique.

**Grackle noseband** => cross-over noseband

**grains**
grains
Hartfutter
granos

**granddaughter**
petite-fille
Enkelin *f*
nieta

**grandsire**
deuxième père ; grand-père
Großvater *m*
abuelo

**grandson**
petit-fils
Enkel *m*
nieto

**Grand Prix de Dressage**
Grand prix de dressage
Grand Prix de Dressage ;
 Olympia-Dressurprüfung *(die ~)* ; Große
 Olympische Dressurprüfung
Gran Premio Olímpico de Doma

**grass**
herbe
Gras
hierba ; yerba

**grass foal** => weanling

**gravel** => abscess (in a hoof)

**gray** => grey

**graze** *v* ; pasture *v*
brouter ; pâturer ; paître
grasen
pastar ; pacer

**grazing grounds** => pasture

**grease for hoofs** => hoof grease

**greater trochanter (of the femur)**
grand trochanter
großer Rollhügel ; großer Umdreher
trochanter mayor

**great metatarsal** => metatarsal bone (large /
 third ~)

**green fodder**
fourrage vert ; vert
Grünfutter *ne*
forraje verde

**grey** *Brit* ; gray *US*
gris
Schimmel *m veränderlich, dunkel geboren* ; grau
tordo
   Varying mosaic of white and coloured hairs growing
from a dark hide. With the age, the coat becomes lighter
and changes from patterns and shades, as the percentage
of white hairs increases. If the colour is permanent it
will rather be described as roan.
   Poils noirs (ou presque) et blancs (ou presque), mélan-
gés sur une peau foncée. Le qualificatif de gris peut
s'appliquer aussi bien aux chevaux dont la couleur de la
robe n'est pas permanente et devient de plus en plus
pâle avec l'âge, qu'à ceux dont la robe est permanente,
ce qui n'est pas le cas pour « grey ».

**greyhoundy** => herring gut

**grinders** => molars ; molar teeth

**grinding surface** => dental table

**grind the teeth** *v*
grincer des dents
knirschen (mit den Zähnen ~)
rechinar las dientes

**groom** ; lad *(1)*
palefrenier *f: palefrenière*
Pferdepfleger
mozo de caballos ; palafrenero ; caballerizo
   *criados*
   1) r: A lad looks after racehorses, rides them out and
accompanies them to race meetings.  *s.a. stable boy*

**groom** *v*
panser
putzen
limpiar

**grooming**
pansage
Pflege *(die ~)* ; Putzen *ne*
aseo ; limpieza

**ground work** => work in hand

**grulla ; grullo** => mouse-dun ; mouse-coloured

**gut** => intestine

**gymkhana**
gymkhana
Gymkhana
gymkhana

**habit**
habitude
Angewohnheit *f*
habito

**hack**
cheval de promenade
Promenadenpferd ; Hack *m*
caballo de paseo
   class.: Type of refined riding horse with good conformation, manners and action.

**hackamore**
hackamore ; jaquima
Hackamore / Hackemore
jáquima
   The true hackamore consists of a bosal, along with a
mecate as reins, a fiador as throat latch which also
prevents the bosal from bumping against the lower jaw,
and a lightweight latigo headstall that may be slit to be
passed over an ear. It may also be made more secure by
a cavesada as a browband.
   Le véritable hackamore comporte un bosal. On désigne
parfois sous le nom de hackamore mécanique une bride
sans mors qui agit sur le chanfrein le plus souvent par
l'intermédiaire de branches agissant comme levier.

**hacking** => pleasure

**Hackney (horse)** *breed*
hackney
Hackney
hackney
   Race d'origine britannique.

**haematoma** *Brit* ; hematoma *US*
hématome
Hämatom *ne* ; Bluterguß *m*
hematoma
   Hémorragie qui reste sous la peau.

**haematuria** *Brit* ; hematuria *US*
hématurie
Harnblutung *f* ; Hämaturie *f*
hematuria
Présence de sang dans les urines.

**haemorrhage** *Brit* ; hemorrhage *US*
hémorragie
Blutverlust *m* ; Hämorrhagie *f*
hemorragia

**hair follicle**
follicule pileux
Haarfollikel ; Haardrüsengrübchen
folículo piloso
Les follicules pileux assurent la régénération des poils du cheval.

**hair (a ~)**
poil (un ~)
Haar
pelo

**half-bred**
demi-sang
Halbblut *ne* ; Halbblüter *m*
media sangre ; cruzado ; mestizo
A horse with only one parent being considered as purebred. Also applies to a thoroughbred horse that is not eligible for entry in the « General Stud Book ».

**half-brother** *(1)*
demi-frère *(1)* ; frère utérin
Halbbruder
medio hermano ; hermanastro
1) Usually applied only for horses having the same dam.
1) Se dit habituellement uniquement pour des chevaux qui ont la même mère.

**half-halt**
demi-arrêt ; demi-parade *anc*
halbe Parade *(die ~)* ; Halber-Arrêt
media parada ; semi parada
Suite à l'action de tout le corps du cavalier afin de provoquer un bref instant de rassemblement, de « suspension » ou « d'arrêt (parade) », pour augmenter / reprendre l'attention et l'équilibre du cheval.

**half-pass** *n*
appuyer *n*
Traversale *f*
apoyo
The horse travels sideways and forwards, head slightly turned in the direction of the movement, shoulders preceding the haunches.
Exercice dans lequel le cheval se déplace latéralement, les antérieurs et les postérieurs sur deux pistes distinctes.

**half-pass** *v*
appuyer *v*
seitwärts treten
apoyar

**half-pass in canter** *n*
appuyer au galop *n*
Galopptraversale
apoyo al galope

**half-pirouette**
demi-pirouette
Kurzkehrtwendung *(die ~)* ; halbe Pirouette
media pirueta
Executed through 180 degrees, around the inside hindleg.
Pivot de 180 degrés, autour d'un postérieur qui doit demeurer le plus immobile possible.

**half-sister** *(1)*
demi-soeur *(1)* ; soeur utérine
Halbschwester
media hermana ; hermanastra
1) Usually applied only to horses having the same dam.
1) Se dit habituellement uniquement pour des chevaux qui ont la même mère.

**half-volt ; half volte**
demi-volte
Kehrtvolte *f* ; halbe Volte
media vuelta
La moitié d'une volte, on revient reprendre la piste, à main opposée.

**halt** *n*
arrêt
Halten *ne*
parada ; alto

**halt** *n*
parade
Parade
parada
The horse has come to an halt on the bit and in good balance.
Arrêt, en équilibre, du cheval, comme à l'intérieur ou au milieu de sa marche.

**halt** *v* ; stop *v*
arrêter
anhalten
parar ; pararse

**halter** ; head halter / collar / stall
licol ; licou
Stallhalfter *ne* ; Halfter
ronzal ; cabestro ; almartigón

**hame**
attelle
Kumtbügel *(der ~)*
horcate

**hammer (of the ear)**
marteau (de l'oreille) ; malleus
Hammer
martillo

**hammer (shoeing / driving / nailing ~)**
brochoir ; marteau de maréchal-ferrant ; mailloche *(1)*
Beschlaghammer *m* ; Hufbeschlaghammer *m*
martillo de herrador ; clavor
Pour enfoncer les clous. 1) Parfois présentée comme n'ayant pas d'échancrure (nommée « oreilles » ou « panne ») servant à arracher ou à couper les clous en les tordant.

**hand**
main *Can.*
Hand *f*
mano
   A 4-inch (10.16 cm) unit measuring the height of a horse.
   Mesure (valant 4 pouces ou 10,16 cm) de la taille d'un cheval.

**handicap**
handicap
Handicap
handicap
   May be a weight or time handicap, or design the race for which a weight handicap has been fixed.
   Peut être un handicap de poids ou de temps qui sert à niveler les chances entre les concurrents. Peut désigner la position d'un cheval à la barrière de départ d'une course.

**handicap weight**
poids de handicap
Ausgleichsgewicht
peso de handicap

**handiness of the horse**
maniabilité du cheval
Durchlässigkeit *f*
manejabilidad del caballo

**hands (action of the ~)**
mains (action des ~)
Zügelhilfen *f pl*
riendas (ayuda de ~) ; manos (acción de ~)
   One of the natural aids for riding or driving a horse.
   Une des aides naturelles pour solliciter un cheval.

**hand service**
saillie assistée ; monte en main
Sprung aus der Hand
monta a mano

**hanging rein** ; floating rein
rêne flottante ; rêne en guirlande
loser Zügel
rienda suelta

**hang out the tongue** *v*
sortir la langue
Zunge herausstrecken (die ~)
arrastrar la lengua ; sacar la lengua

**Hanover horse; Hanoverian (horse)** *breed*
hanovrien
Hannoveraner
hannoveriano
   Race d'origine allemande.

**hardy** *pl: bardies*
tranche(t) (d'enclume)
Abschrot ; Abschröter *m*
tajadera
   A cutting off tool mounted in the anvil and used to cut hot or cold stock.

**hardy / hardie hole** ; toolhole
oeil porte-outils ; oeil carré ; mortaise
Loch *(das ~)*
ojo (para los suplementos)
   A square hole in the face on an anvil.
   Trou carré dans la table d'une enclume.

**hard hat** => cap (hunting / skull / jockey's ~)

**hard mouth** ; poor mouth
bouche dure ; fort en bouche *adj*
hartes Maul
boca dura
   A mouth more or less insensible to the bit.
   S'applique au cheval peu sensible à l'action du mors.

**harmonious use of aids**
accord des aides
Zusammenwirken der Hilfen
acuerdo de ayudas
   Complémentarité et équilibre entre les différentes aides pour obtenir le mouvement recherché. Les aides ne doivent surtout pas avoir des effets antagonistes les unes par rapport aux autres, ce qui ne peut que créer de la confusion.

**harness** => tack ; tackle

**harnessed team**
attelage
Gespann *ne*
arueses ; jaeces ; enganche ; tiro
   Ensemble des chevaux attelés à une voiture.

**harnessing**
attelage
Anspannung des Wagenpferdes *(die ~)*
atalaje
   The actions performed or ways used to harness horses.
   Action ou manière d'atteler.

**harness-maker**
bourrelier ; harnacheur
Riemer ; Geschirrmacher
talabartero ; guarnicionero
   Fabricant de harnais. Le mot harnacheur peut aussi s'utiliser pour celui qui harnache les chevaux.

**harness (up)** *v* ; put the reins on a horse *v* ; put on the harness *v*
harnacher
aufschirren
aparejar

**haunch** => hip

**haunches-in** ; quarters-in
hanches en dedans
Hanke-herein
grupa adentro

**haute école**
haute école
hohe Schule
alta escuela
   Travail des allures relevées: passage, piaffé, pirouette, levade etc.

**haw** => nictitating membrane

**hay**
foin
Heu
heno

**hay bag / net**
filet à foin
Heunetz *ne*
red para heno

**hay bale**
balle de foin
Heubündel *ne*
paca de heno

**hay rack**
râtelier (à fourrage)
Heuraufe *(die ~)*
pesebre ; comedero

**head**
tête
Kopf *m* ; Haupt *ne*
cabeza

Composée de trente-quatre os différents. On peut lui identifier deux parties: le crâne et la face.

**headpiece** ; crownpiece
têtière
Kopfstück *ne* ; Genickstück ; Nackenriemen
testera ; nuquera

**headstall** => bridle

**head cap** => hood

**head halter / collar / stall** => halter

**head to the wall** => travers

**healing**
guérison ; cicatrisation
Abheilung *f* ; Heilung
curación ; sanando

On parle de guérison d'une maladie et de guérison ou de cicatrisation d'une plaie.

**heart**
coeur
Herz
corazón

Son poids varie généralement autour de quatre kilos et demi, chez certains chevaux de course il peut atteindre sept kilos.

**heart muscle** => cardiac muscle

**heat** => trial

**heat** ; estrus *US* ; oestrus *Brit*
chaleur(s) ; oestrus
Brunst *f*
estro ; celo ; calores

**heaves** => broken wind

**heavy draught / draft horse**
trait lourd (cheval de ~)
schwere Zugpferd
caballo de tiro pesado

**heavy horse**
cheval lourd
schweres Pferd *(der ~)*
caballo pesado

**heavy neck** => bull neck

**heavy on the forehand**
sur les épaules
Vorhand (auf der ~)
sobre las manos

Se dit du cheval dont l'avant-main supporte une trop grande proportion de son poids.

**hedge** ; brush (jump) ; hurdle
haie
Buschhürde *f* ; Hürde
seto

**heel** *anat*
talon *anat*
Tracht *(der ~)*
talón
  *s.a. bulb (of a heel)*

**height measurement**
mesure de hauteur
Höhenmaß *ne*
medidas de alzada

**height of rump**
hauteur à la croupe
Kreuzbeinhöhe
alzada a la grupa

**helmet** => cap (hunting / skull / jockey's ~)

**hematoma** => haematoma

**hematuria** => haematuria

**hemorrhage** => haemorrhage

**herd**
harde
Herde
manada ; caballada

**herding instinct**
instinct grégaire
Herdentrieb *m*
instinto gregario

**hereditary defect** => inborn defect

**heredity**
hérédité
Erblichkeit *f*
herencia

**herring gut** ; greyhoundy *adj*
ventre de levrette ; ventre retroussé ; levretté
  (ventre / cheval ~)
Windhundbauch *m* ; aufgeschürzte Bauch *(der ~)*
barriga de pescado / anguilla

Said of a horse having a mean body running upwards from girth to quarters.

Trop maigre à l'arrière, la ligne inférieure remonte vers le haut à l'arrière.

**he-ass** => donkey stallion

**he-mule** => mullet

**high jump**
saut en hauteur
Hochspringen
salto de altura

**high ringbone**
forme du paturon ; forme haute
Krongelenkschale *f*
sobrehueso de la cuartilla

Occurring around the pastern joint.

Implique l'articulation entre les deux premières phalanges.

**high withers**
garrot saillant
hoher Widerrist
cruz alta

**hind-cannon bone** => metatarsal bone (large / third ~)

**hind-legs**
membres postérieurs ; bipède postérieur
Hinterbeine
patas traseras

**hind leg / limb** ; pelvic limb
membre postérieur ; jambe postérieure / de derrière ; postérieur ; membre pelvien
Hinterglied(maße) ; Hinterbein *ne* ;
Beckengliedmaße
remo trasero ; miembro posterior ; pierna posterior / trasera

**hinny** ; bardot ; jennet *(1)* ; genet *(1)*
bardot ; bardeau
Maulesel *m*
mulo

Offspring of a horse or pony stallion and a female donkey. 1) Also a small Spanish horse and a type of horse
(an ambling hack) known in the twelfth century. *s.a.*
*mullet and other entries*

Engendré d'un cheval et d'une ânesse.

**hinny (female ~)**
bardot femelle ; bardote
Mauleselin *f*
mula (roma) ; burdégana
*s.a. other entries*

**hinny (horse ~)**
bardot (mâle)
Maulesel (männlicher ~) *m*
burdégano ; macho romo ; mulo (romo)
*s.a. other entries*

**hip** *(1)* ; haunch *(2)*
hanche
Hüfte *f*
anca

1) Corresponding to the front and side area of the pelvis. 2) The area around the hip, including the upper
thigh, this is the term used when describing the
movements of the horse (haunches-in etc.).

Correspondant, dans l'usage courant, à la région de la
bordure antérieure et de la bordure externe de l'os coxal
(Regio tuberis coxae). Peut aussi être considérée comme
la région comprise entre le sommet de la croupe, la
fesse et le flanc.

**hippology**
hippologie
Hippologie ; Pferdekunde
hipología

**hip joint**
articulation de la hanche ; art. coxo-fémorale
Hüftgelenk *ne*
articulación coxofemoral / del anca

**hip socket** => acetabulum

**hitch** *v*
atteler
anspannen
enganchar

**hitching ring** => paddock

**Hobbie** => Connemara (pony)

**hobby-horse**
cheval de bataille *sens figuré*
Steckenpferd ; Kampfparole *f*
caballo de batalla

**hock** ; tarsus
jarret ; tarse
Sprunggelenk *ne* ; Fußwurzel
corvejón ; tarso ; jarrete ; garrón

Région de la jambe postérieure, entre la jambe et le canon. Dans le sens strict le mot jarret désigne la région
du tarse (Regio tarsi NAV) et le mot tarse (Tarsus
NAV) le premier segment du squelette du pied.

**hock** => engage (the haunches)

**hock hygroma** => capped hock

**hog-back** => arch-back

**hollow-back** => saddle-back

**hollow of the flank**
creux du flanc
Hungergrube
planicie del ijar

**hollow wall**
fourmilière
lose Wand *(die ~)* ; hohle Wand
hormiguillo

Cavité qui s'est formée entre la corne et la partie vivante du pied, elle est le plus souvent sous la paroi mais
peut aussi être sous la sole.

**Holsteiner; Holstein (horse)** *breed*
holstein
Holsteiner
caballo de Holstein

Race d'origine allemande.

**hood** *(1)* ; head cap *(2)*
capuchon *(1)* ; cagoule *(1)* ; bonnet *(2)*
Kopfstück
capucha

1) A cloth covering for the head only or for the head
and neck. 2) A cloth covering for the head only.

1) Protège, en tout ou en partie, la tête et l'encolure. 2)
Couvre la tête seulement.

**hoof**
sabot
Huf *m*
casco

**hoofcare ; hoof care** => care of hooves

**hoof cancer** => canker

**hoof grease** ; grease for hoofs
graisse à sabots
Huffett *ne*
grasa para cascos ; crema para el casco

**hoof knife** ; hoof parer ; drawing knife
rénette ; reinette ; rainette ; couteau de maréchal-ferrant ; couteau anglais *Fr*
Hufmesser ; Rinnmesser
legra (cuchillo de ~) ; cuchilla (inglesa) ; cuchillo
herrero

Used to pare the sole, and for many other works in the
horn. *s.a. sole knife*

Couteau à extrémité repliée, servant principalement à
tailler la corne de la sole et de la fourchette.

**hoof parer** => hoof knife

**hoof pick**
cure-pieds
Hufkratzer *(der ~)*
piquete para el casco

**hoof tester(s)**
pince exploratrice ; pince à sonder
Hufuntersuchungszange *f*
pinza de palpación / testar ; pinza de casco
 Large pincers used to detect soreness in deeper structures of the foot.
 Large paire de pinces utilisée pour localiser une douleur dans le pied du cheval.

**hooks**
crochets
Kinnkettenhaken *m*
ganchos
 Located on the branches of a curb bit.
 Sur les branches d'un mors de bride, ils servent normalement à attacher la gourmette.

**horizontal croup** => flat croup

**horn** *anat*
corne *anat*
Horn *ne*
cuerno

**horn (of an anvil)** ; beak ; bick
bigorne (d'une enclume)
Horn *ne runden*
cuerno (del yunque)

**horn (of a saddle)** *west.*
corne (de la selle) *west.*
Sattelhorn *ne*
cacho ; cuerno
 The prominent projection on the pommel of western
saddles and some Australian stock saddles.
 La différence entre la corne et le pommeau (lui-même
désigné aussi parfois comme étant le gosier) n'a pas
toujours été faite en français.

**horse**
cheval *pl: chevaux*
Pferd *ne*
caballo
 Species « Equus caballus » include all modern domes-
ticated horses and some closely related feral and wild
counterparts.
 Le cheval domestique, de l'ordre des ongulés, famille
des équidés. Il est apparu il y a environ un million
d'années.

**horseback riding** ; equitation
équitation
Reiten *ne* ; Reiterei *f*
equitación

**horseflies**
taons ; tabanidés ; mouches des chevaux
Bremsen *f pl* ; Stechbremsen
tábanos ; tabarros ; moscas de caballo

**horsehair (a ~)**
crin (un ~)
Roßhaar *ne*
crin
 Chacun des longs poils de la crinière et de la queue.

**horseman** => horse person

**horsepower** *pl: same*
cheval vapeur *pl: chevaux vapeur*
Pferdestärke *f*
caballo de vapor

**horseradish**
raifort
Meerrettich *m*
rábano blanco

**horseshoe** ; shoe
fer (à cheval)
Hufeisen *ne*
herradura (de caballo) ; herraje *amer*

**horseshoeing** ; shoeing
ferrure ; ferrage
Hufbeschlag *m*
herraje

**horseshoer** ; farrier ; plater ; smith (shoeing-~)
maréchal-ferrant *pl: maréchaux-ferrants*
Beschlagschmied *m* ; Hufschmied ;
 Hufbeschlagschmied
herrador ; ferrador ; herrero *amer*

**horsetail** ; Equisetum *pl: equisetums / equiseta* ;
 fox tail ; mare's tail
prêle
Schachtelhalm *m*
equiseto ; cola de caballo
 A plant with a hollow jointed stem and looking like a
horse's tail. Horses eating a lot of E. arvense or E.
palustre develop thiamin deficiency.

**horsewhip** => whip

**horse-bay** => stall (standing ~)

**horse-breeding**
élevage chevalin / de chevaux
Pferdezucht
cría caballar

**horse-doctor** => equine veterinarian

**horse-drawn**
hippomobile ; tiré par des chevaux
Pferden gezogen (von ~)
hipomóvil ; tirado por caballos

**horse cloth** => blanket (horse ~)

**horse dealer / trader**
commerçant de chevaux ; maquignon
Pferdehändler
comerciante de caballos

**horse family** => equines (the ~)

**horse improvement**
amélioration de la race chevaline
Verbesserung der Pferde
mejora de caballos

**horse litter** => mule chair

**horse meat**
viande de cheval
Pferdefleisch
carne de caballo

**horse person** ; horseman
homme de cheval *pl: hommes de chevaux*
Pferdemann
persona a caballo ; hombre del caballo
 *s.a. expert*

**horse pox ; horsepox**
variole équine
Pferdepocken *f pl*
viruela equina

**horse show** *hd*
concours hippique *att*
Fahrturnier *ne*
concurso hípico
  L'expression n'est pas précise et peut inclure toutes les compétitions impliquant des chevaux.

**horse show** *class.*
concours hippique *équitation*
Reitturnier *ne*
concurso hípico ; concurso de equitación
  L'expression n'est pas précise et peut inclure toutes les compétitions équestres.

**horse show** *hj*
concours hippique *cs*
Reitturnier *ne*
concurso hípico ; concurso de saltos
  L'expression n'est pas précise et peut inclure toutes les compétitions équestres, elle est souvent utilisée pour désigner spécifiquement les concours de sauts d'obstacles.

**horse tail**
queue-de-cheval *pl: queues-de-cheval*
Pferdeschwanz *m*
cola de caballo

**horse team, two abreast**
attelage à deux chevaux (de front)
Zweiergespann ; Zweigespann ; Zweispänner
tronco (de dos) caballos

**horse trial** ; event
concours complet
Vielseitigkeitsprüfung
concurso completo ; prueba completa / militar
  May be one, two or three-day event. The three tests are, in their usual order: dressage, speed and endurance, and jumping. The speed and endurance is divided into four phases: roads and tracks, steeplechase, a further section of roads and tracks, and cross-country.
  Peut être d'un, deux ou trois jours. Comporte, dans l'ordre habituel: une épreuve de dressage, une épreuve de fond et une épreuve d'obstacles. L'épreuve de fond comporte quatre phases: un parcours routier, un parcours de type steeple, un deuxième parcours routier et un parcours de type cross-country, plus serré que le steeple.

**hound**
chien de meute
Hund
perro de caza ; mastín

**hounds (the ~)** ; pack
meute (la ~)
Meute
jauría ; perrada ; perrería

**house fly ; housefly**
mouche commune / domestique
Stubenfliege
mosca

**humerus**
humérus
Oberarmknochen ; Humerus
húmero
  The arm bone.
  L'os du bras, entre la scapula et le radius, il est attaché au thorax par des muscles.

**Hungarian Anglo-Arab horse** => Gidran

**hunter (field ~)**
cheval de chasse (à courre)
Jagdpferd
caballo de caza / cacería

**hunting saddle**
selle de chasse
Jagdsattel
silla de cacería / cazamiento

**hunting whip** ; hunt crop
fouet de chasse
Hetzpeitsche
fuete de caza ; látigo de caza

**huntsman**
piqueux ; piqueur
Huntsman *m* ; Hundsmann
maestro de los perros
  The hunt official in charge of hounds. *s.a. master of the hunt*
  c. à courre: Responsable de l'entretien des chiens et de leur conduite à la chasse.

**hunt crop** => hunting whip

**hurdle** => hedge

**hurdle(s) race**
course de haies
Hürdenrennen
carrera de salto
  The hurdles are smaller in size than in steeplechasing.
  Course sur des haies de dimensions réduites.

**hyoid apparatus / bone**
appareil hyoïdien ; os hyoïde
Zungenbein
hueso hioides

**hypodermis** => subcutis

**hypophysis** ; pituitary gland
hypophyse ; glande pituitaire
Hypophyse
hipófisis ; glándula pituitaria

**icterus** => jaundice

**idiopathic laryngeal hemiplegia** =>
  laryngeal hemiplegia / paralysis

**ileum**
ileum ; iléon
Krummdarm ; Ileum
íleon
  Partie de l'intestin grêle.

**ilium**
os ilium
Darmbein *ne*
ilion

**illness** => disease

**immobility**
immobilité
Stillstehen
inmovilidad
Standing still for a certain time, as part of a test.
Immobilité temporaire commandée lors d'une épreuve.

**immunity**
immunité
Ansteckungsfestigkeit *f*
inmunidad
Resistance of an organism against an infection.
Ensemble de facteurs protégeant l'organisme contre une infection ou une intoxication.

**impulsion**
impulsion
Schwung *(der ~)*
impulsión
The overall impetus and energy that the horse is putting in forward / upward movements, coming from the hindquarters through the pelvis and back of the horse.

**impulsion control**
contrôle de l'impulsion
Kontrolle des Schwungs
control de la impulsión

**inactive leg** ; passive leg
jambe passive
passiver Schenkel
pierna pasiva

**inattentive**
inattentif
unaufmerksam
desatento

**inborn defect** ; hereditary defect
tare héréditaire
Erbfehler *m*
defecto hereditario / innato

**inbreeding** ; close breeding
accouplement consanguin
Inzucht *f* ; Verwandtschaftszucht
endogamia ; procreación en consanguinidad
The mating of closely related animals.

**inbreeding test**
test de consanguinité
Inzuchttest *m*
prueba de consanguinidad

**incestuous breeding**
accouplement incestueux
Inzestzucht *f*
procreación incestuosa

**inch**
pouce
Zoll
pulgada ; pulgarada
Unité de mesure équivalente à 2,54 centimètres.

**incisive bone**
os incisif ; os intermaxillaire *anc*
Zwischenkieferbein
hueso incisivo ; hueso premaxilar
Il est creusé de cavités destinées à recevoir les incisives supérieures.

**incisors**
incisives
Schneidezähne *m*
incisivos
In the growth order and from the midline outward: centrals, laterals and corners.
Leur ordre de croissance correspond à leur disposition à partir du milieu de la mâchoire: les pinces, les mitoyennes et les coins.

**incorrect seat**
mauvaise assiette
falscher Sitz
asiento falso

**independence of the aids**
indépendance des aides
unabhängig von Hilfen
independencia de las ayudas
Les aides doivent s'exercer indépendamment les unes des autres, sans entraîner tout le corps dans leur mouvement, ou produire d'autres mouvements indésirables que le cheval interpréterait quand même comme des signaux ou qui le contraindraient quand même de quelque façon.

**index** => indicator

**indicator** ; rating ; index
indice
Index *m*
índice

**indoor arena**
manège intérieur ; manège couvert
Reitbahn *f* ; Reithalle
pista cubierta ; arena cubierta ; picadero

**infection** ; taint
infection
Ansteckung *f* ; Infektion *f*
infección

**infectious**
infectieux
ansteckend
infeccioso

**inflammation**
inflammation
Entzündung *f*
inflamación

**influenza (equine ~)** *abbr: EI* ; flu (equine ~)
grippe équine ; influenza
seuchenhafte Husten *(der ~)* ; Influenza (des Pferdes) *f*
gripe (caballar / equina) ; influenza (equina)
Infection virale contagieuse localisée surtout dans les bronches et les poumons, surveillance et repos sont nécessaires, la guérison peut prendre jusqu'à six mois.

**injury**
blessure
Verletzung *(die ~)*
herida

**injury to the coronet (overreach / self ~)**
atteinte à la couronne
Krontritt *(der ~)*
grietas

**inner rein**
rêne intérieure
innerer Zügel
rienda interna ; rienda de adentro

**insecticidal** => insecticide

**insecticide** *n* ; insecticidal *adj*
insecticide *n & adj*
Insektenvernichtungsmittel *ne* ;
 insektenvernichtend *adj*
insecticida *n & adj*

**inseminate** *v*
inséminer
besamen
inseminar

**inside leg**
jambe intérieure
innere Fuß
pierna interior / interna ; pierna de adentro

**instinct**
instinct
Unterbewußtsein *ne* ; Instinkt *m*
instinto

**interbreeding** => cross-breeding

**intermandibular region / space**
auge ; région intermandibulaire
Gefäßeinschnitt *m*
garganta ; fauces
 Espace compris entre les deux branches de la mâchoire
inférieure (i.e. les deux mandibules).

**intermittent limping**
boiterie intermittente
intermittierendes Hinken *(das ~)*
cojera intermitente

**internal parasite** ; endoparasite
parasite interne ; endoparasite
Endoparasit *m*
endoparásito

**International Equestrian Federation**
Fédération équestre internationale *abr: F.E.I.*
Internationale Reiterliche Vereinigung *(die ~)* ;
 Internationaler Reitverband *(der ~)*
Federación Ecuestre Internacional
 L'appellation 'Fédération Équestre Internationale' (la
plupart du temps sans accent sur le E), et l'acronyme
FEI sont utilisés en différentes langues.

**interosseus muscle** => suspensory ligament

**interparietal bone**
os interpariétal
Zwischenscheitelbein
hueso interparietal

**intestine** ; gut
intestin
Darm *m*
intestino

**in-and-out (obstacle / combination)**
double à une foulée (obstacle ~) ; saut de puce
in-out Kombination *(die ~)*
dentro y fuera (obstáculo)

**in-foal mare** => mare in foal

**in-toed** => toed-in

**in at the knees** => knock-kneed

**iodine**
iode
Jod *ne*
yodo

**iris**
iris
Regenbogenhaut ; Iris
iris

**Irish bank**
banquette irlandaise
irische Bank *(die ~)*
banqueta irlandesa

**Irish hunter** *breed*
irlandais *race*
irischer Hunter
media sangre irlandés ; hunter irlandés

**iron**
fer
Eisen *ne*
hierro

**iron grey** => blue roan

**iron (stirrup-~)** => stirrup

**isabella** => palomino

**ischial tuber**
tubérosité ischiatique
Sitzbeinhöcker *m*
tuberosidad isquiática

**ischium** *pl: ischia* ; pinbone
os ischium ; ischium *pl: ischia* ; ischion
Sitzbein *ne*
isquion

**itching** ; pruritus
démangeaison ; prurit
Hautjucken ; Pruritus
prurito

**jack** => donkey stallion

**jacket** ; silks (racing ~) ; coat
casaque
Rennjacke
colores
 With colours and patterns, worn by a jockey during a
race.
 Veste en soie aux couleurs vives que porte un jockey
pour la course.

**jaundice** ; icterus
jaunisse ; ictère
Gelbsucht *(die ~)*
ictericia

**jaw**
mâchoire
Kiefer *m* ; Kinnbacken *m*
quijada

**jejunum**
jejunum ; jéjunum
Leerdarm
yeyuno
 Partie de l'intestin grêle.

**jennet** => hinny

**jenny-ass ; jenny** ; she-ass
ânesse
Eselin *f* ; Eselstute *f*
burra ; asna

**jib** => refuse

    => refusal

**jig** *v*
trottiner
zackeln
trotinar

    Allure précipitée, trot très raccourci.

**jockey** *r* ; driver *br* ; rider *tr* ; reinsman *br*
jockey *c* ; conducteur *ca*
Jockey / Jockei *m* ; Rennreiter ; Fahrer *m br*
jockey ; conductor *br* ; vaquerillo *Mexico*

**jockey boot** ; racing boot
botte (à revers) de jockey
Rennstiefel ; Jockeystiefel
bota para jockey

**jockey seat**
position de course
Rennsitz
asiento de carrera ; asiento para correr

**Jodhpurs ; jodhpurs ; Jodhpur breeches**
culottes Jodhpurs
lange Reithose *(die ~)*
jodhpurs

    The leg is unbuttoned, unlaced and extended down to the ankle, wearing of high boots is thus unnecessary.

**Jodhpur boot**
bottillon ; bottine Jodhpur
Stiefeletten *(die ~)* ; Jodhpurstiefel *m*
botín

    Raising to the ankle level, with elastic sides or a buckle-over front.
    Chaussure montant à la hauteur de la cheville et ne comportant pas de lacets.

**joint**
articulation
Gelenk *ne*
articulación

**jointed** ; broken
brisé ; articulé
gebrochenes (Mundstück) ; geteilt
accionada (embocadura ~)

    Jointed or broken mouth(piece) / bit / snaffle.  *s.a. double jointed*
    Mors ou filet brisé ou articulé: L'embouchure est formée de deux canons articulés ensemble dans le centre.

**joint capsule**
capsule articulaire
Gelenkkapsel
cápsula articular

    Membrane fibreuse doublée à l'intérieur par une membrane synoviale.

**judge**
juge
Richter *(der ~)*
juez

**judges' box**
abri des juges ; mirador des juges
Richterhäuschen *(das ~)*
caseta del jurado

**judging**
jugement
Bewertung *(die ~)*
juicio

**judgment of (external) conformation** ;
  conformation judging
jugement de (la) conformation
Formbeurteilung *f* ; Formbewertung *f*
juzgamiento por conformación

**jugular groove**
sillon jugulaire ; gouttière jugulaire *anc*
Drosselrinne *f*
canal yugular

    Dépression le long du bord inférieur de l'encolure.

**jump** => obstacle

**jump** *v*
sauter
springen
saltar

**jump** *n*
saut
Sprung *m* ; Springen *ne*
salto

**jumper** ; show jumper (horse)
cheval (de saut) d'obstacle(s) ; sauteur
Springpferd
caballo de salto

**jumping**
saut d'obstacles
Springen ; Hindernisspringen
salto de obstáculos

**jumping competition** ; show jumper / jumping
  competition
concours de sauts d'obstacles
Springturnier ; Springprüfung
concurso de saltos de obstáculos

**jumping phase / test** *bt* ; stadium jumping *US bt*
épreuve (de saut) d'obstacles *cc*
Jagdspringen *ne*
prueba de saltos en pista ; fase de (concurso de)
  salto

**jumping rump** => goose rump

**jumping saddle**
selle de saut ; selle d'obstacle
Springsattel
silla de salto

**jump off / jump-off**
barrage
Stechen (mit Zeitwertung) *(das ~)*
desempate

**keep the horse on the aids** *v*
encadrer (le cheval entre les aides)
zwischen Schenkel und Zügel stellen
encuadrarlo entre pantorrilla y rienda

**kennel**
chenil
Zwinger
perrera

**Kentucky Saddler / Saddlebred** =>
American Saddlebred

**keratin**
kératine
Keratin *ne*
queratina

**kick** *v*
ruer
schlagen ; ausschlagen ; streichen
cocear ; dar coces ; patear

**kick** *n*
ruade
Ausschlag(en) ; Schlag *m*
coz

**kidney**
rein
Niere
riñón

**kill** *v hunting*
servir l'animal *c. à courre*
Abfangen des Wildes
matar

**kimblewick bit** ; Spanish snaffle ; Spanish
jumping bit
mors espagnol ; mors kimblewick
Springkandare
freno de palanca corta
  This bit is considered as a member of the pelham group.

**knee** ; carpus
genou *pl: genoux* ; carpe
Vorderknie *ne* ; Vorderfußwurzel *(die ~)* ;
Handwurzel
rodilla ; carpo
  *s.a. stifle*
  Compris entre l'avant-bras et le canon. Nous lui donnons sans doute le nom de genou par analogie avec le nôtre, mais en fait il correspondrait plutôt à notre poignet. Son articulation implique le radius, les os du carpe et les trois métacarpiens. Les mouvements de l'articulation se font pour la plus grande part entre la rangée supérieure des os du carpe et le radius (l'articulation antébrachio-carpienne).

**knee-narrow** => knock-kneed

**knee-wide** ; bandy-legged (in the forelimb) ;
wide at the knees ; bowlegged / bow-legged (in
the forelimb)
cambré des genoux
knieweit ; vorne faßbeinig
abierto de rodillas
  L'adjectif « cambré » qualifie habituellement plutôt les genoux que le cheval.

**knee action**
action du genou
Knieaktion *(die ~)*
acción de la rodilla

**knee bones** => carpal bones

**knee cap (boot)** ; knee cup / boot
genouillère ; botte de devant de genou
Kniekappe *(die ~)*
rodillera

**knee cup / boot** => knee cap (boot)

**knee insert** => knee roll

**knee pad** => knee roll

**knee roll** ; knee insert ; knee pad
insertion pour le genou
Kniewulst *(der ~)* ; Kniepausche *(die ~)*
rollo
  Packing or pad forming part of the front of the flap of the saddle and used for greater security.
  Bourrelet (matelassure du quartier de la selle) permettant de caler et de supporter le genou du cavalier.

**knee spavin** => carpitis

**knee sprung** => over at / in the knees

**knighthood** => chivalry

**knock-kneed** ; knee-narrow ; in at the knees
serré des genoux
knieeng ; X-beinig
cerrado de rodillas

**knock-knees** ; genu valgum ; carpus varus
genoux de boeuf
Ochsenknie
patizambo *adj*
  Inward angulation of the knees, standing closer to each other than the rest of the limb.
  Déviation des articulations vers l'intérieur; les genoux étant plus proches l'un de l'autre que le reste du membre.

**knock down an obstacle** *v*
renverser un obstacle
Hindernis umwerfen (ein ~)
derribar un obstáculo ; arrollar un obstáculo ; botar un obstáculo

**knuckling (over)** ; overshot fetlock ; upright
pastern ; cocked ankle
bouleture *n*
steile Fessel
cuartilla erguida
  Mild cases, in which the fetlock has not luxated or knuckled over, are described as upright or straight. « Cocked ankle » is a term sometimes considered equivalent to « knuckled over ». However, in a severe case where the horse walks on the front of the hoof, the foot will no longer be cocked up on the toe. *s.a. club foot*
  Quand le boulet est trop en avant, presque ou à la verticale avec le paturon (ang. « upright pastern » esp. « cuartilla erguida ») ou en avant de celle-ci.

**kur** ; freestyle dressage
kur ; présentation à volonté
Kür
reprise libre

**lacrimal bone**
os lacrymal
Tränenbein *ne*
hueso lacrimal

**lacrimal gland**
glande lacrymale
Tränendrüse
glándula lacrimal

**lactating mare** ; mare with foal at foot
jument suitée
Stute mit Fohlen bei Fuß ; Mutterstute mit
  Saugfohlen
yegua lactante ; yegua madre con potro lactante ;
  yegua con su potro ; yegua con rastra
  Se dit d'une jument qui allaite.

**lad**  => groom

**lady's mount**
cheval de dame ; cheval d'amazone
Damenpferd
caballo de damas

**lady rider**
cavalière
Reiterin ; Amazone
amazona

**lame** ; limping
boiteux
lahm
cojo ; rengo ; manco

**lameness**
boiterie
Lahmheit
cojera ; renguera ; claudicación

**lame, left // right fore**
boiteux de l'antérieur gauche // droit
vorne links // rechts lahm
cojo en la pierna izquierda // derecha delantera

**laminitis (acute ~)**
fourbure aiguë ; laminite
Hufrehe (akute ~)
laminitis ; dermatitis aguda del casco
  Inflammation of the sensitive laminae of the hoof.
  s.a. founder
  Inflammation du tissu podophylleux du sabot.

**land** v
recevoir (se ~)
fußen ; landen
llegar
  Touching the ground after jumping an obstacle.
  Toucher le sol après avoir sauté un obstacle.

**landau**
landau
Landauer m
landó
  Véhicule à 4 roues.

**landing**
réception
Landung (die ~)
caída ; llegada
  Landing after passing over an obstacle.
  Réception au sol après être passé au-dessus d'un obstacle.

**landing side (of an obstacle)**
côté de la réception
Landeseite (bei Hindernis) (die ~)
lado de recepción ; lugar de contacto ; costado
  de la recepción
  Côté opposé au côté de la battue.

**large intestine**
gros intestin
Dickdarm
intestino grueso
  Comprend le caecum, le gros côlon, le côlon descendant et le rectum.

**larva**
larve
Larve f
larva

**laryngeal hemiplegia / paralysis** ; roaring ;
  idiopathic laryngeal hemiplegia abbr: ILH
cornage m
Kehlkopfpfeifen ne ; Pfeifen ne ; Rohren ne
hemiplejía laríngea ; roncador adj & n
  The roaring is the abnormal noise made during the respiration, due to laryngeal hemiplegia (commonest
  cause) or bilateral paralysis.
  Bruit lié à une paralysie des muscles qui agissent sur
  une ou les deux corde(s) vocale(s), n'étant plus
  tendue(s) la(les) corde(s) vocale(s) vibre(nt) avec le
  passage de l'air de la respiration.

**laryngitis**
laryngite
Kehlkopfentzündung f
laringitis

**larynx**
larynx
Larynx ; Kehlkopf m
laringe
  Ensemble complexe formant un bref conduit qui fait
  communiquer le pharynx avec la trachée. Entre autres, il
  agit sur le débit de l'air et est l'instrument principal de
  la phonation.

**lasso** ; rope
lasso
Lasso (der ~)
lazo

**lateral aid**
aide latérale
einseitige Hilfe (die ~)
ayuda lateral
  Aide qui n'agit que d'un côté du cheval, l'expression
  pourra aussi désigner l'action simultanée de deux aides
  (ce sont habituellement la main et la jambe qui sont
  citées) du même côté du cheval, on parle ainsi souvent
  d'aides latérales.

**lateral cartilage of the foot**  => fibrocartilage
  of the third phalanx

**lateral cartilage of the third phalanx**  =>
  fibrocartilage of the third phalanx

**lateral digital extensor muscle**
muscle extenseur latéral du doigt ; muscle extenseur latéral des phalanges anc
seitliche Zehenstrecker
músculo extensor digital lateral

**lateral pair**
bipède latéral
seitliche Beinpaar *(das ~)*
bípedo lateral
  Paire de membres formée par les deux membres du même côté.

**latissimus dorsi muscle**
muscle grand dorsal
großer Rückenmuskel
músculo gran dorsal

**lead rope**
laisse (en fibre tressée)
Anbindestrick *m* ; Führstrick *m geflochten*
cuerda

**lead (on / at the right // left ~)**
main (à ~ droite // gauche)
Hand (auf der rechten // linken ~)
mano (a ~ derecha // izquierda)
  L'on manoeuvre « à main droite » lorsque l'antérieur droit du cheval est le plus en avant dans la foulée de galop, ou lorsque le déplacement ou le changement de direction se fait dans le sens du mouvement des aiguilles d'une montre.

**lean (heavily) on the hand / bit** *v* ; bore *v*
appuyer (lourdement) sur la main / le mors (s'~)
Zügel legen *(sich auf den ~)*
apoyar en el freno
  *s.a. pull*

**left foreleg** ; near foreleg *old*
antérieur gauche
linkes Vorderbein *(das ~)*
mano izquierda

**leg**  => gaskin
     => limb

**leg-yielding**
cession à la jambe
Schenkelweichen *(das ~)* ; Übertragung auf die Beine
cesión a la pierna

**leg marking**  => white marking on a limb / leg

**length**
longueur (de cheval)
Pferdelänge
cuerpo ; echada

**lengthen**  => extend

**lengthening (of strides)**
allongement (d'allure)
Strecken
alargamiento
  Accroissement de l'amplitude de la foulée, sans accélération de celle-ci.

**lengthen the reins** *v*
allonger les rênes
Zügel verlängern ; Leinen verlängern *(die ~)*
  *att/bd*
soltar las riendas

**length of the head**
longueur de la tête
Kopflänge
longitud de la cabeza

**lens**
cristallin ; lentille
Linse
cristalino

**leopard** *coat*
léopard *robe*
Tigerschecke *(der ~)*
leopardo
  Horse that is mainly white with coloured spots in his coat. If the background colour is not white, that colour should be specified in the description (e.g. sorrel leopard). A « patterned leopard » shows spots that seem to flow out of the flank (sometimes called raindrops).

**letter**  => marker letter

**levade**
levade
Levade
lanzada
  Assis sur ses postérieurs, le cheval élève son avant-main, les antérieurs étant pliés.

**levator muscle of upper lip**
muscle releveur de la lèvre supérieure
Heber der Oberlippe
elevador del labio superior

**levy** ; take out
tantième ; prélèvement
Gewinnanteil *m* ; Tantieme *f*
gravamen
  Taxe ou autre pourcentage prélevé sur le montant des transactions (paris etc.).

**lice** *pl*
poux *pl*
Läuse *f pl*
piojos

**licking block**  => salt lick

**ligament**
ligament
Band *ne pl: Bänder*
ligamento

**ligamentum nuchae**  => nuchal ligament

**lightness**
légèreté
Leichtigkeit
ligereza
  High degree of responsiveness to the aids.

**light bay**
bai clair
Hellbraune *m*
bayo pálido
  Bay of a light red / yellow body colour.  *s.a. buckskin*
  Robe baie dont la teinte principale est jaunâtre ou d'un rouge pâle.

**light chestnut** ; sorrel *(1)*
alezan clair
Hell-Fuchs / Hellfuchs *m* ; Lichtfuchs
alazán claro
  1) Darkest shades of sorrel.
  Robe pâle, proche de café au lait.

**light draught horse**
cheval de trait léger ; cheval d'attelage léger
leichtes Zugpferd *(das ~)* ; leichtes Wagenpferd
caballo de tiro ligero

**light mouth** => soft mouth

**limb** ; leg
membre ; jambe ; patte
Bein *ne* ; Glied *ne*
remo ; extremidad ; pata ; pierna
Au sens large le mot jambe désigne chacun des quatre
membres du cheval.

**limbs (the ~)**
membres (les ~)
Gliedmaßen
miembros

**limb faults**
défauts des membres
Gliedmaßenfehler
defectos de los miembros

**limp** *v*
boiter
lahmen ; lahm gehen ; hinken
cojear ; renguear

**limping** => lame

**lineage** ; strain ; bloodline
lignée
Blutlinie *f* ; Blutstrom *m*
línea de sangre ; línea de procedencia
*s.a. pedigree*

**line breeding ; linebreeding**
élevage en lignée ; sélection en lignée
Linienzucht
cría en líneas
The mating of individuals in the same family but not
closely related.

**line crossing**
croisement entre lignées
Zuchtlinienkreuzung
cruzamiento entre líneas

**line of the course**
tracé du parcours
Linienführung des Parcours
trazado de recorrido

**liniment** ; brace
liniment
Einreibemittel *ne* ; Liniment(um) *ne*
linimento

**link (mouthpiece with ~)** => double jointed
mouthpiece

**linseed** ; flax seed ; flax-seed
graine de lin
Leinsamen
linaza

**linseed oil**
huile de lin
Leinöl
aceite de linaza / lino

**Lipitsa / Lipizza horse** => Lipizzaner

**Lipizzaner** *breed* ; Lipitsa / Lipizza horse
lipizzan
Lipizzaner
lipizano
Race de chevaux qui descend des andalous, fortement
associée avec l'École espagnole de Vienne. Le nom
vient de Lipica (prononcé lipizza) près de Trieste en
Italie.

**lipstrap**
fausse gourmette
Scherriemen
falsa barbada ; correa labial

**lips (of the mouth)**
lèvres (de la bouche)
Lippen
labios

**litter** ; bed ; bedding
litière
Streu *(die ~)* ; Strohbett ; Einstreu
litera ; cama

**liver**
foie
Leber
hígado

**liverpool**
liverpool (obstacle comprenant un ~) ; bidet (obstacle sur ~)
überbauter Wassergraben *(der ~)*
liverpool

**liver chestnut**
alezan brûlé
Dunkelfuchs *m* ; Brandfuchs
alazán tostado
Darkest chestnut coat, deep brown and reddish colour.
La plus foncée des robes alezanes, d'une couleur
brun-roux qui rappelle celle du café torréfié.

**lockjaw** => tetanus

**loin(s)**
rein(s)
Lende *f* ; Lendenpartie *f* ; Niere(n) *f* ; Nierenpartie *f*
lomo(s) ; riñón(/ones)
Lower back (lumbar) area of the horse.
Région lombaire: délimitée par le dos, la croupe, les
hanches et les flancs; soit autour des vertèbres lombaires.

**longeing line** ; longe / lunge (line)
longe
Longe
cuerda (larga)

**longe whip** => lunge(ing) whip

**longe / lunge (line)** => longeing line

**longissimus (dorsi) muscle**
muscle longissimus dorsi
langer Rückenmuskel
músculo largo dorsal ; músculo longissimus dorsi
Includes Musculus longissimus capitis, l. atlantis, l.
cervicis, l. thoracis and l. lumborum.
Inclut Musculus longissimus capitis, l. atlantis, l. cervicis, l. thoracis et l. lumborum.

**long-distance ride** ; raid
longue randonnée ; raid *(1)*
Distanz-Ritt / Distanzritt *m* ; Dauerritt
raid

   1) Fr: Randonnée de plusieurs semaines.

**long digital extensor muscle** => common
  digital extensor muscle

**long pastern**
long jointé *adj*
lang gefesselt *adj* ; lange Fessel
cuartilla larga ; larga de cuartilla *adj*
   Quand le paturon est trop long.

**long pastern bone** => proximal phalanx

**long rein**
longue rêne
lange Zügel
rienda larga

**long rein (on / at a ~)**
rênes longues (les ~)
langen Zügel (am ~)
riendas largas (con ~)
   e.g.: walk on a long rein
   par ex.: pas, les rênes longues

**loose box** => box (stall)

**lope** => canter

**lop-eared**
oreillard ; mal coiffé ; clabaud
Schlappohren (Pferd mit ~)
oreja péndula / gacha / caída *n*
   Horse with ears tending to flop downwards.
   Dont les oreilles sont à l'horizontale.

**lorry / lorrie horse** => dray horse

**louse egg** ; nit
lente
Kopflausei *ne* ; Nisse *f*
liendre
   Oeuf de pou.

**louse (biting ~)** *pl: lice*
pou *pl: poux*
Haarling *m pl: Haarlinge* ; Laus *f*
piojo

**lower jaw** => mandible

**lower lip**
lèvre inférieure
Unterlippe
labio inferior

**lower thigh** => gaskin

**low ringbone**
forme coronaire ; forme basse
Hufgelenkschale *f*
sobrehueso de la corona
   At the coffin joint. May be due to a fractured extensor
process of the coffin bone.
   Implique l'articulation entre la 2ième et la 3ième phalange. On distingue parfois une forme de l'éminence
pyramidale (du processus extenseur).

**lucerne** => alfalfa

**lumbar vertebrae**
vertèbres lombaires
Lendenwirbel
vértebras lumbares
   Le cheval en a 5 (fréquemment chez les chevaux ara-
bes) ou 6. Elles forment la charpente osseuse de la
région des reins et leur mouvement est beaucoup plus
ample que celui des vertèbres thoraciques.

**lung**
poumon
Lunge
pulmón
   Formé de tissu élastique, il est formé de plusieurs mil-
lions d'alvéoles.

**lunge(ing) whip** ; longe whip
chambrière
Bahnpeitsche
látigo largo ; huasca larga ; látigo de picadero

**lunge / longe** *v*
longer
longieren
trabajar a la cuerda ; darle cuerda

**lungworm ; lung worm**
strongle respiratoire
Lungenwurm *(der ~)*
lombriz del pulmón
   Horses and donkeys can be parasitized by
Dictyocaulus arnfieldi and affected by coughing.

**Lusitanian horse** *breed* ; Portuguese horse
lusitano *race*
Lusitano
lusitano

**lymph**
lymphe
Lymphe
linfa
   A liquid collected from tissues in all parts of the body
and returned to the blood via the lymphatic system.
   Son apparence varie selon la partie de l'organisme où
elle est élaborée. Elle collecte les substances nutritives
absorbées par la muqueuse intestinale et les déchets de
diverses cellules de l'organisme.

**lymphangitis**
lymphangite
Lymphangitis *(die ~)*
linfangitis
   Inflammation in the lymphatic system.
   Infection microbienne dans le système lymphatique.
En pratique elle ne frappe la plupart du temps que les
membres postérieurs qui peuvent devenir énormément
gonflés.

**lymphatic system**
système lymphatique
Lymphsystem
sistema linfático
   Sometimes named the white blood system.
   Composé des vaisseaux lymphatiques et des ganglions
lymphatiques. Il se déverse dans le confluent des veines
jugulaires, au voisinage immédiat du coeur.

**lymphatic vessel**
vaisseau lymphatique
Lymphgefäß
vaso linfático

**lymph node**
ganglion lymphatique ; noeud lymphatique
Lymphknoten
ganglio linfático

Any of the lymphoid organs along the course of lymphatic vessel, they are the main of lymphocytes, removing noxious agent and critical in antibody formation.
Les ganglions lymphatiques filtrent la lymphe et en détruisent les germes et corpuscules nocifs.

**made** => well-schooled (horse)

**mahogany chestnut** => dark chestnut

**maintenance ration**
ration d'entretien ; ration de base
Erhaltungsration *f* ; Grundration
ración de conservación / mantenimiento / sostenimiento

**maize** => corn

**make a higher bid** *v*
enchérir ; surenchérir
hinauftreiben (den Preis ~) ; verteuern
pujar ; sobrepujar

Miser une somme supérieure à l'offre courante lors d'une vente aux enchères.

**make a horse stand correctly** *v*
placer (un cheval) d'aplomb
korrekt hinstellen (ein Pferd ~)
colocar (un caballo) bien parado

**male line** ; sire family
lignée mâle
väterliche Linie *(die ~)* ; männliche Linie
línea masculina / paterna

Line of male ancestors of a horse (from sire to sire on a direct genealogical line from male to male only). *s.a. pedigree*
Lignée des ascendants mâles (de père en grand-père paternel en arrière-grand-père paternel etc.) d'un individu.

**mandible** ; lower jaw
mâchoire inférieure ; mandibule
Unterkiefer ; Mandibel ; Kinnbacke
mandíbula

En fait et dans le sens strict, la mâchoire inférieure est formée de deux mandibules.

**mane**
crinière
Mähne *f*
crin ; crinera ; melena

**manège figures** => school figures

**manger** => feed tub

**mange mite**
acarien psorique ; sarcoptide ; sarcoptoïdé
Räudemilbe *f*
arador de (la) sarna

**mange (horse ~)**
gale (des équidés)
Räude *f*
sarna ; roña

Skin disease caused by mites.
Dermatose d'origine parasitaire.

**manner of handling / holding reins**
tenue des rênes
Zügelhaltung ; Zügelführung *att/bd* ; Haltung der Leinen *(die ~)*
manejo de las riendas

**manure**
fumier
Mist *m*
estiércol

**mare**
jument
Stute *f* ; Mähre *f*
yegua

Female horse aged four or five (according to disciplines and interpretations) and over.
Femelle de quatre ou cinq ans (selon les disciplines et les interprétations) et plus.

**Maremma / Maremmana horse** *breed*
maremme ; cheval de Maremme ; toscan
Maremmenpferd
maremmano ; toscano

Race italienne.

**mare's tail** => horsetail

**mare in foal** ; in-foal mare
jument gestante ; jument pleine
tragende Stute ; trächtige Stute
yegua llena ; yegua en gestación ; yegua preñada

**mare keeping**
élevage de juments
Stutenhaltung
yeguada

**mare with foal at foot** => lactating mare

**marker letter** ; letter
point de repère ; lettre
Bahnpunkt *(die ~)*
señal (de referencia)

Dans une carrière ou un manège, utilisé(e) surtout pour la reprise de dressage.

**marking**
marque
Abzeichen *ne*
marca

Spot, area etc., usually white, in the coat of a horse.
Tache, habituellement blanche, (balzane, liste etc.) apparaissant dans la robe d'un cheval.

**marking of the course**
jalonnement du parcours
Markierung der Reitbahn / des Parcours
jalonamiento del recorrido

**marking system** => scheme of marking

**martingale**
martingale
Martingal *ne*
martingala ; gamarra

**masseter muscle**
muscle masséter
äußerer / großer Kaumuskel
músculo masetero

**master of hounds / foxhounds** => master of the hunt

**master of the hunt** ; master of hounds / fox-hounds *abbr. MFH*
maître d'équipage
Jagdherr *m*
maestro de la caza
  The master of the hunt, should he hunt the hounds himself, may also be the huntsman. *s.a. huntsman*
  Personne qui assume la direction et la responsabilité d'une chasse à courre.

**maternal family / line** => female line

**mate (horses)** *v*
accoupler (des chevaux)
paaren
aparear ; acoplar

**mating** => breeding

**maxilla** => upper jaw

**maxillary sinus**
sinus maxillaire
Kieferhöhle (Ober...)
seno maxilar

**meadow fescue**
fétuque des prés
Wiesenschwingel
festuca pratensis

**measles** => cysticercosis

**measuring stick**
canne hippométrique ; toise à potence
Meßstock ; Stockmaß *ne*
metro

**measuring tape**
ruban à mesurer
Meßband *ne* ; Bandmaß *ne*
cinta métrica

**meconium**
méconium
Kindspech *ne*
meconio
  Ensemble des débris accumulés dans l'intestin du poulain au cours de la gestation.

**medial head of the deep digital flexor muscle** *hindlimb*
muscle fléchisseur médial du doigt *membre postérieur* ; m. fléchisseur interne / tibial / oblique des phalanges *anc*
schiefer Zehenbeuger
músculo flexor oblicuo de las falanges

**medication** => medicine

**medicine** ; medication ; drug *medicinal*
médicament ; remède
Medikament *ne*
medicamento ; medicina ; remedio

**medium canter**
galop moyen
Mittelgalopp
galope medio

**medium trot** ; ordinary trot
trot moyen
Mitteltrab
trote medio / ordinario
  Differences are sometimes made between « medium » and « ordinary » paces.

**medium trot sitting**
trot moyen assis
freier Arbeitstrab ausgesessen
trote ordinario sentado

**medium walk** ; ordinary walk
pas moyen / ordinaire
Mittelschritt *(der ~)* ; Gebrauchsschritt
paso medio / ordinario
  Differences are sometimes made between « medium » and « ordinary » paces.
  Des différences sont parfois faites entre les allures « moyennes » et les allures « ordinaires ».

**mesentery ; mesenterium**
mésentère
Gekröse *ne* ; Mesenterium *ne*
mesenterio ; redaño
  Membrane qui suspend une grande partie de l'intestin grêle à la voûte de l'abdomen.

**metacarpal bone (large / third ~)** ;
  forecannon bone ; cannon bone (fore...)
os métacarpien principal ; métacarpe (troisième os du ~) ; os du canon (antérieur)
vorderes Röhrbein *(das ~)*
tercer metacarpiano

**metacarpophalangeal //
  metatarsophalangeal joint** => fetlock joint

**metacarpus**
métacarpe
Metakarpus / Metacarpus *m*
metacarpo
  Segment du squelette du membre antérieur, formé des os métacarpiens.

**metal curry comb**
étrille en métal
Stahlstriegel *(der ~)*
almohaza (de metal) ; rasqueta *amer.*

**metatarsal bones**
os du métatarse (les ~) ; métatarses (les ~) ; métatarsiens (les os ~)
Metatarsalien
huesos metatarsianos
  Os des canons des membres postérieurs: un métatarsien principal (III) et deux métatarsiens rudimentaires (II ou médial, et IV ou latéral) pour chaque membre.

**metatarsal bone (large / third ~)** ; hind-cannon bone ; shannon bone ; shank ; great metatarsal *old* ; cannon bone (hind-~)
os métatarsien principal ; métatarse (troisième os du ~) ; os du canon (postérieur)
Hinterschienbein *ne*
gran metatarsiano ; tercera metatarsiano

**metatarsus**
métatarse
Metatarsus *m*
metatarso
  Deuxième segment du squelette du pied, formé par les os métatarsiens.

**metre / meter**
mètre
Meter
metro
Unit of linear measure equal to 3.2808 feet.
Unité de mesure équivalente à 3,2808 pieds an-
glo-saxons.

**middle phalanx** ; short pastern bone *old* ; os
coronae *old* ; second phalanx
phalange intermédiaire ; os de la couronne ;
deuxième / seconde phalange
Kronbein *ne*
segunda falange ; hueso corona
Son articulation inférieure est à l'intérieur du sabot.

**mildew** ; mold *US* ; mould *Brit*
moisissure
Moder *m* ; Schimmel *m*
moho

**mild steel**
acier doux
Flußstahl *m* ; Flußeisenstahl
acero dulce / blando

**mile**
mille
Meile
milla
Unité de mesure équivalente à 8 furlongs, 5280 pieds
ou 1,6093 kilomètres.

**milk foal** ; suckling (foal)
poulain // pouliche de lait ; poulain // pouliche
non-sevré(e)
Saugfohlen
potrillo // potrilla lactante

**milk teeth** ; deciduous teeth ; temporary teeth
dents de lait
Milchzähne *m* ; Fohlenzähne
dientes de leche

**milk (set of) teeth**
première dentition ; dentition de lait
Milchgebiß
primera dentición

**mineral lick** => salt lick

**miniature horse**
cheval miniature
Zwergpferd
caballo enano

**molars ; molar teeth** ; grinders
molaires
Backenzähne (hintere ~) *m*
molares
Le cheval en possède vingt-quatre.

**molasses** *US* ; treacle *Brit*
mélasse
Melasse *(die ~)*
melaza

**mold** => mildew

**molt** => shedding

**Monday morning sickness / disease** =>
azoturia

**moonblindness ; moon blindness** =>
equine recurrent uveitis

**Morgan** *breed*
morgan
Morgan Horse
morgan
Chevaux de taille moyenne, race originaire des E.U..

**mould** => mildew

**moult ; moulting** => shedding

**mounting step** ; block (horse ~)
montoir
Aufsteigblock
apeadero
Bloc ou piédestal servant à monter sur le cheval plus
aisément.

**mount (a horse)** *v* ; ride (a horse) *v*
monter (à / un cheval) ; chevaucher
bereiten ; reiten
montar (a caballo) ; cabalgar

**mouse-dun ; mouse-coloured** ; grulla ;
grullo ; blue-dun
souris *adj*
Mausgrau *ne mausgraue Farbe* ; mausgrau *adj* ;
Mausfalbe *m Mausgrau mit Aalstrich*
ratonero ; pelo de rata
Light blue or soft grey, with black points, almost always with primitive marks.
Poils gris uni, crins et extrémités noirs, très souvent
avec des zébrures et une raie de mulet.

**mouth**
bouche
Maul *ne* ; Mund *m*
boca

**mouth(piece)**
embouchure
Gebiss / Gebiß *ne*
embocadura
Stricto sensu, the part of the bit which goes in the
mouth.
Au sens strict, la partie du mors qui entre dans la
bouche du cheval, en pratique ce mot désigne souvent le
mors.

**movement**
mouvement
Bewegung
movimiento

**mucosa**
muqueuse
Schleimhaut
mucosa
Inner layer of different organs and body cavities.
Membrane interne de différents organes et cavités du
corps.

**mud guard** ; fender *br*
garde-boue
Kotflügel *(der ~)*
guardabarros

**muleteer** ; mule driver
muletier *n*
Maultiertreiber *m* ; Maultierführer *m*
mulero ; muletero
Personne qui conduit des mulets.

**mule chair** ; horse litter
cacolet
Tragkorb *m*
asiento para caballería

**mule driver**  => muleteer

**mule (female ~)** ; she-mule
mule
Maultier (weibliches ~) *ne*
mula
    Female offspring of a donkey stallion and a horse or
pony mare.
    Femelle du mulet, engendrée d'un âne et d'une jument.

**mule (male ~)**  => mullet

**mullet** ; mule (male ~) ; he-mule
mulet
Maultier (männliches ~) *ne*
mulo
    Male offspring of a donkey stallion and a horse or
pony mare. *s.a. hinny*
    Mâle engendré d'un âne et d'une jument.

**muscle-relaxant drug**
myorelaxant
muskelrelaxierende Medikament *(das ~)*
miorelajante

**mustang ; Mustang**
mustang
Mustang
mesteño ; mestengo ; mustango ; mustang
    Appellation générale pour les chevaux d'Amérique
mi-sauvages, mi-domestiqués, tenant des chevaux
apportés par les colons et des descendants de ceux
apportés par Colomb aux Antilles et par Cortés au
Mexique en 1519, c'est ce dernier qui a réintroduit les
chevaux sur le continent américain.

**muzzle**
muselière
Maulkorb
bozal
    Protective, bucket-like, covering for the nose of the
horse.

**muzzle** ; apex of the nose
museau ; bout du nez
Nasenspitze *f*
morro ; hocico
    Au-dessus de la lèvre supérieure et entre les naseaux.

**myocardium**  => cardiac muscle

**myoglobinuria (paralytic ~)**  => azoturia

**nail prick / tread** ; puncture wound (sole // frog
~)
clou de rue
Nageltritt *m* ; Stichwunde *(die ~)*
clavos ; herida podal por pinchazo
    Penetration of the sole by a sharp object to the depth of
the sensitive laminae.
    La sole est traversée par un clou ou par tout autre corps
étranger produisant une blessure similaire.

**nail (horseshoe ~)**
clou (à ferrer)
Hufnagel *m*
clavo (de herrar)

**narrow at the chest** ; both legs coming out of
one hole (having ~) ; narrow in front
serré de poitrail / poitrine
brusteng
apretado de delante
    Front legs set very closely at the top.

**narrow chest**
poitrine étroite
schmale Brust *(die ~)*
pecho angosto

**narrow in front**  => narrow at the chest

**nasal bone**
os nasal
Nasenbein *ne*
hueso nasal

**national stud**
haras national
Hauptgestüt *ne* ; Landgestüt
parada de sementales del Estado

**Nations' Cup** ; Prix des Nations
Prix des nations
Grand Prix der Nationen ; großer Preis der
  Nationen
Copa de las Naciones

**natural aid**
aide naturelle
natürliche Hilfe
ayuda natural
    Une des suivantes: les jambes, les mains, l'assiette et la
voix.

**natural obstacle**
obstacle naturel
Naturhindernis
obstáculo natural
    Obstacle construit avec des éléments dits naturels
(troncs, eau, fosses, etc.) auxquels on laisse leur
apparence sans couleurs vives et autres composantes qui
donneraient un air artificiel à l'obstacle.

**natural place for the saddle to sit**  =>
  saddle site

**natural service**
saillie naturelle ; monte naturelle
Natursprung *m*
monta natural

**navel** ; umbilical scar ; umbilicus
nombril ; ombilic
Nabel
ombligo

**navicular bone**  => distal sesamoid bone

**navicular disease / lameness / bursitis** ;
  podotrochleitis
naviculaire (maladie ~) ; ulcère corrosif de l'os
  naviculaire
Strahlbeinlahmheit *f* ; Podotrochlitis *f* ; chronische
  Hufrollenentzündung *(die ~)*
enfermedad (del) navicular
    A corrosive ulcer on the navicular bone. Podotroch…
points more specifically to the inflammation of the
podotrochlear bursa.
    Affection de l'os naviculaire à l'endroit où le tendon
du fléchisseur profond des phalanges coulisse sur lui.
Les termes commençant par podotroch… réfèrent plus

spécifiquement à l'affection de la bourse podotrochléaire.

## Near Eastern equine encephalomyelitis
=> Borna disease

**near foreleg** => left foreleg

**near to the ground** => well let down

**neck**
encolure ; cou
Hals *m*
cuello

S'étend de la tête jusqu'aux épaules et au poitrail. Le terme encolure est le plus approprié.

**neck of uterus** => cervix of uterus

**necrosis of the lateral cartilage(s)** => quittor (of horses)

**neigh** *v* ; whinny / whinney *v*
hennir
wiehern
relinchar
*see whinny (n) or neigh (n)*

**neigh** *n (1)* ; whinny ; whinney *n (2)*
hennissement
Wiehern
relincho

1) Loud and sometimes prolonged, the common call between horses that are not near. 2) A gentle neigh, denoting pleasure or expectancy. The word whinny is sometimes used for the common call in a situation of separation.

Le hennissement proprement dit est un appel qui est produit la bouche ouverte et qui porte loin, correspondant en général à une situation de séparation.

**nematode** ; roundworm ; threadworm
nématode ; ver rond
Rundwurm *(der ~)*
nematodo

Any individual organism of the class Nematoda.
Ver parasite, cylindrique, appartenant à la classe des Némathelminthes.

**nephritis**
néphrite
Nephritis *f* ; Nierenentzündung *f*
nefritis

Inflammation des reins.

**nerve** *pl: nerves*
nerf *pl: nerfs*
Nerv *m pl: Nerven*
nervio

**nerve-blocking**
anesthésie d'un nerf
Nervenblockade *f* ; Schmerzausschaltung am Nerv *(die ~)*
bloqueo nervioso

**nerving** => neurectomy

**nervous**
nerveux
nervös
nervioso

**neurectomy** ; nerving
névrectomie ; neurectomie
Neurektomie *f Nervenresektion*
neurectomía

**New-Forest (pony)** *breed*
new-forest
New Forest Pony
new forestal

Race de poneys, originaire du sud de l'Angleterre.

**nictitating membrane** ; haw ; third eyelid
membrane nictitante ; troisième paupière ; corps clignotant
dritte Augenlid *(das ~)* ; Blinzhaut *f* ; Nickhaut
párpado interno ; membrana nictitante ; tercer párpado

**nipper(s) (hoof ~)** ; trimmer / cutter (hoof ~) ; cutting nipper
pince coupante / à parer ; rogneuses ; cisailles ; tenailles à corne ; tricoises à parer
Hufbeschneidzange *f* ; Hufbeschlagzange
tenaza de corte

Used to cut the surplus growth of the wall.

**nit** => louse egg

**non-striated muscle** => smooth muscle

**Norman trotter** => French trotter

**noseband**
muserolle
Nasenriemen
muserola

Bande, en une ou deux pièce(s), passant sur le chanfrein et se bouclant sous l'auge. Elle empêche le cheval d'ouvrir trop largement la bouche, elle peut aussi servir à mettre de la pression sur le chanfrein du cheval.

**nose fly** => bot fly (horse ~)

**nose (bridge of the ~)** => bridge of the nose

**nostril**
naseau *pl: naseaux* ; narine
Nüster *f pl: Nüstern*
ollar *pl: ollares* ; nariz *pl: narices*

**nuchal ligament** ; ligamentum nuchae
ligament nuchal ; ligament de la nuque ; ligament cervical *anc*
Nackenband
ligamento de la nuca

**numnah** => saddle pad

**nutmeg** => flea-bitten grey

**oats**
avoine
Hafer
avena

**obedience**
obéissance
Gehorsam
obediencia

**obstacle** ; jump *n*
obstacle
Hindernis *ne*
obstáculo

**obstacle judge**
juge aux obstacles
Hindernisrichter
juez de obstáculos

**occipital bone**
os occipital
Hinterhauptbein
hueso occipital

**occipital foramen**  => foramen magnum

**occult spavin** ; blind spavin
éparvin aveugle
unsichtbarem Spat
esparaván oculto
 A bone spavin in which there is no external enlargement.
 Qui ne présente pas de déformation extérieure.

**oedema** *Brit* ; edema *US*
oedème
Ödem *ne* ; wässerige Schwellung
edema
 An abnormal accumulation of fluid in the cavities and intercellular spaces of the body.
 Infiltration d'un tissu par une abondance de liquide séreux.

**oesophagus** *Brit* ; esophagus *US*
oesophage
Speiseröhre ; Ösophagus
esófago
 Tuyau qui s'étend du pharynx à l'estomac. Ses fibres musculaires lui impriment un mouvement de vagues qui amènent le bol alimentaire jusqu'à l'estomac.

**oestrus**  => heat

**offending**
fautif
schuldig ; schuldhaft
culpable

**offspring**
rejeton
Nachkomme
prole

**oil glands**  => sebaceous glands

**Oldenburg (horse)** *breed*
oldenbourg ; oldenburg
Oldenburger
oldenburg ; oldenburgo
 Race qui doit son nom à sa région d'origine en Allemagne.

**olecranon**
olécrane / olécrâne
Ellbogenhöcker *m* ; Olekranon
olécranon
 Extrémité supérieure de l'ulna, formant la base du coude du cheval.

**Olympic Games**
Jeux olympiques
olympische Spiele *(die ~)*
Juegos Olímpicos

**one-horse draught**
attelage à un cheval
Einergespann *ne* ; Einspänner *m*
tiro de un caballo

**on the aids** ; between legs and hands
bien encadré ; entre mains et jambes
an den Hilfen ; zwischen Hand und Schenkel
entre las manos y las piernas

**on the bit (horse ~)**
en main (cheval ~)
Gebiss gestellt *(an das ~)* ; gezähmtes Pferd ;
 Gebiss sein ; eifrig *adj*
en la mano / rienda (caballo ~)
 On peut aussi dire que le cheval est bien mis, qu'il est dans la main, etc.

**open-front boot**
guêtre ouverte
Gamasche *(die ~)*
bota frente abierto
 A jumper tendon support boot.
 Guêtre pour la protection des tendons des sauteurs, ouverte à l'avant.

**open ditch**
fossé ouvert
Graben *(der ~)*
foso abierto ; zanja abierta
 Fossé comportant une haie devant et une barrière du côté de la réception.

**optic nerve**
nerf optique
Sehnerv *m* ; Optikus ; Augennerv
nervio óptico

**orbital arch**  => superciliary arch

**orbit (eye ~)**  => eye socket

**ordinary trot**  => medium trot

**ordinary walk**  => medium walk

**ossify** *v*
ossifier (s'~)
verknöchern (sich ~) ; Knochen werden (zu ~)
osificarse

**osteitis**
ostéite
Knochenentzündung *f* ; Ostitis *f*
osteítis
 Inflammation d'un os.

**os calcis**  => calcaneus

**os coronae**  => middle phalanx

**os pedis**  => distal phalanx

**os suffraginis / saffragenous**  => proximal
 phalanx

**otitis**
otite
Ohrenentzündung *f* ; Otitis *f*
otitis

**outbreeding** ; outcrossing
accouplement éloigné / régulier
Fremdzucht
cruzamiento abierto
 The mating of unrelated or distantly related individuals.
 Accouplement de reproducteurs non-apparentés ou apparentés de loin.

**outcrossing**  => outbreeding

**outer covering (of the eye)** => sclera

**outer rein** => outside rein

**outside rein** ; outer rein
rêne extérieure
äußerer Zügel
rienda exterior ; rienda de afuera

**out at the hocks** => bandy-legged (in the hindlimb)

**ovarian cyst**
kyste ovarien
Eierstockzyste *f*
quiste ovárico

**ovary** *pl: ovaries*
ovaire
Eierstock *m*
ovario

**overreach** *v*
atteindre (s'~) ; attraper (s'~) *en talons* ; couper (se ~) ; tailler (se ~) ; toucher (se ~)
greifen (sich ~)
sobrepasar
The striking of a hind toe on the back of a front leg (usually on the heel of the same side).
Lorsque la pince du membre postérieur atteint le pied antérieur du même côté. Bien que les auteurs ne soient pas unanimes, l'expression s'atteindre (en talons) semble la plus adéquate. On dit aussi qu'un cheval s'atteint au coude (« elbow hitting ») ou au genou (« knee hitting »).

**overreach boot** => bell boot

**overshot fetlock** => knuckling (over)

**overshot jaw** => brachygnathia ; brachygnathism

**over-bent**
encapuchonné
überzäumt
encapotado
The lower head is approaching the chest, behind the vertical dropping from the upper part of the head to the ground.

**over at / in the knees** ; buck-kneed ; knee sprung
brassicourt (genou / cheval ~) ; arqué (genou ~)
vorbiegig ; bockbeinig
bracicorto ; corvo
Anterior deviation of the carpal joint.
Déviation de l'articulation du genou vers l'avant: vu de côté, le genou est trop en avant, par rapport à l'axe du membre.

**over the bit** => above the bit

**owner**
propriétaire
Besitzer(in) *m(f)*
propietario ; dueño

**ownership**
propriété
Besitz *m* ; Besitzung *f* ; Besitztum *ne* ; Eigentum *ne*
propiedad

**oxer**
oxer
Oxer *m*
oxer ; doble valla con seto
Could be an hedge with a rail on one side. Usually a « double oxer »: at least two poles on two different stands and possibly with a hedge between them. Literally, rails prevent oxen from eating the hedge.

**pace** => gait
=> amble

**pacer** => ambler

**paces** => gaits

**pack** => field
=> hounds (the ~)

**pack animal**
animal de bât / somme
Tragtier ; Lasttier ; Saumtier
animal de carga

**pack horse ; packhorse**
cheval de bât ; cheval de somme
Packpferd *ne* ; Tragpferd ; Saumpferd
caballo de carga / albarda

**pack saddle**
bât
Bastsattel ; Saumsattel ; Tragsattel
albarda

**paddle** *v* ; wing out *v* ; dish *v*
billarder ; cagneux en marche (être ~) ; faucher
fuchteln
bracear
When moving forwards, the foot of one or both of the forelegs is throw outwards while in the air, and then taken back inwards to its landing position.
Lorsque le cheval se déplace vers l'avant, le pied au soutien décrit un demi-cercle vers l'extérieur.

**paddock** ; hitching ring *hj hd*
paddock
Paddock *m*
paddock
An enclosed area where horses are detained (hr) or walked and viewed by the public (tr) just prior to a race, or in which they are warmed-up and/or waiting just before their participation (hj & hd). *s.a. other entry for paddock*
Enclos à accès restreint où les chevaux sont rassemblés (ca) ou paradés (ct), ou encore dans lequel ils attendent tout juste avant leur participation à une compétition (cs & att).

**paddock boot** ; ankle boot
botte d'écurie ; bottine
Schuh ; Schnürstiefel
botín

**pail**
seau
Eimer *m* ; Kübel *m*
cubo

**paint(ed) (horse)** => pinto ; pintado

**palate**
palais
Gaumen *m*
paladar

**palatine bone**
os palatin
Gaumenbein
hueso palatino

**palfrey**
palefroi
Paradepferd
palafrén
   Cheval de parade des grands seigneurs au Moyen-Âge.

**palomino** ; isabella *(1)*
palomino
Palomino
palomino
   Golden with lighter mane and tail, occasionally with pink skin or a few black hairs, but without the red tint of the chestnuts. 1) In North America this term is proposed to be restricted to very light cream coloured palominos with non-blue eyes.
   Alezan doré ou café-au-lait, à crins lavés.

**pancreas**
pancréas
Bauchspeicheldrüse *f* ; Pankreas
páncreas

**panel (saddle ~)**
matelassure
Sattelkissen ; Kissen ; Polsterung
almohadilla
   The cushion between the tree and the horse's back.
   Partie rembourrée de la selle qui repose sur le dos du cheval.

**parade** ; post parade *r*
parade ; défilé
Parade *(die ~)*
desfile
   r: A parade of the horses in front of the public, on their way to the starting gate.
   c: Passage des concurrents devant le public, avant la course.

**parasite**
parasite
Parasit *m*
parásito
   *s.a. internal parasite*

**parasympathetic nervous system**
système nerveux parasympathique ; parasympathique
parasympathisches Nervensystem
sistema nervioso parasimpático
   Partie du système nerveux autonome, a des effets contraires à ceux du sympathique.

**parenchyma**
parenchyme
Parenchym *ne* ; Parenchyma
parénquima

**pare (a hoof)** *v* ; trim *v* ; dress *v*
parer (un sabot)
Huf richten
rebajar un casco ; recortar un casco

**parietal bone**
os pariétal
Scheitelbein
hueso parietal

**pari-mutuel**
pari mutuel
Rennwette
apuestas mutuas
   Le principe de base est le suivant: les parieurs détenant les mises gagnantes empochent les montants des mises perdantes, après déduction des prélèvements des organisateurs et des pouvoirs publics.

**parotid gland**
parotide (glande ~)
Ohrspeicheldrüse *f* ; Parotis *f*
parótida
   Glande salivaire située sous l'oreille, le long de la branche montante de la mâchoire inférieure.

**parrot mouth / jaw** => brachygnathia ; brachygnathism

**parturition** => foaling

**Paso Fino** *breed*
paso fino *race*
Paso Fino
paso fino
   The horses are shown at three gaits: paso fino, paso corto and paso largo.

**passage**
passage
Passage *(die ~)*
passage; pasaje
   Trot écourté et relevé, très rassemblé, soutenu et cadencé.

**passive leg** => inactive leg

**pastern**
paturon
Fessel *f*
cuartilla
   Partie comprise entre le boulet et la couronne.

**pastern joint** ; proximal interphalangeal joint
articulation du paturon ; première art. interphalangienne ; art. interphalangienne proximale
Krongelenk ; zweites Zehengelenk
primera articulación interfalangiana ; articulación de la cuarta
   Implique les deux premières phalanges.

**pasture** ; grazing grounds
pâturage ; pacage *(1)*
Weide *f* ; Koppel *f* ; Koppelweide *f*
pasto ; pasturaje ; dehesa
   1) Le pacage sera souvent une prairie naturelle pauvre ou de richesse moyenne.

**pasture** => graze

**pasture** *v* ; take to pasture *v*
faire paître
weiden
apacentar ; pastar

**patella**
rotule
Kniescheibe *(die ~)* ; Patella
rótula
   Dans la partie avant de l'articulation du grasset, cet os s'articule sur l'extrémité inférieure du fémur.

**paw the ground** *v*
piaffer *v*
scharren ; stampfen
piafar

Action du cheval qui frappe le sol d'un, ou des deux, antérieur(s), sans avancer.

**peacock-neck** => arched neck

**pedal bone** => distal phalanx

**pedal joint** => coffin joint

**pedigree**
pedigree
Stammbaum ; Pedigree
pedigrí ; pedigree

Pedigree, lineage and ancestry, these terms are sometimes presented as equivalents. However, you may follow a particular bloodline or lineage on a pedigree, which is a recorded portion of a horse ancestry. Lineage and bloodline include both ancestors and descendants.

Pedigree, lignée, ascendance, ces mots sont parfois utilisés indifféremment. Le mot pedigree a toutefois un sens généalogique plus concret et est ainsi souvent représenté sur papier. On peut consulter le pedigree d'un cheval, dans lequel n'est identifiée qu'une partie de ses ancêtres (son ascendance), et y suivre, à titre d'exemple, une partie de la lignée de sa grand-mère paternelle. La lignée inclut à la fois les ancêtres et les descendants.

**Pegasus**
Pégase
Pegasus *m*
Pegaso

**pelham bit**
mors pelham ; pelham
Pelham ; Pelhamgebiß ; Pelhamkandare
freno para dos riendas ; pelham ; pollero

Son embouchure peut-être articulée ou non, il comporte des branches et deux paires d'anneaux porte-rênes, une au niveau du canon et une au bas de la branche inférieure. Il comporte aussi des anneaux pour la gourmette et la fausse-gourmette.

**pelvic limb** => hind leg / limb

**pelvis**
pelvis ; bassin
Becken *ne*
pelvis

Constitué par les deux os coxaux et le sacrum.

**pelvis angle**
angle du bassin
Beckenwinkel
ángulo de la pelvis

**penalty point**
point de pénalité
Strafpunkt
punto de penalidad

**penalty table**
barème des pénalités
Richtverfahren (nach Fehlerpunkten)
baremo de penalizaciones

**penicillin**
pénicilline
Penicillin *ne*
penicilina

**penis**
pénis ; verge
männliches Glied ; Rute ; Penis
pene

**pepsin**
pepsine
Magenferment *ne* ; Pepsin *ne*
pepsina

**Percheron** *breed*
percheron
Percheron
percherón

Race de chevaux de trait lourd français, elle tire son nom de sa région d'origine en Normandie.

**pericardium**
péricarde
Herzbeutel ; Perikard
pericardio

**perineum**
périnée
Damm *m* ; Perineum *ne*
perineo

**periodic ophthalmia** => equine recurrent uveitis

**periople**
périople
Saumband
periopoles

Band of soft, rubbery horn near the coronet. Dried periople will form the stratum externum of the wall.

Genre de vernis qui s'étale sur le sabot à partir du bourrelet périoplique. Il protège la paroi contre une trop forte évaporation de son humidité.

**periosteum**
périoste
Periost ; Knochenhaut
periostio

Membrane fibreuse, dont le rôle est très important, qui recouvre les os, sauf sur leurs faces articulaires et aux points d'insertion des muscles et des tendons.

**periostitis ; periosteitis**
périostite
Knochenhautentzündung *f*
periostitis

Inflammation of the periosteum.
Inflammation du périoste.

**peritoneum**
péritoine
Bauchfell *ne* ; Peritoneum *ne* ; Peritonäum *ne*
peritoneo

**peritonitis**
péritonite
Peritonitis *(die ~)* ; Bauchfellentzündung *(die ~)*
peritonitis

**permanent teeth**
dents de remplacement ; dents d'adulte
Ersatzzähne *m pl* ; bleibende Zähne ;
  Dauerzähne
dientes permanentes

**permanent (set of) teeth**
dentition d'adulte
Dauergebiß
segunda dentición

**Peruvian paso / ambler** *breed* ; Caballo de Paso Peruano
ambleur péruvien
Caballo de Paso (Peruano)
paso peruano (caballo de ~) ; caballo aguililla
  Race péruvienne, la taille standard est de 1,45 à 1,55 mètres au garrot. L'association nationale de l'ambleur péruvien a été formée un peu après la deuxième guerre mondiale.

**pest (insect)**
insecte nuisible
Schädling *m*
insecto dañino

**petrous part (of temporal bone)**
rocher ; partie pétreuse (de l'os temporal)
Felsenteil *m*
hueso petroso del temporal

**phalange**  => phalanx

**phalangeal exostosis**  => ringbone ; ring bone ; ring-bone

**phalanx** ; phalange
phalange
Zehenknochen
falange

**pharynx**
pharynx
Rachen *m* ; Schlundkopf *m* ; Pharynx *m*
faringe
  Section of the alimentary canal between the mouth and the oesophagus, which also serves, except during swallowing, to connect the nasal passages with the larynx.
  Tunnel entre la bouche et l'oesophage qui fait passer les aliments dans ce dernier. Il permet aussi de faire circuler l'air entre les fosses nasales et le larynx.

**phlebotomy**  => blood-letting

**phosphorus**
phosphore
Phosphorverbindung *f*
fósforo

**photophobia**
photophobie
Lichtempfindlichkeit *f*
fotofobia
  Excessive sensitivity to sunlight.
  Sensibilité excessive de l'oeil à la lumière solaire.

**piaffé ; piaffer ; piaffe**
piaffé ; piaffer *n*
Piaffe *f*
piafe ; piaffer
  Trot rassemblé sur place.

**pica** ; allotriophagia ; depraved appetite
pica *m* ; allotriophagie
Allotriophagie *f* ; perverser Appetit
pica ; alotriofagia
  Craving for unnatural articles of food, often caused by a nutritional deficiency.
  Modification des habitudes alimentaires qui amène le cheval à ingérer des substances telles que du crottin ou de la terre.

**pick out a foot** *v*
curer un pied / sabot
Huf auskratzen *(der ~)* ; Huf ausräumen
limpiar un casco

**piebald**
pie noir
Rapp-Schecke *f oder m*
pío negro
  The body coat consists of large irregular patches of black and white. *s.a. other entry*
  Cheval pie, noir et blanc, dont la couleur de fond (qui domine) est le blanc.

**piebald**
noir pie
Rapp-Schecke *f oder m* ; Schwarz-Schecke
pío negro
  The body coat consists of large irregular patches of black and white. Black is the foremost colour in « noir pie ». *s.a. other entry*
  Cheval pie, noir et blanc, dont la couleur de fond (qui domine) est le noir.

**pied (horse)**  => pinto ; pintado

**pigeon-toed**  => toed-in

**pigeon breast**
poitrail de chèvre
Ziegenbrust
pecho de pichón
  Having a sternum that seems to project in front of the shoulders.

**pigment**
pigment
Farbstoff *m* ; Pigment *ne*
pigmento

**pillars**
piliers
Pilaren
pilares
  For working the horse between the pillars.
  Pour le travail du cheval entre les piliers.

**pinbone**  => ischium

**pincer**  => central incisor

**pincers**  => central incisors

**pincer(s) (farrier's ~)**  => puller (shoe ~)

**pincher(s)**  => puller (shoe ~)

**pinto ; pintado** ; paint(ed) (horse) ; calico ; pied (horse) *(1)*
pie *adj & n m* ; pinto *adj & n*
Schecke *f oder m* ; Scheck *m* ; scheckig *adj*
pintado ; pinto ; picazo ; pío
  Body marked in large patches of white and another colour. s.a. piebald, skewbald, tobiano, overo and sabino. 1) When the body presents only a few small

patches of white on a solid colour, the horse might be designed as pied chestnut, pied black etc.

Deux couleurs, dont le blanc, en plaques homogènes. Si le blanc domine on dira que le cheval est pie et de cette autre couleur (pie noir etc.); si l'autre couleur domine on placera cette autre couleur devant le mot pie (noir pie etc.).

**pinworm (horse ~)** ; seatworm
oxyure
Pfriemenschwanz des Pferdes *(der ~)*
oxiuro

**pin-toed** => toed-in

**pin firing (scars)**
pointes de feu
Punktbrennen *ne*
puntas de fuego

**piroplasmosis** => babesiasis ; babesiosis

**pirouette**
pirouette
Pirouette *(die ~)*
pirueta (sobre el tercio posterior) ; pirueta directa

A complete turn of the horse on himself. In the pirouette, forefeet and outside hind foot are moving around the inside hind foot which must be limited to a minimal horizontal displacement.

Tour sur lui-même que le cheval exécute, au pas ou au galop. Dans la pirouette, les antérieurs et le postérieur extérieur pivotent autour du postérieur intérieur.

**pirouette at a canter**
pirouette au galop
Pirouette im Galopp
pirueta a galope

**pirouette renversée** => reversed pirouette

**pisiform bone** => accessory carpal bone

**pituitary gland** => hypophysis

**place a bet** => bet

**plait** *v* ; braid *v*
tresser
einflechten
trenzar

**plaited mane** ; braided mane
crinière tressée
geflochtene Mähne
crinera trenzada

**plank(s)**
palanque(s)
Planke(n) *(die ~)*
tablas (barrera / valla de ~)

The word plank will normally identify a flat piece used in the gate type obstacle called planks or sometimes plank jump.

Le mot palanque (au singulier) est utilisé pour désigner chacune des planches superposées composant l'obstacle (de type barrière) qu'il sert aussi à désigner. Utilisé au pluriel, le mot sert aussi parfois à désigner ce même obstacle.

**plantain**
plantain
Wegerich *m*
llantén ; plantaina

**plantar cushion** => digital cushion

**plan of the course**
plan du parcours
Parcoursskizze
croquis de recorrido ; plano del recorrido ; plano por el curso

**plasma (blood ~)**
plasma (sanguin)
Blutplasma *ne*
plasma

Sérum sanguin qui a été séparé des corpuscules qui y baignent normalement.

**plater** => horseshoer

**pleasure** ; hacking
plaisance ; promenade (équitation de ~)
Promenadenreiten ; Spazierenreiten
paseo a caballo

Pleasure classes are presented in some western riding competitions. Hack classes are held in some classical (hj) riding competitions.

Des classes de plaisance sont tenues dans certains concours d'équitation western.

**pleura**
plèvre
Brustfell ; Pleura
pleura

**pleuritis ; pleurisy**
pleurésie
Brustfellentzündung *f* ; Rippenfellentzündung
pleuresía

**plough horse**
cheval de labour
Ackerpferd *ne*
caballo de labor

**pneumonia**
pneumonie
Lungenentzündung
neumonía ; pulmonía

**podotrochleitis** => navicular disease / lameness / bursitis

**point of hip**
pointe de la hanche
Hüfthöcker *m*
punta del anca ; joroba del lomo

**point of hock**
pointe du jarret
Hacke *(die ~)* ; Sprungbeinhöcker *m*
punta del corvejón

Correspondant au sommet du calcaneus.

**point of shoulder**
pointe de l'épaule
Bugspitze *f*
punta del hombro

Saillie de l'articulation scapulo-humérale.

**point (of a nail)**
pointe (d'un clou)
Stift *m*
punta ; puntilla

**poker**
tisonnier
Feuerhaken *m*
atizador

**pole** => rail

**poll**
nuque
Genick *ne* ; Nacken *m*
nuca

**polo**
polo
Polo(spiel)
polo

**polo boot**
botte de polo
Polostiefel
bota para polo

**polo helmet**
casque de polo
Polohelm
casco

**polo pony**
poney de polo
Polopferd
caballo de polo ; póney de polo

Called ponies even when of horse size, because the rules originally limited their sizes.

**polo saddle**
selle de polo
Polosattel
silla de polo

**pommel**
pommeau
Vorderzwiesel *m* ; Sattelknopf *m*
borrén delantero ; batilla ; perilla ; cabecilla

**pommel horse**
cheval d'arçons
Sprungpferd *ne*
potro (con arzón)

**pony**
poney
Pony ; Kleinpferd
póney ; jaca ; poni / pony

Equine measuring up to around 14-14,2 hh, depending on the breed or discipline, except for polo ponies to which no height limit applies and to Arabs, which are always called horses.

**poor mouth** => hard mouth

**popped knee** => carpal hygroma

**porcelain whIte**
blanc porcelaine
Porzellan-Schimmel
blanco porcelana

Robe qui a une teinte bleuâtre due à la coloration de la peau que l'on devine sous les poils.

**port**
liberté de langue ; dégagement de langue ; passage de langue
Zungenfreiheit *(die ~)*
portalón ; libertad de la lengua

The raised section in the middle of a mouthpiece.
Forme donnée au canon du mors, pour accommoder la langue du cheval.

**portal vein**
veine porte
Pfortader *f*
vena porta

**Portuguese horse** => Lusitanian horse

**position of the rider**
position du cavalier
Haltung des Reiters
posición del jinete

**post** => stand (of an obstacle)

**posting trot** ; rising trot
trot enlevé ; trot à l'anglaise *anc*
leichter Trab
trote levantado ; trote a la inglesa

**post and rail (vertical fence)**
stationata
Staccionata *f* ; Rick *ne*
barrera fija

Obstacle vertical fait de barres superposées, d'aspect assez massif.

**post parade** => parade

**post (to the trot)** *v*
enlever (s'~ au trot)
leichttraben
levantar (al trote

**poultice**
cataplasme
Breiumschlag
emplasto

**poultice boot**
botte à cataplasme ; botte pour le traitement des pieds ; soulier médical
Krankenschuch
bota de medicación

**powdered grey** => dark grey

**preferred** => favourite / favorite

**premolars ; premolar teeth**
prémolaires
vordere Backenzähne
premolares

**prepuce** => sheath

**president of the jury**
président du jury
Obmann
presidente del jurado

**presternal region** => breast

**price**
prix
Preis *m*
precio

Prix à payer, valeur en argent à verser lors d'une transaction etc.

**pricking** => quicking

**pritchel (hot work ~)**
poinçon emporte-pièce ; perce-trou
Austreiber *m* ; Durchtreiber
sacabocados ; taladro ; taladrador

Used to shear the bottom of the nail hole after the stamp have been used to form the countersunk for the nail head.

**Prix des Nations** => Nations' Cup

**Prix St. George**
Prix Saint Georges
St. Georg Preis
premio San Jorge

**prize**
prix
Ehrenpreis *m*
premio (de honor)

Prize, other than money, to be won: a cup, a plate etc.
Prix, autre que de l'argent, que l'on peut remporter: coupe, plaque, objet d'art etc.

**prize**
prix
Preis *m*
premio

Un enjeu, un concours ou un prix que l'on peut remporter.

**prize (cash / money ~)**
prix (en argent) *à remporter*
Geldpreis
premio (en dinero)

**proceed** => break into

**production assessment**
jugement de la production
Leistungsbeurteilung *f* ; Leistungsbewertung *f*
apreciación de la producción

**progeny test(ing)**
épreuve sur / de la descendance
Nachkommenprüfung
análisis de progenie ; prueba de (la) descendencia

Testing the potential on an animal by assessing the qualities of his progeny.
Appréciation des qualités d'un reproducteur à la lumière de celles de ses descendants.

**prognathism / prognathia (mandibular ~)**
prognathisme / prognathie (mandibulaire) ; bec de perroquet inversé ; gueule de singe
Hechtgebiss *ne* ; vorstehender Unterkiefer
prognatismo (de la mandíbula)

Abnormal protrusion of the lower jaw.
Lorsque la mâchoire inférieure dépasse la mâchoire supérieure.

**program** => programme

**programme** *Brit* ; program *US*
programme
Programm *ne*
programa

**prostate**
prostate
Vorsteherdrüse ; Prostata
próstata

**protein**
protéine
Protein *ne*
proteína

**proximal interphalangeal joint** => pastern joint

**proximal phalanx** ; long pastern bone *old* ; os suffraginis / saffragenous *old* ; first phalanx
phalange proximale ; première phalange ; os du paturon
Fesselbein *ne*
primera falange ; hueso cuartilla / cuarta

**proximal sesamoid bones** ; sesamoid bones (proximal ~)
os grands sésamoïdes ; sésamoïdes (os grands ~) ; grands sésamoïdes (os ~)
Gleichbeine *ne*
sesamoideos proximales

Small, pyramid-shaped bone forming the back of the fetlock joint, beneath the flexor tendons.
Petits os en forme de pyramide qui sont au nombre de deux dans le boulet, ils s'articulent étroitement sur la partie postérieure de l'os du canon. Les tendons fléchisseurs des phalanges coulissent sur eux (à la surface du scutum proximal).

**pruritus** => itching

**pterygoid bone**
os ptérygoïde
Flügelbein
hueso pterigoides

**pubis (bone)**
os pubis
Schambein *ne*
hueso pubis

**puissance jumping**
épreuve de puissance *cs*
Mächtigkeitsspringprüfung *(die ~)*
prueba de potencia ; salto de potencia

**pull** *v*
tirer (sur la main)
pullen
jalar (a mano)

**puller (shoe ~)** ; pull off(s) ; pincher(s) ; pincer(s) (farrier's ~)
tenailles à arracher ; tricoises à déferrer
Hufeisenabnehmzange *(die ~)* ; Abnehmzange (für Hufbeschlag)
tenaza de descalzar

**pull off(s)** => puller (shoe ~)

**pull off the shoe** => unshoe

**pull the mane** => thin the mane

**pulmonary alveolus**
alvéole pulmonaire
Lungen Alveolen
alveolo pulmonar

The tiny space where oxygen is presented to the blood in the lungs.
Minuscule terminaison à l'extrémité des voies aériennes dans les poumons.

**pulp tooth**
pulpe dentaire
Zahnmark *ne*
pulpa dental

**pulse**
pouls
Puls *m*
pulso

**puncture wound (sole // frog ~)** => nail
prick / tread

**punter** => bettor

**pupil**
pupille
Pupille *f* ; Sehloch *ne*
pupila

**purebred ; pure bred**
pur-sang ; pur sang *adj et n m inv*
Vollblut *ne* ; Vollblüter *m* ; vollblütig *adj*
pura sangre

Le terme est parfois utilisé imprécisément pour désigner les thoroughbreds (i.e. les pur-sang anglais).

**pus**
pus
Eiter *m*
pus

**pus pocket** => abscess (in a hoof)

**put a horse to sleep** => destroy a horse

**put off the harness** => unharness

**put off the pack saddle** *v*
débâter
abbasten
desalbardar

**put on the harness** => harness (up)

**put on the pack saddle** *v*
bâter
basten
enalbardar

**put the reins on a horse** => harness (up)

**pylorus**
pylore
Magenpförtner ; Pylorus
píloro

**quadrille**
quadrille
Reiter-Quadrille *(die ~)*
cuadrilla

**qualification**
qualification
Qualifikation *(die ~)*
calificación

**quarry**
gibier ; animal
Wild ; jagdbare Tier
presa

**quarters-in** => haunches-in

**quarters out** => renvers

**quicking** ; pricking *(by the farrier)*
piqûre
Nagelzwang *(der ~)* ; Vernageln
pinchazo

Penetration of a sensitive structure by a horseshoe nail.
Piqûre, dans la chair vive ou très près de celle-ci, du clou à ferrer.

**quiet**
calme
ruhig
calmo ; quieto

**quittor (of horses)** ; necrosis of the lateral cartilage(s)
javart cartilagineux
Hufknorpelfistel
gabarro cartilaginoso

Infection of the fibrocartilage(s) of the third phalanx.
Plaie, à l'arrière de la couronne, dans laquelle un (les) cartilage(s) complémentaire(s) de la troisième phalange est (sont) attaqué(s).

**rabies**
rage
Tollwut *f*
rabia

Infection virale mortelle dont le diagnostic ne peut être certain qu'après le décès. Elle peut affecter tous les animaux à sang chaud et est contagieuse.

**rabies rhabdovirus / virus**
virus de la rage
Tollwut-Virus *ne*
virus de la rabia

**races (the ~)** ; turf *(1)*
courses (les ~)
Rennsport
carreras (las ~)

1) Turf is sometimes used as a general term for Thoroughbred horse-racing at gallop, and sometimes as a specific term for such racing on a grass track.

**race course** => race track ; racetrack

**race horse ; racehorse**
cheval de course(s)
Rennpferd
caballo de carrera(s)

**race over jumps**
course à obstacles ; course d'obstacles
Hindernisrennen
carrera de obstáculos

Terme général pour toutes les courses comportant des obstacles devant être sautés.

**race track ; racetrack** *facility* ; race course
hippodrome ; piste de course ; champ de courses
Rennbahn ; Pferderennbahn
hipódromo

Bien que ces termes soient souvent utilisés indifféremment, il faut faire attention de ne pas toujours confondre la piste elle-même avec l'ensemble de l'hippodrome. De plus, un champ de courses peut véritablement être un champ aménagé.

**racing boot** => jockey boot

**racing gallop** ; run *n US*
galop de course
Renngalopp ; Rennbahngalopp
galope de carrera
  A diagonal four-beat gait.

**racing saddle**
selle de course
Rennsattel
silla de carrera

**radius**
radius
Speiche ; Radius
radio
  Os principal de l'avant-bras, entre l'articulation du coude et celle du carpe.

**raid** => long-distance ride

**rail** ; bar ; pole
barre ; perche
Stange *f*
barra
  Longue pièce de bois servant à édifier des obstacles, ou simplement déposée sur le sol.

**rasp** *v*
râper
raspeln
limar ; escofinar ; raspar

**rasp** *n*
râpe
Hufraspel *(die ~)*
escofina ; raspa ; lima
  La râpe utilisée en maréchalerie est souvent une « râpe-lime », râpe d'un côté et lime de l'autre.

**rating** => indicator

**rat tail**
queue de rat
Rattenschweif
cola de rata
  Qui n'est couverte que de quelques crins.

**rear** *v*
cabrer (se ~)
steigen ; bäumen (sich ~) ; aufbäumen (sich ~)
encabritarse ; empinar
  For a horse, to raise himself on his hind legs.

**rearer** => breeder (up)

**rearing**
cabrer *n* ; cabrade
Steigen
encabritamiento

**rear end**
arrière-main ; arrière-train
Hinterteil ; Hinterhand *f* ; Nachhand
tercio posterior / trasero ; cuartos traseros
  Croupe, fesse, membres postérieurs et queue.
  Arrière-main est une expression plus adéquate pour un cheval monté et arrière-train pour un cheval attelé.

**recessive**
récessif
rezessiv
recesivo

**rectum**
rectum
Mastdarm ; Rektum
recto
  Dernier des compartiments de l'intestin, s'étend du côlon descendant à l'anus.

**redwater fever** => babesiasis ; babesiosis

**red mange** => sarcoptic mange

**red roan** => bay roan

**reed fescue** => tall fescue (grass)

**refusal** ; jib *n*
refus
Verweigerung ; Refus
rehúse

**refuse** *v* ; jib *v (1)*
refuser
verweigern
rehusar
  1) To jib is to refuse to go forward, to pass a certain point or to jump.

**registry (of a breed)** => stud-book (general ~)

**regularity** *(1)* ; consistency *(2)*
régularité
Gleichmäßigkeit
regularidad
  1) Applies to the pace. 2) Applies to the performances.

**rein**
rêne ; guide
Zügel *m*
rienda
  *s.a. reins*

**reins**
rênes ; guides *(1)*
Zügel
riendas
  Long straps attached to the bit and used to guide the horse with the hands.
  Courroies fixées au mors et que l'on tient en main pour diriger le cheval. 1) En attelage, on utilise souvent le mot guides.

**reins**
enrênement(s)
Hilfszügel
riendas
  Ensemble des rênes, fausses rênes, rênes fixes, chambon, gogue etc., qui servent à guider le cheval ou à lui imposer un port de tête.

**reinsman** => jockey

**rein-back** => back

**rein-back** ; **reinback** *n*
reculer *n*
Rückwärtsrichten *ne* ; Zurücksetzen des Gespanns *(das ~) att/bd*
reculada

**remove the shoe** => unshoe

**renal artery**
artère rénale
Nierenschlagader *f*
arteria renal

**renvers** ; tail to the wall ; quarters out
renvers ; croupe au mur ; croupe en dehors
Renvers ; Kruppe-heraus ; Kruppe-zur-Wand
grupa al muro ; grupa a fuera

**resistance** ; defence *(1)*
résistance ; défense *(1)*
Widerstand gegen die Hilfen *(der ~)* ;
  Widersetzlichkeit *f*
defensa ; resistencia
    Any attempt by a horse to disobey the rider. 1) The action by which the horse is disobeying or resisting.
    1) Action par laquelle le cheval résiste à la demande du cavalier.

**respiratory system**
appareil respiratoire
Atmungssystem *ne*
aparato respiratorio

**retina**
rétine
Netzhaut *f* ; Retina *f*
retina
    Sensory membrane lining the back surface of the eye's interior. The lens focuses an image on the retina, which in turn transmits it to the optic nerve.

**reversed pirouette** ; pirouette renversée
pirouette renversée
Wendung auf der Vorhand *(die ~)*
pirueta inversa ; pirueta sobre el tercio anterior
    The hindlegs describe a complete circle, at the walk, around a foreleg which is acting as a pivot.
    Tour complet qui s'exécute, au pas, autour d'un des antérieurs.

**reward** *v*
récompenser
belohnen
premiar

**rhinopneumonitis (equine viral ~)** *abbr:*
  *EVR*
rhinopneumonie (virale du cheval) ; rhume
Rhinopneumonie des Pferdes *(die ~)*
rinoneumonitis equina viral
    Maladie contagieuse due à l'herpèsvirus équin de type 4.

**rib**
côte
Rippe *f*
costilla

**ribs**
côtes
Rippen *f pl*
costillas
    Le cheval en a 18 paires.

**rib (bone)**
côte (os d'une ~) ; os costal
Rippenbein *ne*
hueso costal

**rice**
riz
Reis
arroz

**rickets**
rachitisme
Rachitis *f*
raquitismo
    Carence en vitamine D.

**rider** ; equestrian *n f: equestrienne*
cavalier *f: cavalière*
Reiter *m f: Reiterin*
jinete ; caballista

**rider**  => jockey

**ride astride** *v*
monter à califourchon
rittlings aufsitzen
montar a horcajadas

**ride at the walk** *v*
monter au pas
Schritt reiten
montar al paso

**ride bareback** *v*
monter à cru / à poil
reiten ohne Sattel ; ohne Sattel reiten
montar a pelo

**ride side-saddle** *v*
monter en amazone
reiten im Damensattel ; im Damensitz reiten
montar a la amazona ; montar a mujeriegas
    La cavalière assise les deux jambes sur le côté gauche du cheval.

**ride (a horse)**  => mount (a horse)

**ride (trail ~)**
randonnée
Tour
paseo

**ridgling ; ridgeling ; risling**  => cryptorchid

**riding aid**  => aid

**riding aids**  => aids

**riding boot**
botte d'équitation
Reitstiefel ; hohe Stiefel
bota para montar

**riding boot (laced ~)** ; field boot
botte d'équitation (~ avec lacets / ~ de campagne)
Feldstiefel *m*
bota campera / de campo

**riding coat** ; riding jacket
veste / veston d'équitation
Reitrock *m*
chaqueta de montar ; saco de montar

**riding horse**  => saddle horse

**riding instructor**
instructeur d'équitation
Reitlehrer
instructor de equitación ; profesor de equitación

**riding jacket**  => riding coat

**riding master** ; écuyer *(1)*
écuyer
Reitmeister *(1)* ; Ecuyer
caballerizo ; maestro de equitación
  1) Particularly associated with the Cadre Noir.

**riding pony**
poney de selle
Reitpony
jaca de silla

**riding school**
école d'équitation
Reitschule *f*
picadero ; escuela de equitación

**riding technique**
technique d'équitation
Reittechnik
técnica de montar

**riding to the right // left**
équitation à main droite // gauche
reiten (auf der rechten // linken Hand ~)
equitación a mano derecha // izquierda

**riding whip** => crop

**rig** => cryptorchid

**ringbone ; ring bone ; ring-bone** ;
  phalangeal exostosis
forme
Schale *f* ; Ringbein *ne*
sobrepie // sobremano

**rings (of a bit)**
anneaux (du mors)
Ringe ; Zügelringe
anillos ; argollas
  They can be flat or wire, fixed to the cheeks or loose.
  Ils peuvent être plats ou arrondis, fixes sur les branches ou mobiles.

**ringworm** ; dermatophytosis ; trichophytosis *(1)*
  ; tinea *(2)*
teigne ; trichophytose *(1)*
Ringelflechte *(die ~)*
tiña
  Very superficial infection that is highly infectious but causing almost no injury to animals. 1) Caused by fungi of the genus Trichophyton. 2) Term uncommonly used in animals.
  Maladie contagieuse de la peau, sans grande conséquence. Les poils disparaissent par petites plaques. 1) Causée par des fungi du genre Trichophyton.

**ring martingale** => running martingale

**rising trot** => posting trot

**roach-back** => arch-back

**roads and tracks** *ht*
parcours routier *cc*
Wegestrecke *(die ~)*
caminos y pistas

**roaring** => laryngeal hemiplegia / paralysis

**robe** => coat (colour)

**rolled grains**
grains aplatis
gequetschtes Getreide
granos laminados / aplastados

**roller bit**
mors à molette
Kandare mit Walzen ; Rollengebiß
freno con rodadura
  There can be a single roller as centre piece or attached as a player on the bit (mainly among the western curb bits), or a few rollers set round the mouthpiece itself (mainly in the classical riding snaffles, called « roller mouth » or « cherries »). The « Magenis snaffle » has slits in the mouthpiece into which are set the rollers.

**roman nose** ; convex face
busqué(e) (cheval / tête ~) ; chanfrein convexe
Rammskopf *m*
cabeza acarnerada ; nariz acarnerada / romana

**rope** => lasso

**rosette** ; cockade
ruban ; rosette
Schleife *(die ~)*
roseta

**roughage**
fourrage grossier
Rauhfutter / Raufutter *ne*
forraje grosero

**round**
manche ; ronde *n*
Durchgang *m* ; Umlauf *m*
manga

**roundworm** => nematode

**rubber curry comb**
étrille en caoutchouc
Gummistriegel
almohaza de hule / goma

**rug** => blanket (horse ~)

**rump** => croup

**run** => racing gallop

**runaway horse** => bolting horse ; bolter

**running martingale** ; ring martingale
martingale à anneaux
Jagdmartingal ; Ringmartingal
martingala de anillas / anillos ; tijerilla
  Divisée en deux devant le poitrail, elle se termine par des anneaux dans lesquels passent les rênes.

**run-out** *n*
dérobade
Ausbrechen *ne*
escapada

**run away** => bolt

**run out** *v*
dérober (se ~)
vorbeilaufen
zafarse
  Avoiding an obstacle to be jumped, by passing to either side of it.
  Lorsqu'un cheval détourne par la gauche ou la droite, l'obstacle qu'il devrait normalement sauter.

**rye**
seigle
Roggen *m*
centeno

**saber-legged** => sickle-hocked

**sacral tuber**
tuber sacrale ; angle de la croupe *ostéologie*
Kreuzhöcker *m*
tuberosidad sacra

**sacral vertebrae**
vertèbres sacrées / sacrales
Kreuzwirbel
vértebras sacras
  The horse have 5 fused sacral vertebrae forming the sacrum.
  Au nombre de 5 chez le cheval, elles sont soudées et forment le sacrum qui est la base de la croupe.

**sacroiliac joint**
articulation sacro-iliaque
Kreuzdarmbeingelenk
articulación sacroilíaca

**sacrum**
sacrum (os ~)
Kreuzbein *ne*
sacro (hueso ~)
  La hauteur maximale de la croupe correspond au plus haut des processus épineux du sacrum. L'os sacrum, formé par les vertèbres sacrales soudées, est solidement uni aux os coxaux et forme avec eux le bassin. Le sacrum reçoit ainsi l'impulsion des membres pelviens et la transmet au reste du corps.

**saddle**
selle
Sattel *m*
silla (de montar) ; montura

**saddle** *v*
seller
satteln
ensillar

**saddler**
sellier
Sattler
sillero ; guarnicionero ; talabartero

**saddlery; saddler's shop**
sellerie
Sattlerei
talabartería ; guarnicionería ; guadarnés ; monturía

**saddle-back** ; hollow-back ; dipped back
dos ensellé ; dos négligé ; dos concave ; dos creux
gesenkter Rücken ; Senkrücken *m* ; Sattelrücken
dorso ensillado ; espalda hueca / hundida
  Depressed vertebral column, behind the withers only in light cases.
  Plus ou moins concave, le dos négligé est peu concave. La dépression de la colonne vertébrale se limite à l'arrière du garrot dans les cas légers.

**saddle blanket** *west. (1)* ; saddle pad *west. (2)*
tapis de selle *west.*
Satteldecke *(1)* ; Westernpad *(2)*
manta sudadera
  With a western saddle, a difference is made since actual blankets (1) and pads (2) are used, sometimes all together.
  1) couverture servant comme tapis de selle, 2) coussin (tapis coussiné / matelassé).

**saddle blanket** => saddle pad

**saddle cloth** => saddle pad

**saddle horse** ; riding horse
cheval de selle
Reitpferd *ne* ; Sattelpferd
caballo de silla
  Cheval que l'on monte, ou qui est d'une taille permettant normalement de l'utiliser pour la selle.

**saddle pad** => saddle blanket

**saddle pad** *class.* ; saddle cloth *class.* ; saddle blanket *class. & west.* ; numnah
tapis de selle *class.*
Satteldecke *f class. (1)* ; Schabracke *f class. (2)*
sudadero ; mantilla ; manta ; pelero
  Made with two basic shapes: 1) English-saddle-like. 2) about rectangular, blanket-like.

**saddle room**
sellerie (de l'écurie)
Sattelkammer
cuarto de monturas

**saddle site** ; natural place for the saddle to sit
emplacement de la selle
Sattellage
colocación de la montura

**saddle sore**
plaie de selle
Satteldruck *(der ~)*
herida de la silla ; matadura ; pasmudo *amer*

**saddle (harness ~)**
sellette ; selle *att*
Sellette / Selett *ne* ; Sättelchen *ne* ; Oberblatt *ne*
sillín

**sad grey** => dark grey

**safety margin**
innocuité
Harmlosigkeit *f*
innocuidad

**saliva**
salive
Speichel
saliva

**salivary gland**
glande salivaire
Speicheldrüse
glándula salivar
  Parotid, mandibular, sublingual and buccal glands.

**salt**
sel
Salz
sal

**salt lick** ; mineral lick ; licking block
bloc à lécher ; pierre à lécher
Salzleckstein *(der ~)* ; Leckstein
piedra de sal ; bloque de sal ; lamedura ; salegar

**salute**
salut
Gruß *(der ~)*
saludo

**sample**
échantillon
Muster *ne* ; Probe *f* ; Probestück *ne*
muestra

**sandcrack / sand crack** ; crack (hoof ~)
seime *f*
Hornspalt(e) *m(f)*
raza ; cuarto ; fisura del casco ; rajadura de arena ; grieta en el casco

Crack running downward the hoof, will cause lameness if deep enough to touch the laminae. It may be
referred to according to its location: toe, quarter, heel or
bar (sand)crack.

Fissure longitudinale de la muraille du sabot. Elle
pourra faire boiter si elle atteint la partie vivante du
pied.

**sarcoptic mange** ; red mange
gale sarcoptique / sarcoptinique ; gale du corps
Kopfräude *(die ~)*
sarna sarcóptica

**scapula** ; shoulder blade
scapula ; omoplate *anc* ; scapulum *anc*
Schulterblatt ; Skapula
omóplato ; escápula

L'os de l'épaule, sa partie inférieure s'articule avec
l'humérus, il n'est relié au thorax que par des muscles.

**scapular spine** => spine of the scapula

**scapula(r) cartilage** ; cartilage of prolongation
cartilage scapulaire ; cartilage de prolongement
Schulterblattknorpel
cartílago de la escápula

Au sommet de l'omoplate, au niveau du garrot, les tra-
pèzes s'y attachent.

**scent** *hunting*
trace ; empreinte
Witterung ; Spur
rastro ; olfato ; huella ; pista

Chasse à courre: Odeur ou piste laissée par le gibier et
que les chiens suivent.

**scheme of marking** ; marking system
barème (de notation)
Beurteilungsverfahren ; Richtverfahren
baremo de nota

**schooling** => training

**schooling level**
degré de dressage
Dressurgrad *m*
grado de doma

**school air / pace**
air d'école
Schulgang
aire de escuela

**school a horse** *v*
dresser un cheval
einreiten ; einfahren *att/hd*
adiestrar ; amaestrar ; domar

**school figures** ; manège figures
figures de manège
Hufschlagfiguren
figuras escuelas

**sclera** ; outer covering (of the eye)
sclérotique
weiße Augenhaut ; Sklera
esclerótica

**scour(s) ; scouring** => diarrhoea

**scratches**
crevasses
Mauke *f*
rasguños ; raspaduras

Chapped skin in the hollow of the heel.
Gerçures dans le pli du paturon.

**scrotum**
scrotum
Hodensack *m* ; Skrotum ; Geschröte *ne*
escroto ; bolsa

**scurry jumping (with time factor)** ; competition against the clock *hj*
épreuve au chronomètre *cs* ; épreuve contre la
montre *cs*
Zeitspringen
prueba contra el reloj

**seatworm** => pinworm (horse ~)

**seat (of a rider)**
assiette (du cavalier)
Sitz *m*
asiento

Manière d'être « assis » à cheval, de préférence de façon stable, avec une assiette liante qui suit les
mouvements du cheval.

**seat (of a saddle)**
siège (d'une selle)
Sitzfläche *f* ; Sattelsitz *m* ; Sitz *m*
asiento

**sebaceous glands** ; oil glands
glandes sébacées
Haarbalgdrüsen ; Talgdrüsen
glándulas sebáceas

Secrete the necessary oils to keep the hide pliable and
resistant.
Sécrètent le sébum, une huile de protection pour la
peau.

**sebum**
sébum
Talg
sebo

**second horse** *hunting*
cheval de rechange / relais *c. à courre*
Ersatzpferd
segundo caballo

**second phalanx** => middle phalanx

**second thigh** => gaskin

**selenium**
sélénium
Selen *ne*
selenio

**self-injury**
atteinte
Einhauen *ne*
alcance

Self-injury by brushing, forging, overreaching or
speedy cutting.
Blessure à une jambe du cheval provoquée par le fait
que ses membres se touchent.

**semen** => sperm

**semicircular canals**
canaux semi-circulaires (de l'oreille)
Bogengänge
conductos semicirculares

**seminal vesicle** => vesicular gland

**semiwild horse**
cheval semi-sauvage ; cheval demi-sauvage
halbwildes Pferd
caballo semi-salvaje

**sensible / sensitive mouth** => soft mouth

**serpentine**
serpentine
Schlangenlinie *(die ~)*
serpentina
Série de demi-cercles alternés dans l'une et l'autre direction.

**serum**
sérum
Serum
suero

**serve** => cover (a mare)

**service** ; covering of mare
saillie ; monte
Deckakt *m* ; Sprung *m*
monta ; corto ; cubrición
On utilise plutôt le terme saillie pour désigner un acte d'accouplement en particulier, et le terme monte pour désigner cette action de façon plus collective par ex.: service de monte, période de monte, monte publique.

**service season**
saison de monte
Decksaison *f*
época de cubrición / monta

**service station** ; covering station
station de monte
Deckstation *f* ; Beschälstation
estación de monta / cubrición ; parada de cubrición

**service / serving hobbles** => breeding
hopples / hobbles

**sesamoid bones (proximal ~)** => proximal
sesamoid bones

**shadow roll ; shadow blind**
cache-ombrages ; cache-vue
Nasenschoner
rollo de sombra

**shaft**
brancard ; limon ; montant *Can.* ; ménoire *Can.* ; timon *(1)*
Schere *(die ~)*
varal
Either of the two pieces between which a horse is hitched to a vehicle.
Chacune des pièces entre lesquelles on attelle un cheval à une voiture. 1) En courses attelées le terme timon est parfois utilisé pour désigner les brancards.

**shaft girth / strap** => belly band

**Shagya (Arab) horse** *breed*
shagya arabe
Shagya
árabe shagya
Race d'origine hongroise.

**shake the head (up and down)** => bob the
head

**shank** => branch (of a bit)

**shannon bone ; shank** => metatarsal bone
(large / third ~)

**shavings**
copeaux
Späne *(die ~)* ; Schnitzel *(die ~)*
aserrín

**sheath** ; fleece ; prepuce
fourreau ; prépuce
Schlauch *m* ; Vorhaut ; Präputium
prepucio ; vaina

**shedding** ; moult ; moulting ; molt *US* ; changing
of coat
mue
Haarwechsel *(der ~)*
muda

**sheep knee** => calf-knee / calf knee

**sheetwriter** => chart maker

**Shetland (pony) ; Shetlie** *breed*
shetland
Shetlandpony
póney de Shetland
Race d'origine écossaise.

**she-ass** => jenny-ass ; jenny

**she-mule** => mule (female ~)

**shin bone** => cannon bone

**shipping boot**
guêtre de transport ; botte de transport
Transportgamasche *(die ~)*
cañera de viaje ; bota de embarque / transporte

**shoe** *v*
ferrer
beschlagen (Huf ~)
herrar

**shoe** => horseshoe

**shoeing** => horseshoeing

**shoemaker**
cordonnier
Schuhmacher
zapatero

**shoe boil** => capped elbow

**shorten the reins** *v*
raccourcir les rênes
Zügel verkürzen ; Leinen verkürzen *(die ~) att/bd*
cortar las riendas

**short-coupled** ; close-coupled ; compact ;
cobby
compact
derb ; geschlossen
compacto ; apretado

**short pastern**
court jointé *adj*
kurze Fessel
cuartilla corta ; corta de cuartilla *adj*
  Quand le paturon est trop court.

**short pastern bone**  => middle phalanx

**short winded**  => broken winded

**shoulder**
épaule
Schulter *f*
espalda ; hombro
  Corresponding to the scapula area, some interpretations include the humerus.
  Comprise entre le garrot et le bras ou l'avant-bras selon les interprétations, comprend donc la scapula (Regio scapularis NAV), plus l'humérus si on y inclut le bras.

**shoulder-in**
épaule-en-dedans
Schulterherein *ne*
espalda adentro

**shoulder angle**
angle de l'épaule
Schulterwinkel
ángulo de la espalda

**shoulder blade**  => scapula

**shoulder joint**
articulation de l'épaule ; art. scapulo-humérale
Schultergelenk ; Buggelenk *ne*
articulación de la espalda / del hombro

**show jumper (horse)**  => jumper

**show jumper (rider)**
cavalier d'obstacles
Springreiter
jinete de salto

**show jumper / jumping competition**  =>
  jumping competition

**show (a horse) in hand** *v*
présenter (un cheval) en main
Hand vorführen (ein Pferd an der ~)
presentar (un caballo) a la mano

**shuffling gait**
allure basse ; allure rasante
schleppende Bewegung *(die ~)* ; flachen Gang
acción baja
  1° Quand le déplacement vertical du centre de gravité du cheval est peu important. 2° Dans laquelle les pieds se déplacent au ras du sol.

**shuttle bone**  => distal sesamoid bone

**shy** *v*
effrayer (s'~)
erschrecken ; scheuen ; scheu werden
asustarse ; espantarse

**sickle-hocked** ; saber-legged
coudé des jarrets
säbelbeinig
acodado de corvejones
  L'adjectif « coudé » qualifie habituellement plutôt les jarrets que le cheval.

**sickle hock(s)** ; curby conformation
jarret(s) coudé(s) ; jarret(s) à courbe *(1)*
stark gewinkeltes Sprunggelenk
corvejón(/ones) acodado(s) ; pata(s) de sable
  When seen from the side, hocks are bent too strongly at the joint, the lower leg is then angled forwards instead of vertical.
  Vu de côté, angularité excessive de l'articulation du jarret: le cheval devient sous-lui du derrière à partir du jarret. 1) Cette expression signifie que le jarret est prédisposé à souffrir d'une courbe. Bien qu'une tare du nom de courbe ait été mentionnée en français, on la présente, dans les documents plus récents, plutôt comme étant une tare dure de la tubérosité inférieure interne du tibia. Le mot courbe semble utilisé ici comme traduction de « curb ».

**sidesaddle**
selle d'amazone
Damensattel
montura de amazona

**side bone ; sidebone**
forme cartilagineuse
Hufknorpelverknöcherung *(die ~)*
fibrocartílago lateral ; endurecimiento de los cartílagos de las patas
  Ossification of a fibrocartilage of the third phalanx.
  Ossification d'un cartilage complémentaire de la troisième phalange.

**side rein**
rêne fixe
Ausbindezügel
rienda de atar

**side step**
pas de côté
Seitengang *m*
paso de costado

**silent heat**
chaleurs discrètes
stille Brunst
celo silencioso

**silks (racing ~)**  => jacket

**silver eye**
oeil vairon
Kakerlakenauge *ne*
ojiblanco *adj*
  Oeil dont l'iris, dépigmenté, est gris-clair.

**simple change of lead / leg (through the trot)**
changement de pied simple ; changement de galop de ferme à ferme
einfacher Galoppwechsel *(der ~)*
cambio simple de pie ; cambio de galope simple ; cambio de galope con pasos intermedios

**simple obstacle**
obstacle simple
einfaches Hindernis *(das ~)*
obstáculo simple
  Qui se franchit en un seul saut.

**sire**
père ; géniteur
Vater ; Vatertier
padre ; genitor

**sire family**  => male line

**sitting trot**
trot assis
Deutschtraben
trote sentado

**sit too far forward** *v*
devancer le mouvement (du cheval)
vor der Bewegung sitzen
sentarse delante del movimiento

**six-in-hand** => six horse hitch

**six bars** *hj*
six barres (épreuve des ~) *cs*
Barrierenspringprüfung *f*
seis barras

**six horse hitch** ; six-in-hand
attelage de six
Sechsergespann ; Sechsspänner *(der ~)* ;
 Sechserzug *(der ~)*
enganche de seis caballos

**skeletal**
squelettique
skelettartig
esquelético

**skeleton**
squelette
Skelett *ne* ; Knochengerüst
esqueleto

 Comprend de 192 à 205 os (selon les sujets et les interprétations) représentant de 7 à 8 % du poids du corps
chez un cheval moyen.

**skin**
peau
Haut *f*
piel

**skull** ; cranium
crâne
Schädel
cráneo

 1° Partie de la tête qui renferme le cerveau. 2° Squelette de la tête.

**slaughterhouse** ; abattoir
abattoir
Schlachthof *m* ; Schlachthaus *ne*
matadero

**slaughter horse**
cheval de boucherie
Schlachtpferd
caballo para sacrificio

**sledge hammer**
marteau à frapper devant
Vorschlaghammer *m* ; Vorhammer ;
 Zuschlaghammer
martillo de dos manos ; macho de fragua ; combo
 *amer*

 A heavy blacksmithing hammer, weighting 6 pounds
or more it may require both hands.
 Lourd marteau de forgeron, manipulé à deux mains.

**sleeping sickness** => encephalomyelitis
 (equine viral ~)

**sloping croup**
croupe inclinée
abfallende Kruppe
grupa caída
 *s.a. goose rump*
 L'angle souhaité dépend naturellement des disciplines
et des perceptions, mais il devrait être environ d'une
trentaine de degrés avec l'horizon.

**sloping pastern / foot**
bas jointé *adj*
schräge Fessel *(die ~)*
cuartilla angulada
 Pastern / foot with a low angle; if the pastern angle is
lower than the hoof angle, the foot is broken forward.
 Quand le paturon est trop incliné vers le sol. Les défi-
nitions rencontrées varient et manquent de précision, il
n'est ainsi pas clair si l'axe du paturon bas- jointé est
plus à l'horizontale que l'axe du pied correspondant.

**sloping shoulder**
épaule inclinée / oblique
schräge Schulter
espalda inclinada ; hombro angulado

**small intestine**
intestin grêle
Dünndarm
intestino delgado
 Formé du duodénum, du jéjunum et de l'iléum.

**small star**
légèrement en tête
Blümchen *ne* ; kleiner Stern
estrellita

**smegma**
smegma (préputial)
Smegma *ne*
esmegma

**smithy** => farriery

**smith (shoeing-~)** => horseshoer

**smooth muscle** ; non-striated muscle ; visceral muscle
muscle lisse ; muscle viscéral ; muscle à contraction involontaire
glatter Muskel *(der ~)*
músculo liso ; músculo involuntario
 Muscle remplissant une fonction interne ne nécessitant
pas d'intervention directe volontaire du cerveau.

**snaffle-rein**
rêne de filet
Trensenzügel
rienda de filete

**snaffle bit**
mors de filet ; filet
Trense *f* ; Trensegebiß *ne* ; Trensenmundstück *ne*
filete
 A bit consisting of a single mouthpiece, jointed or not.
 Avec une embouchure, rigide ou articulée, aux extrémités de laquelle sont fixés des anneaux.

## snaffle (bridle)
bridon ; bride à filet
Trensenzaum *m* ; Trensenzäumung *f*
brida de filete ; bridón

A bridle with any snaffle bit attached, or designed to receive such a mouthpiece.
Bride légère comprenant un filet simple, ou destinée à en recevoir un.

## snap
fermoir ; mousqueton
Karabinerhaken
cierre

## sock   => white to half-cannon

## sodium
sodium
Natrium *ne*
sodio

## soft mouth ; tender mouth ; sensible / sensitive mouth ; fine mouth ; light mouth
bouche fine / légère / chatouilleuse / tendre / sensible
weiches Maul ; empfindliches Maul ; durchlässiges Maul ; nachgiebiges Maul *(das ~)*
boca sensitiva

Mouth which is delicate to the action of the bit.
Bouche particulièrement sensible à l'action du mors.

## soft palate
voile du palais ; palais mou
weicher Gaumen ; Gaumensegel
velo del paladar

Rideau de chair molle qui, partant du bord postérieur du palais dur, sépare la cavité buccale de la cavité du pharynx. Une fois que l'eau ou les aliments ont passé dans le pharynx, le voile du palais leur interdit de revenir dans la bouche. S'ils devaient alors être rejetés, ils ne pourraient l'être que par les cavités nasales.

## solar plexus
plexus solaire
Sonnengeflecht
plexo solar

Sometimes presented as the celiac plexus and sometimes as a celiacomesenteric plexus.
Désigne habituellement le plexus céliaque.

## sole
sole
Sohle *f* ; Hornsohle ; Hufsohle
suela

## sole knife ; toeing knife
rogne-pied *(1)* ; tranchet *(2)*
Hauklinge *f*
roñeta ; machete

Held in one hand and struck with a hammer, it is used to remove dry and hard layers of sole.  *s.a. hoof knife*

1) Dans le sens traditionnel c'est une simple lame dont une partie est tranchante et sert à couper la corne, on le tient d'une main et le frappe avec un marteau de l'autre, il peut aussi servir à dériver les clous. 2) Formé d'une épaisse lame tranchante d'un côté, épaisse de l'autre et dotée d'un manche, il sert à couper la corne et est manié de la même façon que le rogne-pied.

## sole ulcer   => bruise (of the sole)

## solid fence
obstacle fixe
festes Hindernis ; starres Hindernis
obstáculo fijo

## son
fils
Sohn *(der ~)*
hijo

## sore   => wound

## sorghum
sorgho
Sorghum *ne*
sorgo ; zahína

## sorrel   => light chestnut
                => chestnut

## sound *adj*
sain
gesund
sano

In good condition and showing no significant defects.
Qualifie le cheval en bon état de santé et ne souffrant d'aucune tare qui puisse handicaper ses performances ou son avenir.

## soundness
bon état
Gesundheit *(die ~)*
salud

Bon état de santé et bonne conformation: Le cheval ne souffre d'aucune maladie ou d'aucun défaut qui puisse handicaper ses performances ou son avenir.

## Spanish fly   => blister beetle / fly

## Spanish jumping bit   => kimblewick bit

## Spanish snaffle   => kimblewick bit

## Spanish walk
pas espagnol
spanische Tritt
paso español ; paso castellano

In which the horse raises and extends forelegs.

## spatula (mouthpiece with ~)   => double jointed mouthpiece

## spavin
éparvin
Spat *m*
esparaván

## speculum *pl: specula*
spéculum *pl: spéculums*
Spekulum *ne*
espéculo

## speed
vitesse
Schnelligkeit
velocidad

## sperm ; semen *anat*
sperme ; semence *anat*
Sperma *n* ; Samen *m*
esperma ; semen *anat*

## sphenoid bone
os sphénoïde
Keilbein *ne*
hueso esfenoides

**spinal column; spine** => vertebral column

**spinal cord**
moelle épinière
Rückenmark
médula espinal

**spine**
épine dorsale
Rückgrat *ne*
espina dorsal ; espinazo

**spine of the scapula** ; scapular spine
épine scapulaire ; épine acromienne *anc*
Schulterblattgräte
espina de la escápula

**spinous process**
processus épineux
Dornfortsatz *m*
apófisis espinosa

Their great length on the second to the ninth thoracic vertebrae causes the prominence of the withers.

Saillie osseuse qui s'élève à la verticale, de façon plus ou moins prononcée sur certaines vertèbres.

**splayed foot ; splay-footed** => toed-out

**spleen**
rate
Milz
bazo

Emmagasine des réserves de sang qui peuvent être libérées dans le flot sanguin au besoin.

**splint**
suros
Überbein *ne*
sobrehueso (en la caña) ; sobrecaña

Osteitis, periostosis, exostosis or interosseous desmitis on the cannon, and frequently touching the splint bones (hence the name). A peg splint is located behind the cannon bone and next to the suspensory ligament. A shin splint or shin buck is located on the front of the cannon bone and results from a surface fracture.

Ostéite, périostose, exostose ou inflammation ligamentaire dans la région du canon impliquant souvent les os rudimentaires.

**sponge**
éponge
Schwamm *m*
esponja

**sponsor**
commanditaire
Sponsor *(der ~)*
comanditario

**spread fence / jump**
obstacle large
Weitsprung *m*
salto ancho
*s.a. spread jump*

**spread jump** ; broad jump
saut en largeur
Hochweitsprung *m* ; Weitsprung
salto de anchura
*s.a. spread fence*

**springhalt** => stringhalt

**sprinter**
sprinter
Sprinter
velocista

**spur** *n*
éperon
Sporn *m pl: Sporen*
espuela

**spur** *v*
éperonner
Sporen geben (die ~)
espolear

**square oxer**
oxer carré
Carree-Oxer *m*
oxer cuadrado

Dont les barres supérieures de chacun des éléments sont à la même hauteur.

**stable** => barn

**stable boy / man**
garçon d'écurie
Stallbursche ; Pferdewärter ; Gestütswärter
mozo de cuadra
*s.a. groom and stable fatigue*

**stable fatigue**
garde d'écurie ; surveillant d'écurie
Stallwache
guardia en la caballeriza
*s.a. stable boy*

**stable fly**
mouche de l'étable ; mouche charbonneuse ;
 mouche piqueuse des étables
Stallfliege ; Wadenstecher
mosca de establo

**stabling**
stabulation
Stallfütterung *f*
estabulación

**stadium jumping** => jumping phase / test

**stag-hunting**
chasse au cerf
reiten zu Hirschhunden
caza de ciervo

**stag face** => dished (face)

**stake** => bet

 => bet

**stallion** ; entire (male horse)
étalon ; entier (cheval mâle ~) *n & adj*
Beschäler *m* ; Hengst *m* ; Zuchthengst
caballo entero ; semental (caballo ~) ; padrillo
*amer* ; garañón *amer*

An uncastrated male horse.

**stall (standing ~)** ; horse-bay
stalle (d'écurie) ; entre-deux
Stand *m*
compartimiento

Usually open at the rear, the horse must be tied-up in it.
Compartiment qui n'est pas complètement fermé et dans lequel le cheval doit être attaché.

**stamina**
vigueur ; résistance
Ausdauer *f*
resistencia

The ability to endure a prolonged physical strain.
Capacité à fournir un effort physique durant une période relativement prolongée, sans se fatiguer indûment.

**stance**  => stand(s)

**Standardbred** ; American trotter
standardbred ; trotteur américain
amerikanischer Traber ; American Standard Bred
trotador americano

US originating breed, at the beginning selected only on their capacity of racing a mile, without galloping, within 2:30 minutes (the standard to be met, adopted in 1879).
Race originaire des E.U., les chevaux ont été sélectionnés au début uniquement sur leur capacité à courir un mille, sans galoper, en moins de deux minutes et trente secondes (le standard, adopté en 1879).

**standing jump**
saut de pied ferme
Sprung aus dem Stand
salto a pie firme

**standing martingale** ; fixed martingale ;
  tie-down *west.*
martingale fixe / droite
starre Martingal
bajador (martingala de ~)

**standing stretched**  => camped (out)

**standing under**
sous-lui
unterständig
remitido adelante // de atrás

Standing under in front // behind: Front limbs sloping toward the rear or hind limbs sloping toward the front, being too much under the horse.
Sous-lui du devant // du derrière: Quand, vus de côté, les membres sont trop sous le corps du cheval par rapport à leurs articulations supérieures.

**stand(s)** ; stance
aplomb(s)
Stellung (der Gliedmaßen) *(die ~)* ; Stand *m* ;
  Beinstellung *f*
aplomo(s)

Axe et position des membres sous le tronc du cheval.

**stand level**  => stand square

**stand square** *v* ; stand to attention *v* ; stand
  level *v*
tenir ferme (se ~)
gleichmäßiges stehen auf allen vier Füßen
cuadrarse

Standing with balance (and with attention) on all four legs at the halt.
Arrêté ferme, le cheval se tient en équilibre et carré sur ses quatre membres.

**stand to attention**  => stand square

**stand (of an obstacle)** ; post
chandelier ; support (d'un obstacle)
Ständer *m*
poste

**star**
en tête
Stern *(der ~)* ; Blume *f*
lucero ; estrella ; estrellado

A white mark on the forehead of the horse, it may have any shape (like star, Stern and estrella) or no shape at all.
Marque blanche localisée sur le front du cheval, on la qualifiera selon sa forme et sa grosseur, par exemples: étoile ou pelote.

**starch**
amidon
Stärke *f*
almidón

**start**
départ
Start *(der ~)*
salida ; partida

**starter**  => starting judge

**starting judge** ; starter *br*
juge au / de départ
Starter *(der ~)*
juez de salida

An official supervising the start of a / the participant(s).
Responsable du signal de départ, et, en course, de l'alignement des participants.

**starting line**
ligne de départ
Startlinie
línea de salida

**starting point**
point de départ
Ausgangspunkt *m*
punto de partida

**start at a trot** *v*
partir au trot
antraben
romper al trote ; tomar el trote

**start at a walk**
rompre au pas ; partir au pas
anreiten im Schritt
romper al paso ; tomar el paso

**start at the canter** *v*
partir au galop
angaloppieren
romper al galope ; tomar el galope

**star-gaze** *v*
porter le nez au vent
hoher Nase gehen (mit ~)
despapar

A horse carrying his head very high with the muzzle forward.
Se dit du cheval qui porte la tête très haut, le museau par en-avant.

**stayer**
cheval de fond ; cheval de tenue
Steher
caballo de larga distancia

**steeplechase**
course au clocher ; steeple ; steeple-chase
Jagdrennen
steeple chase
  Steeplechasing takes place over tracks with rather high
obstacles or in the open country.

**steeplechase phase** *ht*
steeple (phase de ~) *cc*
Rennbahn *f*
fase de steeple chase

**step**
pas
Tritt
paso
  Term used mainly for displacements to the side, back-
wards and at the walk. A step is also a complete
movement of a limb in any gait, and the distance
covered by this.
  Terme utilisé surtout pour les déplacements de côté,
vers l'arrière et au pas en général.

**step back**  => back

**step (obstacle)**
piano
Stufen *f pl*
obstáculo escalonado / en escalera
  A jumping obstacle consisting of a series of steps.
  Obstacle formé de deux banquettes soudées, à deux niveaux différents. Le terme est aussi utilisé pour des
obstacles comportant trois niveaux différents.

**sternal ribs**
côtes sternales ; côtes vraies
wahre Rippen
costillas esternales
  Dont les cartilages s'articulent directement sur le sternum.

**sternocephalicus muscle**
muscle sterno-céphalique
Brustkiefermuskel
músculo esternofalico

**sternocostal articulations**
articulations sterno-costales / sterno-chondrales
Brustbein-Rippen-Gelenke
articulaciones esternocostales

**sternum**
sternum
Brustbein *ne* ; Sternum
esternón

**steward**
commissaire (d'un concours)
Kampfrichter
comisario

**stifle**
grasset ; genou *anat*
Knie *ne* ; Hinterknie
babilla
  *s.a. knee*
  Région entre la cuisse et la jambe.

**stifle joint**
articulation du grasset ; art. du genou *anat*
Kniegelenk *ne*
articulación femoro-tibia-rotuliana ; articulación
de la babilla
  Implique le fémur, la rotule et le tibia, elle peut ainsi
être désignée « fémoro-tibio-patellaire ».

**stirrup** *west. & class.* ; iron (stirrup-~) *class.*
étrier
Steigbügel ; Bügel
estribo

**stirrup bar**
porte-étrivière (couteau ~)
Sturzfeder
barra de estribo

**stirrup leather / strap**
étrivière
Steigriemen ; Steigbügelriemen ; Bügelriemen
estribera ; ación ; arción *amer*

**stirrup pad / tread** ; foot pad
coussinet d'étrier
Bügeleinlage *(die ~)*
colchoneta de un estribo

**stirrup (of the ear)**
étrier (de l'oreille) ; stapes
Steigbügel
estribo

**stocking**  => white to above knee // hock

**stock saddle**  => western saddle

**stock tie**
lavallière
Künstlerschleife *f*
chalina ; corbata

**stomach**
estomac
Magen *m* ; Gaster
estómago
  Relativement petit pour la taille du cheval. Ses deux
orifices sont relativement proches et permettent un
transit relativement rapide de l'eau vers l'intestin.

**stone bruise**  => bruise (of the sole)

**stone wall**
mur de pierres
Feldsteinmauer *f* ; Natur-Mauer ; Steinmauer
muro de piedra

**stop**  => halt

**straight bar bit / snaffle** ; straight mouthpiece
rigide (filet / canon ~)
einteiliges Mundstück
recta (embocadura ~)

**straight mouthpiece**  => straight bar bit /
snaffle

**straight shoulder**  => upright shoulder

**strain**  => lineage

**strangles** ; distemper (equine ~)
gourme *f*
Druse *f*
gurma ; papera / papo (del caballo)

Highly contagious infection, caused by Streptococcus equi, characterized by fever, nasal discharge becoming thick pus, lack of appetite and moist cough. The abscesses in lymph glands (retropharyngeal nodes) around throat may become so large as to obstruct the airway (hence the name strangles).

Infection bactérienne contagieuse des voies respiratoires supérieures. Les complications sont nombreuses et elle peut causer la mort. Les symptômes sont: fièvre, augmentation de la fréquence respiratoire, écoulement nasal, agitation et perte d'appétit.

**stratum germinativum (epidermidis Malpighii)**
couche germinative ; stratum germinativum ; couche génératrice du corps muqueux de Malpighi ; couche basale de l'épiderme
Stratum germinativum *Keimzellenschicht*
estrato germinativo

A layer of epithelial cells, directly on the membrane of the dermis / corium, here these cells are not cornified and, in the hoof, their proliferation maintains the growth of the wall.

Elle repose directement sur la membrane du derme / chorion. Les cellule épithéliales non-kératinisées y prolifèrent, remplaçant les cellules plus anciennes et plus ou moins kératinisées, lesquelles s'éloignent ainsi de plus en plus de la partie vivante, dans le pied ceci résulte en l'accroissement (la pousse) de la corne du sabot.

**straw**
paille
Stroh *ne*
paja

**striated muscle** ; voluntary muscle
muscle (à contraction) volontaire ; muscle strié
quergestreift(er) Muskel *(der ~)* ; Skelettmuskel
músculo estriado ; músculo voluntario

Muscle qui obéit directement au cerveau.

**stringhalt** ; springhalt
harper *n & v* ; éparviner ; pas de coq
Hahnentritt *m* ; Zuckfuß *m*
paso de gallo ; arpeo ; arpeado ; mioclonia de las patas traseras

Sporadic disease due to unknown cause, characterized by involuntary repetitive exaggerated flexion of a hock.

Flexion brusque, répétitive et exagérée du jarret, sans cause bien identifiée, mais que l'on attribue parfois à un éparvin, quelquefois nommé « éparvin sec ».

**stripe**
liste
Blesse *f* ; Strichblesse ; Blässe
cordón ; lista

Narrow white marking down the face, not wider than the flat anterior portion of the nasal bones.

Marque blanche étroite localisée sur le chanfrein et pouvant se prolonger jusqu'à la bouche.

**stripe (narrow ~)**
liste (fine / petite)
Strich ; Schnurblesse
cordoncillo

**stroke of the whip**
coup de cravache
Stockhieb
fustazo

**stubborn**
rétif ; têtu
störrisch ; stätisch
reacio ; resabiado ; terco

**stud-book (general ~)** ; registry (of a breed)
registre (général) ; livre généalogique
Zuchtbuch
libro genealógico ; registro de raza

**stud-book ; stud book**
livre de(s) haras ; livre généalogique
Gestütsbuch ; Stutbuch ; Pferdestammbuch
libro genealógico / registro

**stud farm**
dépôt d'étalons
Hengstdepot
depósito de padrillos / sementales

Un centre où des étalons sont rassemblés.

**stud farm** ; breeding farm (horse-~)
haras ; ferme d'élevage
Gestüt *ne* ; Zuchtbetrieb
acaballadero ; criadero (rancho de ~) ; yeguada

Établissement destiné à la reproduction de chevaux, dans un haras on fait de la sélection et on vise l'amélioration de la race.

**stud horse**
reproducteur (mâle) ; étalon reproducteur
Zuchthengst ; Gestüthengst
progenitor (padre)

**stud (horseshoe / screw-in ~)** => calk
(screw-in ~)

**stumble** *v*
buter
stolpern ; straucheln
tropezar

**subcutaneous tissue** => subcutis

**subcutis** ; subcutaneous tissue ; hypodermis
toile sous-cutanée ; hypoderme
Subkutis ; Unterhaut
tejido celular subcutáneo

Attaches the dermis to the deeper structures, it is thin in general. In the foot, it forms the coronary cushion and the digital cushion.

**suckling**
allaitement
Säugen
lactancia

**suckling (foal)** => milk foal

**sugar**
sucre
Zucker
azúcar

**sugar beet pulp**
pulpe de betteraves
Rübennaßschnitzel *m pl*
pulpa de remolacha(s) ; pulpa de betarragas

**sulfonamide** ; sulphonamide
sulfamide
Sulfonamide *ne*
sulfamida

**sulky** ; bike
sulky
Sulky *ne*
sulky

Light two-wheeled cart used for harness racing.
Voiture légère à deux roues, utilisée pour les courses attelées.

**sulphonamide**  => sulfonamide

**summer coat**
poil d'été
Sommerhaar *ne*
pelo de verano

**summer dermatitis / eczema**  => summer sores

**summer sores** ; summer dermatitis / eczema
plaies d'été ; mal d'été
Sommerekzem *ne*
dermatitis estival ; lastimados de verano ; ulceraciones de verano

Sores that are most prevalent during summer months.
Différentes plaies peuvent faire leur apparition, ou être beaucoup plus importantes, durant les mois d'été.

**superciliary arch** ; orbital arch
arcade sourcilière
Augenbogen *m* ; Augenbrauenwölbung *f*
arco superciliar

**superficial gluteal muscle** ; gluteus superficialis m. ; gluteus maximus m. *old*
muscle fessier superficiel ; muscle grand fessier *anc*
oberflächlicher Kruppenmuskel
músculo glúteo superficial

**supplementary ration**
ration supplémentaire
zusätzliche Ration *(die ~)*
ración suplementaria / extra

**suppleness**
souplesse
Geschmeidigkeit
flexibilidad ; soltura

**supple seat**  => good and easy seat

**supraorbital fossa**
salière ; fosse supra-orbitaire
Augengrube *f*
fosa supraorbitaria

Depression above the eye of the horse.
Dépression située au-dessus de l'oeil du cheval.

**suspended phase**  => suspension (moment of ~)

**suspension**
planer
Streckphase *(die ~)*
suspensión

Suspension phase over an obstacle.
Phase au-dessus d'un obstacle.

**suspension (moment of ~)** ; suspended phase ; free flight (moment of ~) *(1)*
suspension (temps de ~)
Schwebemoment
suspensión (tiempo de ~)

During a motion, when a foot or feet, is/are off the ground. 1) At the gallop, when all four feet are off the ground.
Dans un déplacement, moment durant lequel un membre, un bipède, ou, dans le galop, les quatre membres (« free flight »), ne touche(nt) pas le sol.

**suspensory ligament** ; interosseus muscle
ligament suspenseur du boulet ; muscle interosseux (III)
Hängeband
ligamento suspensorio

Entièrement fibreux chez l'adulte; pour le membre antérieur: il commence à l'arrière du genou et au haut du métacarpien principal, il se sépare en deux grosses branches se rattachant au sommet de l'os grand sésamoïde qui leur correspond. Ces bandes présentent aussi une bride fibreuse qui va se rattacher au tendon de l'extenseur dorsal du doigt.

**suture**
suture
Naht *f*
sutura

**swan neck**  => arched neck

**sweat**
sueur ; transpiration
Schweiß
sudor

**sweating**
sudation
Schwitzen *ne*
sudación

**sweat flap (of a saddle)**
faux-quartier (d'une selle)
Schweißblatt *(das ~)*
falso faldón ; hoja falsa

**sweat glands**
glandes sudoripares
Schweißdrüsen
glándulas sudoríparas

**sweat scraper**
couteau de chaleur ; écumoir ; écumoire
Schweißmesser *(das ~)*
raspador para secar

**Swedish oxer**
oxer suédois ; oxer en ciseaux
Scherenoxer
oxer sueco

Dont les barres (toutes ou seulement les supérieures) sont en angle par rapport à l'horizontale, inclinant sur un côté et sur l'autre, formant ainsi un x.

**swelling**
enflure ; tuméfaction
Schwellung
hinchazón

**swinging rail**
bat-flanc
Flankierbaum *m* ; Stallbaum *m*
tranca ; tranquera ; tabla de separación en las
cuadras
Panneau mobile qui sépare deux stalles.

**swingle-tree** ; bar *hd*
palonnier ; bacul *Can.*
Ortscheit *(das ~)* ; Schwengel *(der ~)*
volquete

**switch the tail** *v*
fouailler de la queue
Schweif wedeln (mit dem ~)
menear la cola

**sympathetic nervous system**
système nerveux sympathique ; sympathique
sympathisches Nervensystem
sistema nervioso simpático
Partie du système nerveux autonome, il a des effets
contraires à ceux du parasympathique.

**synovia** => synovial fluid

**synovial bursa**
bourse synoviale
Schleimbeutel ; Synovialbeutel
bolsa sinovial
Poche synoviale placée entre un tendon et l'emplacement sur lequel il passe ou s'appuie.

**synovial fluid** ; synovia
synovie
Gelenkschmiere ; Synovia
sinovia ; líquido sinovial ; fluido sinovial
Liquide visqueux, limpide et jaune clair, servant à la
lubrification des articulations ou des parties de tendons
qui s'appuient sur d'autres structures.

**synovial sheath**
synoviale vaginale
Sehnenscheide
vaina sinovial
Habituellement, une telle membrane accompagne un
ou des tendon(s) pour en faciliter le glissement à
l'intérieur d'une gaine tendineuse.

**syringe**
seringue
Spritze *(die ~)*
jeringuilla ; jeringa

**systole**
systole
Systole *f*
sístole

**table** => face (of an anvil)

**table** *jump*
table *obstacle*
Tisch *m*
mesa

**table surface** => dental table

**tack ; tackle** ; gear ; harness
harnachement ; harnais *(1)*
Geschirr
arreo ; arnés ; jaez
Equipment worn by a horse to be driven, including bridle, girth, collar etc.
Équipement porté par le cheval pour la conduite, y incluant sangle, bride, rênes, collier etc. 1) Le mot harnais
est souvent utilisé dans un sens qui semble exclure la
bride.

**taenia / tenia** *anat*
ténia *anat*
Tänie / Taenie *ne*
tenia
A flat ribbon-like structure, especially the muscles of
the colon.

**taenia / tenia** => tapeworm

**tail**
queue
Schweif *m* ; Schwanz
cola ; rabo

**tailor**
tailleur
Schneider
sastre

**tail-female lineage** => female line

**tail hairs**
crins de la queue
Schweifhaare *(die ~)*
cerdas

**tail head**
naissance de la queue
Schweifansatz *m* ; Schwanzansatz
nacimiento de la cola

**tail to the wall** => renvers

**tail vertebrae** => caudal vertebrae

**tail wrap**
protège-queue ; fourreau de queue
Schweifschoner
venda para la cola

**taint** => infection

**take-off side (of an obstacle)**
côté de la battue
Absprungseite (bei Hindernis) *(die ~)*
lado de partida ; lugar de batida ; costado de la
batida
Côté du départ, par lequel un obstacle est prévu pour
être abordé.

**take a wide turn** => turn wide

**take off impulsion**
élan ; détente
Absprung *m*
lanzamiento
From the take-off point and before the suspension,
pushing in the air over the obstacle.
Action ou moment où le cheval se pousse dans les airs
pour franchir l'obstacle. Il s'agit d'une phase entre la
battue et le planer.

**take off point**
emplacement de la battue d'appel
Absprungstelle *f*
punto de picar / saltar

**take off the halter** *v*
enlever le licou
abhalftern
descabestrar

**take off (stride)**
battue d'appel ; appel *cs*
Anreitephase *f*
batida (de llamada)

**take out** => levy

**take the bridle off** => unbridle

**take to pasture** => pasture

**tall fescue (grass)** ; reed fescue
fétuque élevée
Rohrschwingel
festuca arundinacea

**talus** ; astragalus *old* ; tibial tarsal bone *old*
talus ; astragale *anc*
Talus
tarsotibial ; taba ; astrágalo
    Un des os du tarse.

**tapeworm** ; taenia / tenia
taenia ; ténia ; ver plat segmenté
Bandwurm *m*
tenia ; taenia ; lombriz solitaria
    Internal parasite with elongated flat body, living in the intestines.
    Parasite interne.

**tap root / taproot mare** ; foundation mare
jument de base ; jument-base ; jument-souche ; jument originaire
Stammstute
yegua original
    The earliest known mare in a female line.
    La souche (maternelle) à laquelle une lignée femelle remonte.

**tarsal bones**
os du tarse (les ~)
Fußwurzelknochen
huesos tarsianos
    Il y en a normalement six.

**tarsus** => hock

**tattooing**
tatouage
Tätowierung *f*
tatuaje

**tawny bay** => fawn bay

**team jumping (competition)**
saut par équipes (compétition de ~)
Mannschaftsspringen
salto por equipos

**teaser (stallion)**
boute-en-train ; souffleur (étalon ~) ; étalon d'essai
Probierhengst
incitador ; recelador ; recela ; calentador
    Horse used to test whether or not a mare is in heat.
    Cheval utilisé pour déterminer si les juments sont en chaleur.

**technical delegate**
délégué technique
technische Delegierte *(der ~)* ; technischer Betreuer
delegado técnico

**teletimer** => automatic timing device

**temperament**
tempérament
Temperament *(das ~)*
temperamento

**temperature**
température
Temperatur *(die ~)*
temperatura
    La température rectale normale du cheval est de 37,5°C, elle peut atteindre 40,5°C durant un galop important.

**temple**
tempe
Schläfe *f*
sien
    Région de la tête du cheval, située entre la joue, l'oeil, le front et l'oreille.

**temporal bone**
os temporal
Schläfenbein
hueso temporal
    Base de la région de la tempe.

**temporary teeth** => milk teeth

**tender mouth** => soft mouth

**tendinitis**
tendinite
Sehnenentzündung *f*
tendinitis
    Inflammation of a tendon. *s.a. tendon bow*
    Inflammation d'un tendon.

**tendon**
tendon
Sehne *f pl: Sehnen*
tendón *pl: tendones*
    Cordon fibreux qui prolonge un muscle et le rattache à un os. Il porte habituellement le nom de ce muscle.

**tendon bow**
claquage de tendon
Zerrung
distensión de un tendón ; curva en el tendón
    Usually presented as a chronic tendinitis (affecting both the tendon and its synovial sheath) of flexor tendons, usually of the forelimb.
    Inflammation d'un tendon (tendinite) dans laquelle il n'y a pas seulement la gaine d'affectée (ce qui serait un chauffage de tendon).

**tendon of common digital extensor** =>
    common (digital) extensor tendon

**testicle ; testis**
testicule
Hoden ; Testikel ; Testis
testículo

**tetanus** ; lockjaw
tétanos ; mal de cerf
Wundstarrkrampf *(der ~)*
tétanos ; tétano ; trismo
   Causée par la contamination d'une plaie par Clostridium tetani, une bactérie qui est présente dans l'intestin et les excréments du cheval. La raideur musculaire est particulièrement visible au niveau des mâchoires.

**tetanus immune serum** => antitetanus
   serum

**thigh**
cuisse
Oberschenkel *m*
muslo
   Partie du membre postérieur, dont le squelette est formé par le fémur.

**thigh bone** => femur

**thin the mane** *v* ; pull the mane *v*
éclaircir la crinière
Mähne verziehen *(die ~)*
entresacar la crin ; igualar la crin

**third eyelid** => nictitating membrane

**third phalanx** => distal phalanx

**thoracic cavity** ; chest cavity
cavité thoracique
Brusthöhle *f*
cavidad torácica

**thoracic limb** => forelimb ; foreleg

**thoracic vertebrae**
vertèbres thoraciques
Brustwirbel
vértebras torácicas
   Le cheval en a 18.

**thorax**
thorax
Brustkasten ; Brustkorb ; Thorax
tórax
   *s.a. chest*

**Thoroughbred**
thoroughbred ; pur-sang anglais
englisches Vollblut
pura sangre inglés
   English breed, bred chiefly for racing since the end of the 17th century. The word thoroughbred is the literal translation of the Arabic « Kehilan » meaning pure-bred all through.
   Race d'origine anglaise.

**thoroughpin**
vessigon tendineux de la gaine tarsienne
Kurbengalle ; Sprunggelenksgalle *(die ~)*
hinchazón tarsal
   Inflamed synovial sheath of the deep flexor tendon as it passes just above the hock.
   Vessigon de la gaine du tendon du fléchisseur profond.

**threadworm** => nematode

**three-day event**
concours complet (de trois jours)
Vielseitigkeitsprüfung
prueba de tres días

**throat**
gorge
Kehle *f*
garganta
   Comprise entre l'encolure, l'auge et les ganaches, a pour base anatomique le larynx.

**throatlash ; throatlatch**
sous-gorge ; gorgette *Can. ca*
Kehlriemen
ahogadero ; fiador

**thrombosis**
thrombose
Thrombose *f*
trombosis

**throw the head** => bob the head

**throw the rider** *v* ; unseat *v* ; buck off *v (1)*
désarçonner (le cavalier)
abwerfen (den Reiter ~)
voltear (al jinete) ; derribar (el / al jinete) ; tirar el jinete
   1) To throw the rider by mean of bucking.

**thrush**
pourriture de la fourchette ; échauffement de la fourchette
Strahlfäule *f*
podredumbre de la ranilla
   Degeneration of the frog with a foul-smelling discharge.
   Habituellement la résultante d'une mauvaise hygiène des sabots et de l'action d'une bactérie. L'échauffement de la fourchette précède la pourriture de celle- ci.

**thymus**
thymus
Thymus
timo

**thyroid (gland)**
thyroïde (glande ~)
Schilddrüse *f* ; Thyreoidea *f*
glándula tiroidea ; tiroides

**tibia**
tibia
Tibia ; Schienbein *ne*
tibia
   Os principal de la jambe, de l'articulation du grasset à celle du jarret, cet os est très peu protégé sur sa face interne. La fibula lui est soudée.

**tibial tarsal bone** => talus

**ticket rack**
porte-billets *m inv* ; porte-tickets
Brieftasche (kleine ~) *f*
billetero

**ticks**
tiques
Zecken *(die ~)*
garrapatas

**tick fever** => babesiasis ; babesiosis

**tie-down** => standing martingale

**tighten the girth**  => girth

**time**
temps
Zeit
tiempo

**timekeeper** ; timer
chronométreur ; préposé au chronomètre
Zeitnehmer *(der ~)*
cronometrador

**timer**  => timekeeper

**time allowed**
temps accordé
Mindestzeit
tiempo concedido

**time limit**
temps limite
Höchstzeit
tiempo límite / máximo

**time penalty**
pénalité de temps
Strafpunkt für Zeitüberschreiten
penalidad de tiempo ; falta por / de tiempo

**timothy (grass)**
fléole (des prés) ; phléole ; mil
Timothe ; Wiesenlieschgras
fleo

**tinea**  => ringworm

**toed-in** ; pin-toed ; toeing-in ; pigeon-toed ;
 in-toed
cagneux du pied *adj* ; pied cagneux *n*
zeheneng ; zehenenge Stellung
estevado ; pie de paloma
   One or both feet (toes) pointing inwards, usually because the legs are turning inwards. *s.a. base narrow*
   Quand un pied, ou les deux, reste(nt) tourné(s) en dedans, les pinces convergent l'une vers l'autre.

**toed-out** ; splayed foot ; splay-footed ; foot
 turned out ; toeing-out
panard du pied (cheval ~) ; pied panard
zehenweit ; zehenweite Stellung ;
 Tanzmeisterstellung
izquierdo (caballo ~)
   The hoof points outwards, usually because the whole
limb is rotated slightly. *s.a. base wide*
   Quand le pied reste tourné vers l'extérieur; c'est habituellement tout le membre qui est tourné vers
l'extérieur.

**toeing-in**  => toed-in

**toeing-out**  => toed-out

**toeing knife**  => sole knife

**toe clip**
pinçon en pince
Zehenaufzug
pestaña / agarradera de punta
   A clip on the toe of a horseshoe.

**toe (of a hoof)**
pince (d'un sabot)
Zehe *f* ; Hufzehe ; Zehenteil (des Hufes)
dedo ; pinza de casco ; punta de pie
   The dorsal or anterior portion of the hoof wall.
   Partie antérieure du sabot.

**tongue**
langue
Zunge
lengua

**tongue**  => billet (of a buckle)

**tongue clicking**  => click (of the tongue)

**toolhole**  => hardy / hardie hole

**tooth** *pl: teeth*
dent *pl: dents*
Zahn *m pl: Zähne*
diente *pl: dientes*
   Dans l'ordre d'apparition: dents de lait et dents d'a-
dulte ou de remplacement.

**tooth root**
racine d'une dent
Zahnwurzel
raíz

**top-hat**
haut-de-forme (chapeau ~)
Zylinderhut *m* ; Reithut
sombrero de copa ; chistera

**torsion (of a loop of intestine)**  => volvulus

**torso**  => trunk

**toss the head**  => bob the head

**tournament**
tournoi
Turnier *ne* ; Wettbewerb *m*
torneo

**trace** *hd*
trait *att*
Strang *m* ; Zuggurt *m* ; Zugstrick *m*
tirante
   Courroie de cuir allant du collier au palonnier, par laquelle un cheval tire une charge ou un véhicule.

**trachea** ; windpipe
trachée
Luftröhre *f*
tráquea
   Air passage extending from the larynx to the main
bronchi.
   Long tuyau formé d'anneaux cartilagineux. Il ache-
mine l'air entre le larynx et les bronches.

**track (in a riding arena)**
piste (dans un manège)
Hufschlag *m* ; Spur *f*
pista

**trailer (horse ~)**
remorque (à chevaux)
Pferdetransportwagen ; Anhänger
remolque (para transporte de caballos) ; acoplado

**trainer** ; coach
entraîneur
Trainer
entrenador

**training** ; schooling ; dressage
entraînement ; dressage
Training ; Dressur ; Zureiten
adiestramiento ; amaestramiento ; entrenamiento

The schooling and training of a horse for jumping or such disciplines may be considered being the same thing. For endurance performances however, the term training appears to be more adequate. Dressage stands especially for training in responsiveness, deportment and skills.

Entraînement d'un cheval en fonction d'une discipline. Une fois que le cheval est dressé ou entraîné à se comporter de la façon qu'on attend de lui, ou à exécuter des mouvements particuliers, il pourra encore faire l'objet d'un autre genre d'entraînement. On dit plutôt, par exemple, qu'on entraîne un cheval, pour qu'il acquière la résistance nécessaire, à la course d'endurance.

**training level** => degree of training

**train (a horse)** *v*
entraîner (un cheval)
trainieren
entrenar
*see training*

**Trakehner ; Trakehnen horse** *breed* ; East
  Prussian (horse)
trakehner
Trakehner
trakehner

Race originaire du haras de Trakehnen en Prusse-Orientale.

**tranquillizer**
tranquillisant
Beruhigungsmittel *(das ~)*
tranquilizante

**transition**
transition
Übergang *m*
transición

**transverse process**
processus transverse
Querfortsatz *m*
apófisis transversa

Saillie osseuse de chaque côté d'une vertèbre, plus ou moins marquée selon la région de la colonne vertébrale.

**trappings (horse's ~)** ; caparison
caparaçon
Pferdedecke
caparazón

**travers** ; head to the wall
travers ; tête au mur ; croupe en dedans
Travers
cabeza al muro ; cabeza afuera

**treacle** => molasses

**treble** => triple (combination)

**tree (boot ~)**
embauchoir ; embouchoir
Stiefelblock ; Stiefelleiste
horma de bota

A support inserted, when not being worn, to preserve the shape of leather boots.

Support que l'on introduit dans les bottes de cuir pour les aider à maintenir leurs formes quand elles ne sont pas portées.

**tree (of a saddle)**
arbre (d'une selle) ; arçon
Sattelbaum
fuste

**trial** ; heat
épreuve
Probieren *ne* ; Prüfen *ne*
prueba

**trichophytosis** => ringworm

**tricorne**
tricorne
Dreispitz *m* ; Dreimaster *m*
tricornio ; sombrero de tres picos

A three-cornered hat.

**trim** => pare (a hoof)

**trimmer / cutter (hoof ~)** => nipper(s) (hoof ~)

**trimming (of the hoof)**
parage (de la corne)
Beschneiden (des Hufes) *ne*
cuidado de los cascos

On utilise aussi parfois l'expression parage des sabots.

**triple bar(s)**
barres triples ; spa *(1)* ; barres de spa *(1)*
Tripelbarre *f* ; Triple-Barre
triples de barras ; barra triple

An obstacle made of three bars, widely spread and of increasing height.

Un obstacle dont la hauteur des barres est croissante.
1) Les barres ne sont pas nécessairement au nombre de trois.

**triple (combination)** ; treble
triple (obstacle ~)
dreifache Kombination *(die ~)*
obstáculo triple ; combinación triple

**trochlea of the femur** => femoral trochlea

**trophy**
trophée
Trophäe *f*
trofeo

**trot**
trot
Trab *m* ; Trott *m langsamer, schwerfälliger Trab*
trote

At this gait, the horse moves his left front and right rear legs simultaneously or almost, then the right front and the left rear.

Au trot, le cheval déplace en alternance l'antérieur gauche avec le postérieur droit, puis l'antérieur droit avec le postérieur gauche. En course le trot pourra être à quatre temps, les deux membres déplacés ensemble n'étant pas alors déposés au sol simultanément.

**trot** *v*
trotter ; aller au trot
Trab reiten ; traben
trotar

**trotter** ; trotting horse
trotteur
Traber ; Trabpferd
trotador

**trotting horse**  => trotter

**trot race**
course au trot
Trabrennen
carrera de trote / trotadores ; carrera de los trotones
Mounted trot races are seen in France.
Les courses au trot peuvent être attelées ou montées, ces dernières étant populaires en France.

**trot rising** *v*
trotter enlevé
leichttraben
trote levantado

**true canter / gallop**  => canter / gallop at / on the true lead

**true to type**
conforme au type de la race
typvoll
tira al tipo / a la raza ; representa a su raza

**trunk** ; torso ; barrel (of the horse)
tronc
Rumpf *m* ; Stamm ; Hauptteil
tronco ; torso

**tuber calcis**  => calcanean tuber

**tuber coxae**  => coxal tuber

**turf**  => races (the ~)

**turn** *r*
virage *c* ; tournant *c*
Kurve
curva

**turned-in elbow** ; elbow inclined inwards
coude serré ; coude au corps
angedrückter Ellbogen
codo hacia adentro

**turned-out elbow** ; elbow inclined outwards
coude écarté
abstehender Ellbogen
codo hacia afuera
Un coude écarté correspond souvent à un membre cagneux.

**turned-over neck**  => arched neck

**turnip**
navet
Futterrübe *f*
nabo

**turn on the forehand** *n & v*
tourner sur les antérieurs *n & v* ; pivot sur les antérieurs
Wendung auf der Vorhand / Vorderhand
vuelta sobre el anterior
*s.a. reversed pirouette*

**turn on the haunches / quarters / hocks** *n & v*
tourner sur les postérieurs *n & v* ; pivot sur les postérieurs
Wendung auf der Hinterhand
vuelta sobre el posterior / la grupa

**turn short / sharply** *v*
tourner court
kurz wenden ; scharf wenden
volver corto

**turn wide** *v* ; take a wide turn *v*
tourner large
in großem Bogen wenden
volver ancho

**turn (on the forehand // haunches)** *n & v*
tourner (sur les antérieurs // postérieurs) *n & v* ;
tourner de pied ferme *n & v* ; conversion *(1)*
Wendung (auf der Vorhand // Hinterhand) *(die ~)*
vuelta (sobre el anterior // posterior)
*s.a. pirouette*
Pivot sur les épaules / l'avant-main, ou bien sur les hanches / l'arrière-main. 1) Une conversion peut s'effectuer sur les antérieurs, sur les postérieurs ou encore par une combinaison des deux.

**turpentine**
térébenthine
Terpentin *ne*
trementina ; terpentina *amer*

**tush**  => canine (tooth)

**tushes**  => canine teeth

**two-horse trailer**
remorque (à) deux places ; remorque (pour) deux chevaux
Anhänger *m*
acoplado para dos caballos

**two tracks (on ~)**
deux pistes (sur ~)
zwei Hufschlägen (auf ~)
dos pistas (en / de ~)

**tying-up (syndrome)**  => azoturia

**tympanic cavity**
caisse du tympan
Paukenhöhle
caja del tímpano
Cavité de l'oreille moyenne.

**tympanic membrane**
tympan
Trommelfell
tímpano

**udder (the ~)**
mamelles (les ~)
Euter *ne*
ubre

**ulcer**
ulcère
Geschwür *ne*
úlcera

**ulna** ; cubitus *old*
ulna ; cubitus *anc*
Elle *f* ; Ulna
cúbito

Fusionné à la partie supérieure du radius, sa pointe supérieure (l'olécrâne) forme la pointe du coude.

**ultrasound scanning**
échographie
Ultraschalluntersuchung *(die ~)*
ecografía

**umbilical scar ; umbilicus** => navel

**unbridle** *v* ; take the bridle off *v*
débrider
abzäumen
desembridar

**ungird** *v*
dessangler
losgürten ; abgürten
descinchar

**ungulates (the ~)**
ongulés (les ~)
Huftiere *ne*
ungulados

**unharness** *v* ; put off the harness *v*
déharnacher
abschirren
desaparejar

**unruly horse** ; difficult horse
cheval difficile
schwieriges Pferd
caballo difícil

**unsaddle** *v*
desseller
absatteln
desensillar

**unseat** => throw the rider

**unshoe** *v* ; remove the shoe *v* ; pull off the shoe *v*
déferrer (un pied)
Eisen abnehmen *(das ~)* ; Hufeisen abnehmen
desherrar ; sacar una herradura

**unwilling (horse)**
peu généreux (cheval ~)
unwillig
sin voluntad

**upper jaw** ; maxilla
mâchoire supérieure ; maxillaire
Oberkiefer ; Maxilla
maxilar (superior)

Au niveau des os, la mâchoire supérieure est composée de deux maxillaires et de l'os incisif. C'est donc par extension que l'on assimile maxillaire et mâchoire supérieure; certains auteurs donnent même parfois le nom de maxillaire inférieur à la mâchoire inférieure.

**upper lip**
lèvre supérieure
Oberlippe
labio superior

**upright obstacle** => vertical

**upright pastern** => knuckling (over)

**upright shoulder** ; straight shoulder
épaule droite
steile Schulter
hombro derecho

The angle from the point of the shoulder to the withers is too close to the vertical, inhibiting desirable movement of the front legs.

L'angle de la pointe de l'épaule au garrot est trop à la verticale.

**upside-down neck** => ewe neck

**ureter**
uretère
Harnleiter
uréter

Conduit de drainage du rein vers la vessie.

**urethra**
urètre
Harnröhre
uretra

**urine**
urine
Urin ; Harn
orina

**urticaria**
urticaire
Nesselausschlag *m* ; Quaddelausschlag
urticaria

**uterine horn**
corne utérine / de l'utérus
Gebärmutterhorn ; Uterushorn
cuerno uterino

**uterine tube**
trompe utérine ; oviducte ; trompe de Fallope
Eileiter *m* ; Ovidukt *m*
oviducto

**uterus**
utérus
Gebärmutter *f* ; Uterus
útero ; matriz

**vaccination**
vaccination
Impfung *f*
vacunación

**vaccine**
vaccin
Impfstoff *f*
vacuna

**vagina**
vagin
Vagina ; Scheide
vagina

**van horse** => dray horse

**vaulting** ; voltige
voltige
Voltigieren
volteo ; voltereta

**vein**
veine
Vene *f*
vena
Les veines ramènent le sang depuis les tissus jusqu'au cœur, elles comportent souvent des valvules pour que le sang ne puisse y circuler que dans ce sens.

**ventral border of mandible**
ganache
Ganasche *f*
fance
Saillie formée par le bord inférieur de la mandibule.

**vermicide**   => anthelmintic (drug)

**vertebra** *pl: vertebrae*
vertèbre
Wirbel *m*
vértebra

**vertebral artery**
artère vertébrale
Wirbelarterie *f*
arteria vertebral

**vertebral canal**
canal vertébral ; canal rachidien *anc*
Wirbelkanal
canal vertebral
La moelle épinière y est logée dans la colonne vertébrale.

**vertebral column** ; spinal column; spine
colonne vertébrale ; rachis *anc*
Wirbelsäule ; Rückgrat
columna vertebral

**vertical** ; upright obstacle
vertical (obstacle ~) ; droit (obstacle ~)
steiles Hindernis
obstáculo vertical ; vertical *m*

**vesicant**   => blister ; blistering

**vesicular gland** ; seminal vesicle
glande vésiculaire ; vésicule séminale
Samenblase ; Bläschendrüse ; Vesikulardrüse
vesícula seminal

**vestibule of vagina**
vestibule du vagin
Scheidenvorhof
vestíbulo vaginal

**veterinarian** ; veterinary surgeon
vétérinaire *n*
Tierarzt *m* ; Veterinär *m*
veterinario ; albéitar

**veterinary**
vétérinaire *adj*
tierärztlich
veterinario

**veterinary examination** ; vet check
examen vétérinaire
Verfassungsprüfung *(die ~)* ; tierärztliche
  Untersuchung / Ankaufsuntersuchung
reconocimiento veterinario ; examen (del) veterinario

**veterinary medicine**
médecine vétérinaire
Veterinärmedizin *f*
medicina veterinaria

**veterinary surgeon**   => veterinarian

**vet check**   => veterinary examination

**vice**
vice
Untugend
vicio

**victory**   => win

**visceral muscle**   => smooth muscle

**visceral nervous system**   => autonomic
  nervous system

**vitamin**
vitamine
Vitamin *ne*
vitamina

**voice**
voix
Stimme *(die ~)*
voz

**volte at the walk**
volte au pas
Schrittvolte
vuelta al paso

**volte (to the left // right)**
volte (à gauche // droite)
Volte (Rechts... // Links...)
vuelta (a la izquierda // derecha)

**volte ; volt**
volte
Volte *f*
vuelta
acad: Cercle de 6 mètres de diamètre.

**voltige**   => vaulting

**voluntary muscle**   => striated muscle

**volvulus** ; torsion (of a loop of intestine)
volvulus
Darmverschlingung *m*
vólvulo intestinal

**vomer**
vomer
Vorner ; Pflugscharbein
vómer

**vulcanite**
ébonite
Hartgummi *ne* ; Ebonit *m*
ebonita

**vulva**
vulve
Scham ; Vulva
vulva

**wager**   => bet

**wagerer**   => bettor**

**walk** *v*
marcher (au pas) ; aller au pas
Schritt gehen
marchar al paso ; ir al paso

**walk** *n*
pas
Schritt *m*
paso

**walk on a long rein** *n*
pas, les rênes longues
Schritt am langen Zügel
paso con riendas largas

**walk (over) the course** *v*
marcher le parcours
abgehen
pisar el recorrido ; caminar la cancha / el curso

**wall**
mur
Mauer *f*
muro ; pared
  Vertical obstacle looking like a wall.
  Obstacle vertical imitant un mur.

**wall (of the hoof)**
paroi (du sabot) ; muraille
Hufwand ; Hornplatte ; Hornwand *f*
tapa (del casco) ; pared del casco

**warmblood ; warm-blooded horse**
cheval à sang chaud ; cheval de sang (chaud)
Warmblut *ne* ; Warmblüter *m* ; Warmblutpferd *ne* ;
  Warmblütiger Schlag *m* ; warmblütige Schlag
  *(der ~)*
caballo de sangre (caliente)
  Type of horse with finer bones than the coldblood (the
  overlap being a matter of opinion), usually suitable for
  riding. In some countries the term may be used to
  distinguish horses containing a strain of Arab blood.

**war horse**
cheval de guerre
Kriegspferd ; Schlachtroß
caballo de guerra

**water** *n*
eau
Wasser
agua

**water** *v*
abreuver ; donner à boire
tränken
abrevar ; dar de beber

**waterer**  => water(ing) trough

**water(ing) trough** ; waterer ; drinking trough
abreuvoir
Tränke
abrevadero

**water brush**
brosse de lavage
Waschbürste *(die ~)*
cepillo de agua

**water ditch**  => water jump (open ~)

**water jump (open ~)** ; brook ; water ditch
rivière *cs obstacle* ; fossé d'eau
Wassergraben *m* ; Bach *m*
ría ; foso de agua ; salto de agua

**weakness**
faiblesse
Schwäche
endeblez

**weak back**
dos mou
weiche Rucken
lomo blando

**wean** *v*
sevrer
absetzen ; entwöhnen
destetar

**weaning**
sevrage
Absetzen *ne*
destete

**weanling** ; grass foal
poulain // pouliche sevré(e) ; poulain // pouliche
  d'herbe
Absetzfohlen *ne*
potro destetado // potra destetada ; potrillo destetado // potrilla destetada
  From the weaning to the following January first, the
  horse is then usually considered being a yearling.
  Du sevrage jusqu'au premier janvier suivant, alors que
  le cheval est habituellement considéré avoir un an.

**weaving**
tic de l'ours
Weben
zigzagueo
  A vice, the horse rocks from side to side on his front
  legs. This prevents him from resting properly.
  Tic du cheval qui se balance d'un antérieur à l'autre,
  ce qui empêche un repos adéquat.

**weigh** *v*
peser
wiegen
pesar

**weight aid**  => action of the seat

**weight cloth**
fontes
Bleigewichte
mantilla de peso / plomo ; faldón de pesas ; fundas

**weigh in** *v tr*
peser (après la course) *v ct*
zurückwiegen
pesar

**well-defined hock**
jarret bien sculpté
ausgeprägtes Sprunggelenk
corvejón bien definido

**well-defined knee**
genou bien sculpté
ausgeprägtes Vorderfußwurzelgelenk ; starkes
  Karpalgelenk
rodilla bien definida

**well-schooled (horse)** ; made
dressé (cheval bien ~) ; confirmé
gerittenes Pferd
caballo bien hecho / domado / riendado ; caballo
  enseñado

**well let down** ; well to the ground ; close to the
  ground ; near to the ground
bien descendus ; près de terre
tief am Boden
cerca de la tierra

  Applied to hocks or knees which are set low, resulting
in short cannon bones.
  S'applique aux genoux ou jarrets placés bas, ce qui résulte en un canon court, caractéristique très souhaitable.

**well to the ground**  => well let down

**Welsh pony**
poney welsh
Walespony
póney galés / galense

**western saddle** ; stock saddle
selle western
Westernsattel *m* ; Cowboysattel
montura vaquera

**Weymouth bridle**  => double bridle

**Weymouth (curb bit)**  => curb bit

**wheat**
blé ; froment
Weizen *m*
trigo

**whinny / whinney**  => neigh

**whip** *v* ; horsewhip *v*
cravacher
Reitpeitsche schlagen (mit der ~)
fustigar

**whip**
fouet
Peitsche *f*
látigo

**whiplash**
coup de fouet
Peitschenhieb
latigazo

**whipper-in**
valet-de-chiens
Pikör
mozo de perros

  A huntsman's assistant.
  Il soigne les chiens et les accompagne à la chasse, sous
les ordres du piqueux. Le terme allemand « Pikör »
recoupe aussi différents autres rôles au sein de
l'équipage de chasse.

**white**
blanc
Weiß *ne* ; weiß *adj*
blanco

  Sometimes used to designate a grey horse whose hairs
have turned white with age. *s.a. albino*
  Parfois utilisé pour désigner un cheval gris dont le poil
a blanchi avec l'âge.

**white coronet**
principe de balzane
weiße Kronränder
corona blanca

  Balzane limitée à la hauteur de la couronne et en faisant le tour en totalité.

**white face** ; bald face ; calf face
belle-face *n*
Laterne *f*
careto *n*

**white foaled**
blanc de naissance
Schimmel *m weißgeboren*
blanco (desde el nacimiento)

**white line (of the hoof)** ; white zone
ligne blanche (du sabot)
weiße Linie *(die ~)*
línea blanca

**white marking on a limb / leg** ; leg marking
balzane
weiß Fessel
calzado ; mancha blanca

  Marque blanche habituellement limitée aux extrémités
des membres.

**white to above knee // hock** ; stocking ; full
  stocking
balzane au-dessus du genou // jarret ; balzane
  haut-chaussée
hoch (weiß) gestiefelt (Bein) ; hochgestiefelt weiß
calzado alto

**white to half-cannon** ; sock
balzane mi-canon ; grande balzane
  (mi-chaussée)
halb weiß gestiefelt (Bein) ; halbgestiefelt weiß
medio calzado blanco

**white zone**  => white line (of the hoof)

**white (true ~)**  => albino

**whole colour(ed)**
zain *adj*
ohne (jegliche) Abzeichen ; ganzfarbig ; einfarbig
zaino

  Body, legs, mane, tail and head of the same colour,
with no hairs of any other colour.
  Formée de poils et de crins d'une seule couleur, sans
poils ou marques d'une autre couleur.

**whorl** ; cowlick
épi
Haarwirbel
remolino

  A circle or other irregular setting of coat hair.
  Zone où les poils, changeant de direction, ressemblent
à un petit tourbillon ou prennent une autre forme
irrégulière.

**wide at the chest**
large de poitrine
brustweit
abierto de delante

**wide at the knees**  => knee-wide

**width of chest**
largeur de la poitrine
Brustbreite
anchura del pecho

**width of hips**
largeur aux hanches
Hüftbreite ; Hüftweite
anchura de las ancas / la grupa

**wild horse**
cheval sauvage
wildes Pferd
caballo salvaje

**willing (horse)**
généreux (cheval ~)
leistungsbereit ; willig
voluntario

**win** *n* ; victory
victoire
Sieg *m* ; Siegen *ne*
victoria

**windpipe** => trachea

**wind-sucking**
tic aérophagique (sans appui) ; tic à l'air
Koppen
aerofagia ; tiro

1st: Gulping and swallowing of air, can be accompanied by crib-biting. 2nd: This term may also be applied to drawing of air and expelling it from the reproductive tract by the vulva with each change of intra-abdominal pressure. This can result from a laceration of the vulva or by a closure that is not effective enough.

Tic du cheval qui avale de l'air sans prendre appui avec ses dents sur quelque chose.

**wind gall / puff (articular ~)**
mollette articulaire ; vessigon articulaire
Gelenkgalle (weiche ~)
vejiga articular blanda

**wind gall / puff (tendinous ~)**
mollette tendineuse ; vessigon tendineux
Sehnenscheidengalle (weiche ~)
vejiga tendinosa blanda

Wind gall of a synovial sheath.

**wind gall / windgall** => wind puff / windpuff

**wind puff / windpuff** ; wind gall / windgall
mollette ; molette *f* ; vessigon *m*
Galle (weiche ~) *f* ; Fesselgelenkgalle
distensión sinovial

Protrusion due to excessive fluid in tendon synovial sheaths or joint capsules.

Dilatation exagérée des membranes synoviales, due à un excès de synovie. On parle habituellement de mollette dans la région du boulet et du paturon, et de vessigon dans la région du carpe et du jarret.

**wing out** => paddle

**winker** => blinker

**winner**
vainqueur ; gagnant *n*
Sieger *(der ~)*
vencedor ; ganador

**winter coat**
poil d'hiver ; pelage hivernal
Winterhaar *ne* ; Winterfell
pelo del invierno

**wire (finish ~)** => finish(ing) line

**withdraw** *v*
retirer
zurückziehen
retirar

**withers**
garrot
Widerrist *m*
cruz

Éminence comprise entre l'encolure, les épaules et le dos du cheval.

**wolf tooth**
dent de loup
Wolfszahn
diente de lobo

The first premolar, usually to be removed.

La première prémolaire, elle n'est que rudimentaire quand elle apparaît et est considérée comme une nuisance.

**working canter**
galop de travail
Arbeitsgalopp
galope de trabajo

**working ration**
ration de travail
Arbeitsration *f*
ración para trabajo

**working trot**
trot de travail
Arbeitstrab
trote de trabajo

**work between the pillars** *n*
travail entre (les) piliers
Arbeit in den Pilaren *(die ~)*
trabajo en los pilares

**work in hand** *n* ; ground work
travail à la main
Arbeit an der Hand *(die ~)*
trabajo a la mano

**work in long reins** *n*
travail sur / aux longues rênes
Arbeit am langen Zügel *(die ~)*
trabajo en riendas largas

**work on two tracks** *n*
travail sur deux pistes
Arbeit auf zwei Hufschlägen *(die ~)*
trabajo de dos pistas

**worm** *pl: worms*
ver *pl: vers*
Wurm *m pl: Würmer*
verme *pl: vermes* ; lombriz *pl: lombrices*

**wormer** => anthelmintic (drug)

**worthless horse** *r*
tocard *c* ; toquard
schlechtes Pferd *(das ~)*
caballo de carrera malo

**wound** ; sore
plaie
Verletzung *(die ~)*
herida

**wrap** => bandage

**Württemberg horse** *breed*
wurtemberg ; württemberg
Württemberg
wurtembergués
  Race d'origine allemande.

**X-ray examination**
examen radiographique
Röntgenuntersuchung *f*
radiografía

**yearling (colt // filly)**
poulain // pouliche d'un an ; yearling
Jährling *m*
potrillo // potrilla de un año ; potro // potra de un
  año ; yearling
  Usually and for administrative purposes, the horse is
considered as being one year old, hence a yearling, on
January first following his birth, until January first the
following year.
  Pour les fins administratives et de façon habituelle, le
poulain ou la pouliche est considéré(e) comme ayant un
an le premier janvier qui suit sa naissance.

**yellow body** ; corpus luteum
corps jaune
Gelbkörper *m*
cuerpo lúteo

**zebra**
zèbre
Zebra
cebra

**zebra-dun**  => buckskin

**zero-grazing**
zéro-pâturage
Sommerstallfütterung *f*
pastoreo en reclusión

**zigzag half-pass**  => counter-change of hand

**zygomatic arch**
arcade zygomatique
Jochbeinbogen *m*
filo cigomático

**zygomatic bone** ; cheekbone
os zygomatique
Jochbein
hueso cigomático

# FRANÇAIS

## Index

**à volonté** free choice
**abattoir** slaughterhouse
**abattre un cheval** destroy a horse
**abcès (dans un pied)** abscess (in a hoof)
**abdomen** abdomen
**abducteur** abductor
**abduction** abduction
**aborder un obstacle** approach an obstacle
**abreuver** water
**abreuvoir** water(ing) trough
**abreuvoir automatique** automatic waterer
(floater ~)
**abri des juges** judges' box
**absence de chaleurs** anestrus ; anoestrus
**acarien psorique** mange mite
**accord des aides** harmonious use of aids
**accouplement** breeding
**accouplement consanguin** inbreeding
**accouplement éloigné / régulier** outbreeding
**accouplement incestueux** incestuous
breeding
**accoupler (des chevaux)** mate (horses)
**accul (être à l'~)** bay (to be / stand at ~)
**acculoire** breeching
**acépromazine** acepromazin
**acétabulum** acetabulum
**acheteur** buyer
**acier doux** mild steel
**action** action
**action de l'assiette** action of the seat
**action des jambes** aid of the legs
**action du genou** knee action
**adducteur** adductor
**adduction** adduction
**aérophagie** aerophagia
**agalactie ; agalaxie** galactia
**aide** aid
**aide artificielle** artificial aid
**aide diagonale** diagonal aid
**aide du poids du corps** action of the seat
**aide latérale** lateral aid
**aide naturelle** natural aid
**aides** aids

**air d'école** school air / pace
**airs relevés** airs above the ground
**aisselle** axilla
**ajuster les rênes** adjust the reins
**albinos** albino
**albumine** albumin
**aldéhyde formique** formalin
**alezan** chestnut
**alezan brûlé** liver chestnut
**alezan clair** light chestnut
**alezan doré** golden chestnut
**alezan foncé** dark chestnut
**allaitement** suckling
**allèle** allele
**aller au pas** walk
**aller au trot** trot
**allongement (d'allure)** lengthening (of strides)
**allonger** extend
**allonger les rênes** lengthen the reins
**allotriophagie** pica
**allure** gait
**allure basse** shuffling gait
**allure énergique** good action
**allure rasante** shuffling gait
**allures** gaits
**alvéole pulmonaire** pulmonary alveolus
**amateur** amateur
**amble** amble
**ambler** amble
**ambleur** ambler
**ambleur péruvien** Peruvian paso / ambler
**amélioration de la race chevaline** horse
improvement
**amende** fine
**amidon** starch
**amnios** amnion
**ampoule** blister
**analgésique** analgesic
**analyse de sang** blood examination
**anasarque** anasarca
**andalou** Andalusian
**âne (en général)** donkey
**âne (mâle)** donkey stallion

**anémie** anaemia

**anémie infectieuse équine / des équidés** equine infectious anaemia / anemia

**ânesse** jenny-ass ; jenny

**anesthésie d'un nerf** nerve-blocking

**anesthésique** anesthetic ; anaesthetic

**angle de l'approche** angle of the approach

**angle de l'épaule** shoulder angle

**angle de la croupe** sacral tuber

**angle de la hanche** coxal tuber

**angle du bassin** pelvis angle

**anglo-arabe** Anglo-Arab(ian) (horse)

**anglo-arabe hongrois** Gidran

**anglo-normand** French Saddle (horse)

**animal** quarry

**animal de bât / somme** pack animal

**anneaux (du mors)** rings (of a bit)

**annonceur (officiel)** announcer (house / track ~)

**anoestrus** anestrus ; anoestrus

**ânon** donkey foal

**antérieur** forelimb ; foreleg

**antérieur gauche** left foreleg

**anthelmintique** anthelmintic (drug)

**anti-inflammatoire** anti-inflammatory

**antibiotique** antibiotic

**anus** anus

**aplomb(s)** stand(s)

**aponévrose** aponeurose

**appaloosa** Appaloosa

**appareil hyoïdien** hyoid apparatus / bone

**appareil respiratoire** respiratory system

**appel** take off (stride)

**appel de langue** click (of the tongue)

**apprenti** apprentice

**appui** contact with the bit (horse moving into a ~)

**appuyer** half-pass

**appuyer** half-pass

**appuyer (lourdement) sur la main / le mors (s'~)** lean (heavily) on the hand / bit

**appuyer au galop** half-pass in canter

**arabe** Arab ; Arabian

**arbre (d'une selle)** tree (of a saddle)

**arc costal** costal arch

**arcade** arch

**arcade sourcilière** superciliary arch

**arcade zygomatique** zygomatic arch

**arçon** tree (of a saddle)

**ardennais** Ardennais ; Ardennes (horse)

**ardillon** billet (of a buckle)

**arqué (genou ~)** over at / in the knees

**arrachement** avulsion

**arrêt** halt

**arrêter** halt

**arrière-main** rear end

**arrière-train** rear end

**arrivée** finish

**art** art

**art équestre** art of equestrian riding

**artère** artery

**artère rénale** renal artery

**artère vertébrale** vertebral artery

**artérite virale du cheval** equine viral arteritis

**articulation** joint

**articulation atlanto-axiale** atlanto-axial articulation

**articulation coxo-fémorale** hip joint

**articulation de l'épaule** shoulder joint

**articulation de la hanche** hip joint

**articulation du boulet** fetlock joint

**articulation du coude** elbow joint

**articulation du genou** stifle joint

**articulation du grasset** stifle joint

**articulation du paturon** pastern joint

**articulation du pied** coffin joint

**articulation huméro-antébrachiale** elbow joint

**articulation interphalangienne distale** coffin joint

**articulation interphalangienne proximale** pastern joint

**articulation métacarpo-phalangienne // métatarso-phalangienne** fetlock joint

**articulation(s) du carpe** carpal joint(s)

**articulation sacro-iliaque** sacroiliac joint

**articulation scapulo-humérale** shoulder joint

**articulations sterno-costales / sterno-chondrales** sternocostal articulations

**articulé** jointed

**ascaride** ascarid

**ascaris** ascarid

**ascendance** ancestry

**assiette (du cavalier)** seat (of a rider)

**assiette souple et élastique** good and easy seat

**association d'éleveurs** breeder's association

**asthme** asthma

**astragale** talus

**ataxie** ataxia

**ataxie du poulain** foal ataxia

**atlas** atlas

**atteindre (s'~) ; attraper (s'~)** overreach brush

**atteinte** self-injury

**atteinte à la couronne** injury to the coronet (overreach / self ~)

**attelage** harnessing

**attelage** harnessed team

**attelage à deux chevaux (de front)** horse team, two abreast

**attelage à un cheval** one-horse draught

**attelage de six** six horse hitch

**atteler** hitch

**attelle** hame

**attirail** equipment

**au-dessus de la main** above the bit

**auge** intermandibular region / space
    feed tub

**autre droit (l'~)** back stretch ; backstretch

**avaloire** breeching

**avant-bras** forearm

**avant-main** forehand

**avant-train** forehand

**avoine** oats

**avulsion** avulsion

**axis** axis

**babésiose** babesiasis ; babesiosis

**bacul** swingle-tree

**bai** bay

**bai acajou** cherry bay

**bai-brun** brown

**bai cerise** cherry bay

**bai clair** light bay

**bai doré** golden bay

**bai fauve** fawn bay

**balle** chaff

**balle de foin** hay bale

**ballotade ; ballottade** ballotade

**balzane** white marking on a limb / leg

**balzane au-dessus du genou // jarret** white to above knee // hock

**balzane haut-chaussée** white to above knee // hock

**balzane mi-canon** white to half-cannon

**bandage ; bande** bandage

**banquette** bank

**banquette irlandaise** Irish bank

**barbe** barb

**barbe** chin groove

**bardeau** hinny

**bardot** hinny

**bardot (mâle)** hinny (horse ~)

**bardot femelle** hinny (female ~)

**bardote** hinny (female ~)

**barème (de notation)** scheme of marking

**barème des pénalités** penalty table

**barrage** jump off / jump-off

**barre** rail

**barre (de la bouche)** bar (of the mouth)

**barres de spa** triple bar(s)

**barres triples** triple bar(s)

**barrière** gate

**bas jointé** sloping pastern / foot

**base de la queue** dock

**bassin** pelvis

**bât** pack saddle

**bat-flanc** swinging rail

**bâter** put on the pack saddle

**battre à la main** bob the head

**battue** beat (hoof...)

**battue d'appel** take off (stride)

**baudet** donkey

**baudet** donkey stallion

**bave** foam

**bec de perroquet** brachygnathia ; brachygnathism

**bec de perroquet inversé** prognathism / prognathia (mandibular ~)

**bégayer** bob the head

**belge (trait lourd ~)** Belgian (draft / heavy draught horse)

**belle-face** white face

**benzimidazole** benzimidazole

**betterave** beet

**bicorne** bicorne

**bidet (obstacle sur ~)** liverpool

**bien descendus** well let down

**bien en selle (cavalier ~)** good seat (rider with a ~)

**bien encadré** on the aids

**bigorne** anvil (portable ~)

**bigorne (d'une enclume)** horn (of an anvil)

**billarder** paddle

**biotine** biotin

**bipède antérieur** forelegs

**bipède diagonal** diagonal pair

**bipède latéral** lateral pair

**bipède postérieur** hind-legs

**blanc** white

**blanc de naissance** white foaled

**blanc porcelaine** porcelain white

**blé** wheat

**blessure** injury

**bloc à lécher** salt lick

**boiter** limp

**boiterie** lameness

**boiterie intermittente** intermittent limping

**boiteux** lame

**boiteux de l'antérieur gauche // droit** lame, left // right fore

**bombe (de chasse)** cap (hunting / skull / jockey's ~)

**bon état** soundness

**bonne assiette** good seat

**bonne assiette (cavalier ayant une ~)** good seat (rider with a ~)

**bonnet** hood

**bonnet avec oeillères** blinker hood

**bore** boron

**bosal** bosal

**botte** boot (for horses)

**botte (à revers) de jockey** jockey boot

**botte à cataplasme** poultice boot

**botte d'écurie** paddock boot

**botte d'équitation** riding boot

**botte d'équitation (~ avec lacets / ~ de campagne)** riding boot (laced ~)

**botte de devant de genou** knee cap (boot)

**botte de polo** polo boot

**botte de transport** shipping boot

**botte pour le traitement des pieds** poultice boot

**bottes** boots

**bottier** bootmaker

**bottillon** Jodhpur boot

**bottine** paddock boot

**bottine Jodhpur** Jodhpur boot

**botulisme** botulism

**bouche** mouth

**bouche dure** hard mouth

**bouche faite** full mouth

**bouche fine / légère / chatouilleuse / tendre / sensible** soft mouth

**boucle** buckle

**boulet** fetlock

**bouleture** knuckling (over)

**boulonnais** Boulonnais (horse)

**bourrelet générateur de la corne** coronary band

**bourrelet principal** coronary band

**bourrelier** harness-maker

**bourse synoviale** synovial bursa

**bout du nez** muzzle

**boute-en-train** teaser (stallion)

**box** box (stall)

**brabançon** Belgian (draft / heavy draught horse)

**brabant** Belgian (draft / heavy draught horse)

**brachygnathie (mandibulaire)** brachygnathia ; brachygnathism

**braire** bray

**brancard** shaft

**branche (d'un fer)** branch (of a shoe)

**branche (d'un mors)** branch (of a bit)

**bras** arm (upper / true ~)

**brassicourt (genou / cheval ~)** over at / in the knees

**bréchet** brisket

**bréhaigne** barren

**bricole** breast collar

breast collar / plate

**bride** bridle

**bride à filet** snaffle (bridle)

**bride complète** double bridle

**bride double** double bridle

**brider (un cheval)** bridle (a horse)

**bridon** snaffle (bridle)

**brisé** jointed

**brochoir** hammer (shoeing / driving / nailing ~)

**bronche** bronchus

**bronchiole** bronchiole

**bronchite** bronchitis

**brosse (à panser)** brush

**brosse de lavage** water brush

**brouter** graze

**brucellose** brucellosis

**bull-finch** bull-finch / bullfinch

**bulle** blister

**bursite brucellique du garrot** fistulous withers

**bursite du tarse** capped hock

**busqué(e) (cheval / tête ~)** roman nose

**buter** stumble

**cabrade** rearing

**cabrer** rearing

**cabrer (se ~)** rear

**cabriole** capriole

**cache-oeil** blinker

**cache-ombrages** shadow roll ; shadow blind

**cache-vue** shadow roll ; shadow blind

**cacolet** mule chair

**caecum** cecum / caecum

**cagneux des membres** base narrow

**cagneux du pied** toed-in

**cagneux en marche (être ~)** paddle

**cagoule** hood

**cagoule avec oeillères** blinker hood

**caisse du tympan** tympanic cavity

calcanéum calcaneus

calcaneus ; calcanéus calcaneus

calcium calcium

calme quiet

cambré des genoux knee-wide

cambré des jarrets bandy-legged (in the hindlimb)

campé camped (out)

canal rachidien vertebral canal

canal vertébral vertebral canal

canaux semi-circulaires (de l'oreille) semicircular canals

canine canine (tooth)

canines canine teeth

canne hippométrique measuring stick

canon cannon

canon (antérieur) forecannon

cantharide blister beetle / fly

cap de maure / more black-faced dark head

capacité de transformation des aliments feed (conversion) efficiency

caparaçon trappings (horse's ~)

capelet capped hock

capillaire (vaisseau ~) capillary (vessel)

capriole capriole

capsule articulaire joint capsule

capuchon hood

caractère character

carcinome carcinoma

cardia cardia

carotte carrot

carpe knee

carpite carpitis

carrosse coach

cartilage cartilage

cartilage articulaire articular cartilage

cartilage complémentaire / latéral de la troisième phalange fibrocartilage of the third phalanx

cartilage costal costal cartilage

cartilage de prolongement scapula(r) cartilage

cartilage scapulaire scapula(r) cartilage

cartilage ungulaire fibrocartilage of the third phalanx

casaque jacket

casque de polo polo helmet

casque protecteur cap (hunting / skull / jockey's ~)

casser break (a horse)

castration castration

castrer geld

cataplasme poultice

cathéter catheter

cautère firing

cavalerie cavalry

cavaletti cavaletti

cavalier rider

cavalier d'obstacles show jumper (rider)

cavalier de concours complet event rider

cavalier de dressage dressage rider

cavalière lady rider

caveçon cavesson (lungeing / longeing / breaking ~)

cavité abdominale abdominal cavity

cavité buccale buccal cavity

cavité cotyloïde acetabulum

cavité thoracique thoracic cavity

cément (d'une dent) cement (of a tooth)

centre de gravité centre of gravity

cercle circle

cerveau brain

cervelet cerebellum

cession à la jambe leg-yielding

cestodes cestodes

chaff chaff

chaîne chain

chaînette curb chain

chaleur(s) heat

chaleurs discrètes silent heat

chambon chambons

chambrière lunge(ing) whip

champ de courses race track ; racetrack

chandelier stand (of an obstacle)

chanfrein bridge of the nose

chanfrein convexe roman nose

changement d'allure change of gait / pace

changement de direction change of direction

changement de galop de ferme à ferme simple change of lead / leg (through the trot)

changement de main change of rein

changement de pied change of lead / leg

changement de pied en l'air flying change of lead / leg

changement de pied simple simple change of lead / leg (through the trot)

changer (de main) dans le cercle change of hand in / through the circle

changer de main change rein

changer de pied change of leg

changer de pied en l'air change (of lead) in the air

charbon anthrax

charolais Charolais

chasse au cerf stag-hunting

chasse au renard fox-hunting

chasse au renardeau cubbing ; cub-hunting

chasse sur une piste artificielle / odorante
  drag-hunting

châtaigne chestnut

châtrer geld

chef d'équipe Chef d'équipe

chemise anti-mouches fly sheet (scrim ~)

chenil kennel

cheptel reproducteur breeding stock

cheval horse

cheval (de saut) d'obstacle(s) jumper

cheval à sang chaud warmblood ;
  warm-blooded horse

cheval à sang froid coldblood ; cold-blooded
  (horse)

cheval castré / châtré gelding

cheval d'amazone lady's mount

cheval d'arçons pommel horse

cheval d'attelage cart-horse

cheval d'attelage léger light draught horse

cheval d'extérieur cross-country horse

cheval de bât pack horse ; packhorse

cheval de bataille hobby-horse

cheval de boucherie slaughter horse

cheval de camionnage dray horse

cheval de cavalerie cavalry horse

cheval de chasse (à courre) hunter (field ~)

cheval de concours complet event horse

cheval de course(s) race horse ; racehorse

cheval de cross-country cross-country horse

cheval de dame lady's mount

cheval de dressage dressage horse

cheval de fond stayer

cheval de frise cheval de frise

cheval de guerre war horse

cheval de labour plough horse

cheval de Maremme Maremma / Maremmana
  horse

cheval de promenade hack

cheval de rechange / relais second horse

cheval de roulage dray horse

cheval de sang (chaud) warmblood ;
  warm-blooded horse

cheval de selle saddle horse

cheval de selle américain American
  Saddlebred

cheval de somme pack horse ; packhorse

cheval de tenue stayer

cheval de trait draught horse

cheval de trait léger light draught horse

cheval de troupe charger

cheval demi-sauvage semiwild horse

cheval difficile unruly horse

cheval du Don Don (horse)

cheval emballé bolting horse ; bolter

cheval ibérique Andalusian

cheval lourd heavy horse

cheval miniature miniature horse

cheval sauvage wild horse

cheval semi-sauvage semiwild horse

cheval vapeur horsepower

chevalerie chivalry

chevaucher mount (a horse)

cheville ankle

chien de meute hound

chlore chlorine

chorion dermis

chromosome chromosome

chronomètre à déclenchement automatique
  automatic timing device

chronomètre électronique automatic timing
  device

chronométreur timekeeper

chute fall

cicatrisation healing

cisailles nipper(s) (hoof ~)

clabaud lop-eared

claquage de tendon tendon bow

claquement de langue click (of the tongue)

cloche bell boot

cloche bell

clou (à ferrer) nail (horseshoe ~)

clou de rue nail prick / tread

clydesdale Clydesdale (horse)

cocher coachman

cochlée cochlea

coefficient de consanguinité coefficient of
  relationship

coeur heart

coin corner incisor
  corner

coin du sabot frog

coire dock

col utérin cervix of uterus

colique colic

collier collar

collier de poitrine breast collar / plate

côlon colon

**colonne vertébrale** vertebral column

**colostrum** colostrum

**combinaison (d'obstacles)** combination (of obstacles)

**commanditaire** sponsor

**commerçant de chevaux** horse dealer / trader

**commissaire (d'un concours)** steward

**commission d'appel** appeal committee

**commissure des lèvres** corner of the lips

**compact** short-coupled

**compétition de dressage** dressage competition

**comportement** behaviour

**comprimés / cubes de luzerne** alfalfa pellets / cubes

**concave** dished (face)

**concours complet** horse trial

**concours complet (de trois jours)** three-day event

**concours de dressage** dressage competition

**concours de sauts d'obstacles** jumping competition

**concours hippique** horse show

**concours hippique** horse show

**concours hippique** horse show

**conducteur** jockey

**conducteur (d'un attelage)** driver

**conduit auditif externe** external acoustic / auditory meatus

**conduit déférent** deferent duct

**conduite** behaviour

**confiance** confidence

**confirmé** well-schooled (horse)

**conformation** conformation

**conforme au type de la race** true to type

**congénital** congenital

**conjonctive** conjunctiva

**conjonctivite** conjunctivitis

**connaisseur** expert

**connemara** Connemara (pony)

**consanguinité** consanguinity

**contact** contact

**contre-changement de main** counter-change of hand

**contre-galop** canter counter-lead

**contre-sanglon** girth strap

**contrôle de l'impulsion** impulsion control

**contrôle du cheval** control of the horse

**contusion** bruise

**contusion de la sole** bruise (of the sole)

**conversion** turn (on the forehand // haunches)

**copeaux** shavings

**corde du jarret** common calcanean / calcaneal tendon

**cordonnier** shoemaker

**cornage** laryngeal hemiplegia / paralysis

**corne** horn

**corne (de la selle)** horn (of a saddle)

**corne utérine / de l'utérus** uterine horn

**cornée** cornea

**corps clignotant** nictitating membrane

**corps jaune** yellow body

**corrida** bullfight

**côte** rib

**côte (os d'une ~)** rib (bone)

**côté de la battue** take-off side (of an obstacle)

**côté de la réception** landing side (of an obstacle)

**côtes** ribs

**côtes asternales** asternal ribs

**côtes sternales** sternal ribs

**côtes vraies** sternal ribs

**cou** neck

**cou de taureau** bull neck

**couche basale de l'épiderme** stratum germinativum (epidermidis Malpighii)

**couche génératrice du corps muqueux de Malpighi** stratum germinativum (epidermidis Malpighii)

**couche germinative** stratum germinativum (epidermidis Malpighii)

**coude** elbow

**coude au corps** turned-in elbow

**coudé des jarrets** sickle-hocked

**coude écarté** turned-out elbow

**coude serré** turned-in elbow

**coup de cravache** stroke of the whip

**coup de fouet** whiplash

**coup de hache** dip in front of the withers

**couper (se ~)** overreach

**couper (se ~) ; entrecouper (s'~)** brush

**couronne** coronet

**courroie de reculement** breeching strap

**course à obstacles ; course d'obstacles** race over jumps

**course au clocher** steeplechase

**course au trot** trot race

**course de haies** hurdle(s) race

**course de plat** flat race

**course sur le plat** flat race

**courses (les ~)** races (the ~)

**court jointé** short pastern

**courtaud** docked tail(ed) ; docked

**courtaudé** docked tail(ed) ; docked

Français => English

courtauder dock

courte queue docked tail(ed) ; docked

coussin plantaire digital cushion

coussinet d'étrier stirrup pad / tread

coussinet digital / plantaire digital cushion

couteau anglais hoof knife

couteau de chaleur sweat scraper

couteau de maréchal-ferrant hoof knife

couverture blanket (horse ~)

couverture à mailles fly sheet (scrim ~)

couverture de refroidissement cooler (horse ~)

couvre-sangle girth cover

couvrir cover (a mare)

cow-boy cowboy

crampon calk ; caulk ; calkin ; caulkin

crampon à vis / vissé calk (screw-in ~)

crâne skull

crapaud canker

cravache crop

cravache de dressage dressage whip

cravacher whip

créole Criollo

crête (de l'encolure) crest

creux du flanc hollow of the flank

crevasses scratches

crin (un ~) horsehair (a ~)

crinière mane

crinière tressée plaited mane

crins de la queue tail hairs

criollo Criollo

cristallin lens

crochet canine (tooth)

crochets canine teeth
          hooks

croisement cross-breeding ; crossbreeding

croisement entre lignées line crossing

crottin droppings

crottins droppings

croupe croup

croupe abattue goose rump

croupe au mur renvers

croupe avalée goose rump

croupe en dedans travers

croupe en dehors renvers

croupe en pupitre goose rump

croupe horizontale flat croup

croupe inclinée sloping croup

croupe plate flat croup

cruauté cruelty

cryptorchide cryptorchid

cryptorchidie cryptorchidism ; cryptorchism

cryptorchisme cryptorchidism ; cryptorchism

cubitus ulna

cuillère ; cuiller cup

cuisse thigh

cuivre copper

culeron crupper dock

culottes breeches

culottes de chasse beige breeches

culottes Jodhpurs Jodhpurs ; jodhpurs ; Jodhpur breeches

culottier breeches-maker

cure-pieds hoof pick

curer un pied / sabot pick out a foot

cysticercose cysticercosis

débâter put off the pack saddle

débourrer (un cheval) break (a horse)

débrider unbridle

défaut defect

défauts des membres limb faults

défense resistance

déferrer (un pied) unshoe

défilé parade

dégagement de langue port

déglutition d'air aerophagia

degré de dressage schooling level

déharnacher unharness

délégué technique technical delegate

démangeaison itching

demi-arrêt half-halt

demi-frère half-brother

demi-parade half-halt

demi-pirouette half-pirouette

demi-sang half-bred

demi-soeur half-sister

demi-volte half-volt ; half volte

démonter dismount

dent tooth

dent de loup wolf tooth

dentine dentine

dentition dentition

dentition complète full mouth

dentition d'adulte permanent (set of) teeth

dentition de lait milk (set of) teeth

dents d'adulte permanent teeth

dents de lait milk teeth

dents de remplacement permanent teeth

départ start

dépôt d'étalons stud farm

dermatite dermatitis

dermatose dermatosis

derme dermis

dérobade run-out

dérober (se ~) run out

désarçonner (le cavalier) throw the rider

descendance (la ~) descendants (the ~)

descendant femelle female descendant

descendante female descendant

descendants (les ~) descendants (the ~)

descendre de cheval dismount

déshydratation dehydration

désobéissance disobedience

dessangler ungird

desseller unsaddle

dessinateur de parcours course designer

détente take off impulsion

deux pistes (sur ~) two tracks (on ~)

deuxième / seconde phalange middle
phalanx

deuxième articulation interphalangienne
coffin joint

deuxième père grandsire

devancer le mouvement (du cheval) sit too
far forward

diaphragme diaphragm

diarrhée diarrhoea

disqualification disqualification

distance distance

docile docile

docilité docility

dompter break (a horse)

don Don (horse)

donner à boire water

donner le départ give the signal to start

dopage doping

dos back

dos concave saddle-back

dos convexe arch-back

dos creux saddle-back

dos de carpe arch-back

dos de mulet arch-back

dos du nez bridge of the nose

dos ensellé saddle-back

dos mou weak back

dos négligé saddle-back

double (obstacle / combinaison ~) double
(obstacle)

double à une foulée (obstacle ~) in-and-out
(obstacle / combination)

double brisure (embouchure à ~) double
jointed mouthpiece

dourine dourine

douve (grande ~ du foie) fluke (common liver ~)

drêche (de brasserie) brewer's draff / grains

dressage training

dressage (classique) dressage (classical ~)

dressé (cheval bien ~) well-schooled (horse)

dresser un cheval school a horse

drogue drug

droit (obstacle ~) vertical

droit d'inscription entry fee

duodénum duodenum

eau water

eau noire azoturia

ébonite vulcanite

échantillon sample

échauffement de la fourchette thrush

échographie ultrasound scanning

éclaircir la crinière thin the mane

école d'équitation riding school

écoulement discharge

écourter ; écouer dock

écume foam

écumoir ; écumoire sweat scraper

écureur (automatique) barn cleaner (automatic ~)

écurie barn

écuyer riding master

écuyer de cirque circus rider

eczéma eczema

effet de rênes effect of reins

efficience alimentaire feed (conversion)
efficiency

effrayé frightened

effrayer (s'~) shy

élan take off impulsion

électrolytes electrolytes

élevage breeding

élevage chevalin / de chevaux
horse-breeding

élevage de juments mare keeping

élevage en lignée line breeding ; linebreeding

éleveur breeder (up)

éleveur (-naisseur) breeder

élimination elimination

éliminer cull

émail (d'une dent) enamel (of a tooth)

emballer (s'~) bolt

embauchoir ; embouchoir tree (boot ~)

embouchure mouth(piece)

embrocation embrocation

éminence pyramidale extensor process

**emphysème (pulmonaire)** emphysema (pulmonary ~)

**emplacement de la battue d'appel** take off point

**emplacement de la selle** saddle site

**empreinte** scent

**en arrière de la main** behind the bit

**en dedans de la main** behind the bit

**en main (cheval ~)** on the bit (horse ~)

**en tête** star

**encadrer (le cheval entre les aides)** keep the horse on the aids

**encan** auction (sale)

**encapuchonné** over-bent

**encenser** bob the head

**encéphale** brain

**encéphalomyélite (équine)** encephalomyelitis (equine viral ~)

**enchère** bid

**enchérir** make a higher bid

**enclume** anvil

**enclume (de l'oreille)** anvil (of the ear)

**encolure** neck

**encolure de cerf** ewe neck

**encolure de cygne** arched neck

**encolure épaisse** bull neck

**encolure renversée** ewe neck

**endocarde** endocardium

**endoparasite** internal parasite

**enflure** swelling

**engagement** entry

**engagement (de l'arrière-main)** engagement (of the hindquarters)

**engager (l'arrière-main)** engage (the haunches)

**enlever (s'~ au trot)** post (to the trot)

**enlever le licou** take off the halter

**enrênement(s)** reins

**entier (cheval mâle ~)** stallion

**entraînement** training

**entraîner (un cheval)** train (a horse)

**entraîneur** trainer

**entraves d'accouplement** breeding hopples / hobbles

**entre-deux** stall (standing ~)

**entre mains et jambes** on the aids

**éparvin** spavin

**éparvin (calleux)** bone spavin

**éparvin aveugle** occult spavin

**éparvin mou** bog spavin

**éparviner** stringhalt

**épaule** shoulder

**épaule droite** upright shoulder

**épaule-en-dedans** shoulder-in

**épaule inclinée / oblique** sloping shoulder

**éperon** spur

**éperonner** spur

**épi** whorl

**épiderme** epidermis

**épiglotte** epiglottis

**épine acromienne** spine of the scapula

**épine dorsale** spine

**épine scapulaire** spine of the scapula

**épistaxis** epistaxis

**épithélioma malin** carcinoma

**épithélium** epithelium

**épizootie** epizooty

**éponge** sponge

**éponge** capped elbow

**épreuve** trial

**épreuve (de saut) d'obstacles** jumping phase / test

**épreuve au chronomètre** scurry jumping (with time factor)

**épreuve avec barrage** competition with jump-off

**épreuve contre la montre** scurry jumping (with time factor)

**épreuve de dressage** dressage test

**épreuve de dressage élémentaire** basic dressage test

**épreuve de fond** endurance test / phase (speed and ~)

**épreuve de précision** competition with jump-off

**épreuve de puissance** puissance jumping

**épreuve sur / de la descendance** progeny test(ing)

**équestre** equestrian

**équidés (les ~)** equines (the ~)

**équipement** equipment

**équitation** horseback riding

**équitation à main droite // gauche** riding to the right // left

**équitation d'extérieur** cross country riding

**ergot** ergot

**erreur de parcours** error in the course

**estomac** stomach

**étalon** stallion

**étalon d'essai** teaser (stallion)

**étalon reproducteur** stud horse

**étrier** stirrup

**étrier (de l'oreille)** stirrup (of the ear)

**étrille** currycomb

**étrille en caoutchouc** rubber curry comb

**étrille en métal** metal curry comb

**étriller** curry

**étrivière** stirrup leather / strap

**euthanasier** destroy a horse

**examen radiographique** X-ray examination

**examen vétérinaire** veterinary examination

**exmoor** Exmoor

**exostose** exostosis

**expert** expert

**extérieur (du cheval)** external conformation

**face** face

**faiblesse** weakness

**faire paître** pasture

**famille maternelle** female line

**fanon** fetlock (tuft)

**fascia** fascia

**faucher** paddle

**fausse gourmette** lipstrap

**fausse martingale** false martingale

**fausses côtes** asternal ribs

**faute** fault

**fautif** offending

**faux-quartier (d'une selle)** sweat flap (of a saddle)

**favori** favourite / favorite

**fèces** droppings

**Fédération équestre internationale** International Equestrian Federation

**fell** Fell (pony)

**femelle** female

**fémur** femur

**fer** iron

**fer (à cheval)** horseshoe

**fer à marquer** branding iron

**fer à planche** bar shoe

**fer à traverse** bar shoe

**fer en aluminium** aluminium shoe / plate

**ferme d'élevage** stud farm

**fermoir** snap

**ferrage** horseshoeing

**ferrer** shoe

**ferrure** horseshoeing

**fesse** buttock

**fétuque des prés** meadow fescue

**fétuque élevée** tall fescue (grass)

**feu** firing

**feu liquide** blister ; blistering

**feutre** felt

**fibrocartilage (complémentaire) de la troisième phalange** fibrocartilage of the third phalanx

**fibula** fibula

**fièvre** fever

**figure de.huit** figure (of) eight

**figures de manège** school figures

**fil d'arrivée** finish(ing) line

**filet** snaffle bit

**filet (mince / de bride)** bridoon

**filet à foin** hay bag / net

**filet à olives** egg-butt / eggbutt snaffle

**filet releveur** gag bit

**fille** daughter

**fils** son

**fistule du garrot** fistulous withers

**fjord ; fjoring ; fjordhest** Fjord pony

**flanc** flank

**fléole (des prés)** timothy (grass)

**flexion de la nuque** bend at the poll

**foie** liver

**foin** hay

**follicule pileux** hair follicle

**fontes** weight cloth

**foramen magnum** foramen magnum

**forge** farriery

**forger** forge

**forgeron** blacksmith

**forme** ringbone ; ring bone ; ring-bone

**forme basse** low ringbone

**forme cartilagineuse** side bone ; sidebone

**forme coronaire** low ringbone

**forme du paturon** high ringbone

**forme haute** high ringbone

**formol** formalin

**fort en bouche** hard mouth

**fossé** ditch

**fossé barré** ditch with rail(s)

**fossé d'eau** water jump (open ~)

**fossé ouvert** open ditch

**fossé sec** dry ditch

**fosse supra-orbitaire** supraorbital fossa

**fouailler de la queue** switch the tail

**fouet** whip

**fouet (d'attelage)** driving whip

**fouet de chasse** hunting whip

**fourbure aiguë** laminitis (acute ~)

**fourbure chronique** founder

**fourchette** frog

**fourmilière** hollow wall

fourrage fodder
fourrage grossier roughage
fourrage vert green fodder
fourreau sheath
fourreau de queue tail wrap
fox trotteur Fox trotter (Missouri ~)
fracture d'un os bone fracture
franchir un obstacle clear an obstacle
frère propre full brother
frère utérin half-brother
froment wheat
front forehead
frontal browband
frontière browband
fuite flight
fumier manure
furioso Furioso ; Furioso-North Star (horse)
gag gag bit
gager bet
gageure bet
gagnant winner
gaine de sangle girth cover
gale (des équidés) mange (horse ~)
gale du corps sarcoptic mange
gale sarcoptique / sarcoptinique sarcoptic
  mange
galop gallop
galop (petit ~) canter
galop à droite canter (on the) right (lead)
galop à faux canter on / at the wrong lead
galop à faux canter counter-lead
galop à gauche canter (on the) left (lead)
galop allongé extended canter
galop allongé, demi-assiette extended
  canter, half-seat
galop de course racing gallop
galop de travail working canter
galop désuni disunited canter
galop juste canter / gallop at / on the true lead
galop moyen medium canter
galop rassemblé collected canter / gallop
galop sur le bon pied canter / gallop at / on
  the true lead
galop sur le pied droit canter (on the) right
  (lead)
galop sur le pied gauche canter (on the) left
  (lead)
galoper gallop
galoper (au petit galop) canter
ganache ventral border of mandible
ganglion ganglion

ganglion lymphatique lymph node
gant glove
garçon d'écurie stable boy / man
garde-boue mud guard
garde d'écurie stable fatigue
garrot withers
garrot coupé camel withers
garrot maigre / décharné bony withers
garrot saillant high withers
gastrite gastritis
gastrophile ; gastérophile bot fly (horse ~)
gaz carbonique carbon dioxide
gaze gauze
gène gene
généalogie genealogy
généreux (cheval ~) willing (horse)
génétique genetic
géniteur sire
genou knee
genou stifle
genou bien sculpté well-defined knee
genou creux calf-knee / calf knee
genou de mouton calf-knee / calf knee
genou effacé calf-knee / calf knee
genou renvoyé calf-knee / calf knee
genouillère knee cap (boot)
genoux de boeuf knock-knees
gestation gestation
gibier quarry
gidran Gidran
gland du pénis glans penis
glande lacrymale lacrimal gland
glande pituitaire hypophysis
glande salivaire salivary gland
glande surrénale adrenal gland
glande vésiculaire vesicular gland
glandes sébacées sebaceous glands
glandes sudoripares sweat glands
glome bulb (of a heel)
glycérine glycerin
goitre goitre
gorge throat
gorgette throatlash ; throatlatch
gourme strangles
gourmette curb chain
gouttière jugulaire jugular groove
graine de lin linseed
grains grains
grains aplatis rolled grains
graisse à sabots hoof grease

grand-père grandsire

Grand prix de dressage Grand Prix de Dressage

grand trochanter greater trochanter (of the femur)

grande balzane (mi-chaussée) white to half-cannon

grande volte circle

grands sésamoïdes (os ~) proximal sesamoid bones

grasset stifle

grille (d'un étrier) bottom of a stirrup

grincer des dents grind the teeth

grippe équine influenza (equine ~)

gris grey

gris (de) fer blue roan

gris-bleu blue roan

gris foncé dark grey

gris moucheté flea-bitten grey

gris pommelé dapple(d) grey / gray

gros intestin large intestine

guérison healing

guêtre boot (for horses)

guêtre de transport shipping boot

guêtre ouverte open-front boot

gueule de singe prognathism / prognathia (mandibular ~)

guide rein

guides reins

gymkhana gymkhana

habitude habit

hackamore hackamore

hackney Hackney (horse)

haie hedge

haie barrée brush and rails

hanche hip

hanches en dedans haunches-in

handicap handicap

hanovrien Hanover horse; Hanoverian (horse)

haras stud farm

haras national national stud

harde herd

harnachement tack ; tackle

harnacher harness (up)

harnacheur harness-maker

harnais tack ; tackle

harnais de recul breeching

harper stringhalt

haut-de-forme (chapeau ~) top-hat

haute école haute école

hauteur à la croupe height of rump

hématome haematoma

hématurie haematuria

hémoglobinurie azoturia

hémorragie haemorrhage

hémorragie pulmonaire provoquée par l'exercice epistaxis

hennir neigh

hennissement neigh

herbe grass

hérédité heredity

hippodrome race track ; racetrack

hippologie hippology

hippomobile horse-drawn

hipposandale barrier boot

holstein Holsteiner; Holstein (horse)

homme de cheval horse person

hongre gelding

hongrer geld

hors concours excluded from competition

huile de lin linseed oil

huile de ricin castor oil

huit (de chiffre) figure (of) eight

humérus humerus

hygroma du coude capped elbow

hygroma du genou carpal hygroma

hygroma du tarse capped hock

hypoderme subcutis

hypophyse hypophysis

ictère jaundice

ileum ; iléon ileum

immobilité immobility

immunité immunity

impulsion impulsion

inattentif inattentive

incisives incisors

incurvation flexion

incus anvil (of the ear)

indépendance des aides independence of the aids

indice indicator

infectieux infectious

infection infection

inflammation inflammation

inflexion flexion

influenza influenza (equine ~)

innocuité safety margin

inscription entry

insecte nuisible pest (insect)

insecticide insecticide

insémination artificielle artificial insemination

**inséminer** inseminate
**insertion pour le genou** knee roll
**instinct** instinct
**instinct grégaire** herding instinct
**instructeur d'équitation** riding instructor
**intestin** intestine
**intestin grêle** small intestine
**iode** iodine
**iris** iris
**irlandais** Irish hunter
**irritation** chafing
**isabelle** buckskin
**ischion** ischium
**ischium** ischium
**ivoire (d'une dent)** dentine
**jalonnement du parcours** marking of the course
**jambe** gaskin
    limb
**jambe active** active leg
**jambe avant** forelimb ; foreleg
**jambe intérieure** inside leg
**jambe passive** inactive leg
**jambe postérieure / de derrière** hind leg / limb
**jambières** chaps
**jaquima** hackamore
**jarde** curb
**jarret** hock
**jarret bien sculpté** well-defined hock
**jarret(s) à courbe** sickle hock(s)
**jarret(s) coudé(s)** sickle hock(s)
**jaunisse** jaundice
**javart cartilagineux** quittor (of horses)
**jejunum ; jéjunum** jejunum
**Jeux olympiques** Olympic Games
**jockey** jockey
**joue** cheek
**juge** judge
**juge au / de départ** starting judge
**juge aux obstacles** obstacle judge
**juge auxiliaire** assistant judge
**jugement** judging
**jugement de (la) conformation** judgment of (external) conformation
**jugement de la production** production assessment
**jument** mare
**jument de base ; jument-base** tap root / taproot mare
**jument gestante** mare in foal

**jument originaire** tap root / taproot mare
**jument pleine** mare in foal
**jument poulinière** broodmare ; brood mare
**jument-souche** tap root / taproot mare
**jument suitée** lactating mare
**jument vide** empty mare
**jumenterie** broodmare station
**kératine** keratin
**kur** kur
**kyste** cyst
**kyste ovarien** ovarian cyst
**lâcher son mors** get the tongue over the bit
**ladrerie** cysticercosis
**laisse (en fibre tressée)** lead rope
**laminite** laminitis (acute ~)
**landau** landau
**langue** tongue
**large de poitrine** wide at the chest
**largeur aux hanches** width of hips
**largeur de la poitrine** width of chest
**largeur du front** breadth of the forehead
**larve** larva
**laryngite** laryngitis
**larynx** larynx
**lasso** lasso
**lavallière** stock tie
**légèrement en tête** small star
**légèreté** lightness
**lente** louse egg
**lentille** lens
**léopard** leopard
**lettre** marker letter
**levade** levade
**lèvre inférieure** lower lip
**lèvre supérieure** upper lip
**lèvres (de la bouche)** lips (of the mouth)
**levretté (ventre / cheval ~)** herring gut
**liberté de langue** port
**licol ; licou** halter
**ligament** ligament
**ligament cervical** nuchal ligament
**ligament de la nuque** nuchal ligament
**ligament nuchal** nuchal ligament
**ligament suspenseur du boulet** suspensory ligament
**ligne blanche (du sabot)** white line (of the hoof)
**ligne d'arrivée** finish(ing) line
**ligne d'en face** back stretch ; backstretch
**ligne de départ** starting line

**lignée** lineage
**lignée femelle** female line
**lignée mâle** male line
**limaçon (de l'oreille)** cochlea
**lime (de finition)** file (finishing ~)
**limon** shaft
**liniment** liniment
**lipizzan** Lipizzaner
**liste** stripe
**liste (fine / petite)** stripe (narrow ~)
**liste large** broad stripe
**litière** litter
**liverpool (obstacle comprenant un ~)** liverpool
**livre de(s) haras** stud-book ; stud book
**livre généalogique** stud-book ; stud book
**livre généalogique** stud-book (general ~)
**long jointé** long pastern
**longe** longeing line
**longer** lunge / longe
**longue randonnée** long-distance ride
**longue rêne** long rein
**longueur (de cheval)** length
**longueur de la tête** length of the head
**longueur du corps** body length
**lusitano** Lusitanian horse
**luzerne** alfalfa
**luzerne en comprimés / cubes** alfalfa pellets / cubes
**lymphangite** lymphangitis
**lymphe** lymph
**mâcher le mors** champ (the bit)
**mâchoire** jaw
**mâchoire inférieure** mandible
**mâchoire supérieure** upper jaw
**mailloche** hammer (shoeing / driving / nailing ~)
**main** hand
**main (à ~ droite // gauche)** lead (on / at the right // left ~)
**mains (action des ~)** hands (action of the ~)
**maïs** corn
**maître d'équipage** master of the hunt
**maître de l'arrière-main (être ~)** control the hindquarters
**mal coiffé** lop-eared
**mal d'été** summer sores
**mal de cerf** tetanus
**mal du coït** dourine
**maladie** disease
**maladie de Borna** Borna disease
**maladie du lundi** azoturia

**maladie du sommeil** encephalomyelitis (equine viral ~)
**maladie obstructive respiratoire chronique** asthma
**maladie(s) des chevaux** disease(s) (horse / equine ~)
**malleus** hammer (of the ear)
**mamelles (les ~)** udder (the ~)
**manche** round
**mandibule** mandible
**manège couvert** indoor arena
**manège intérieur** indoor arena
**mangeoire** feed tub
**maniabilité du cheval** handiness of the horse
**maquignon** horse dealer / trader
**marcher (au pas)** walk
**marcher le parcours** walk (over) the course
**maréchal-ferrant** horseshoer
**maremme** Maremma / Maremmana horse
**marquage à froid** freeze branding
**marquage au fer (rouge / chaud)** branding (hot ~)
**marque** marking
**marque (au fer rouge / au feu)** branding (hot ~ mark)
**marteau (de l'oreille)** hammer (of the ear)
**marteau à frapper devant** sledge hammer
**marteau de maréchal-ferrant** hammer (shoeing / driving / nailing ~)
**martingale** martingale
**martingale à anneaux** running martingale
**martingale fixe / droite** standing martingale
**matelassure** panel (saddle ~)
**mauvaise assiette** incorrect seat
**maxillaire** upper jaw
**méat acoustique externe** external acoustic / auditory meatus
**méconium** meconium
**médecine vétérinaire** veterinary medicine
**médicament** medicine
**mélasse** molasses
**melon (chapeau ~)** bowler (hat)
**membrane nictitante** nictitating membrane
**membre** limb
**membre antérieur / de devant** forelimb ; foreleg
**membre pelvien** hind leg / limb
**membre postérieur** hind leg / limb
**membre thoracique** forelimb ; foreleg
**membres (les ~)** limbs (the ~)
**membres antérieurs** forelegs
**membres postérieurs** hind-legs

**meneur** driver

**méningoencéphalite infectieuse du cheval** Borna disease

**méningoencéphalomyélite enzootique** Borna disease

**ménoire** shaft

**menton (houppe du ~)** chin (swelling)

**mère** dam

**mésentère** mesentery ; mesenterium

**mesure de hauteur** height measurement

**métacarpe** metacarpus

**métacarpe (troisième os du ~)** metacarpal bone (large / third ~)

**métatarse** metatarsus

**métatarse (troisième os du ~)** metatarsal bone (large / third ~)

**métatarses (les ~)** metatarsal bones

**métatarsiens (les os ~)** metatarsal bones

**métis** crossbred (animal)

**mètre** metre / meter

**métrite équine contagieuse** contagious equine metritis

**mettre bas** foal

**mettre en selle (se ~)** get in the saddle

**mettre pied à terre** dismount

**meute (la ~)** hounds (the ~)

**mil** timothy (grass)

**milieu (du cheval)** barrel (of the horse)

**mille** mile

**mirador des juges** judges' box

**mise** bid
bet

**mise bas** foaling

**mise en main** bringing in hand

**miser** bet

**moelle épinière** spinal cord

**moelle osseuse** bone marrow

**moisissure** mildew

**molaires** molars ; molar teeth

**mollette ; molette** wind puff / windpuff

**mollette articulaire** wind gall / puff (articular ~)

**mollette tendineuse** wind gall / puff (tendinous ~)

**montant** shaft

**montant (de bride // muserolle)** cheekpiece

**monte** service

**monte en avant** forward seat

**monte en main** hand service

**monte naturelle** natural service

**monter** cover (a mare)

**monter (à / un cheval)** mount (a horse)

**monter (en selle)** get in the saddle

**monter à califourchon** ride astride

**monter à cru / à poil** ride bareback

**monter au pas** ride at the walk

**monter en amazone** ride side-saddle

**monter sur ses grands chevaux** get on one's high horse

**montoir** mounting step

**mordre** bite

**morgan** Morgan

**morphologie** conformation

**mors** bit

**mors à levier** curb bit

**mors à molette** roller bit

**mors de bride** curb bit

**mors de filet** snaffle bit

**mors espagnol** kimblewick bit

**mors kimblewick** kimblewick bit

**mors pelham** pelham bit

**mortaise** hardy / hardie hole

**morve** glanders (equine ~)

**mouche charbonneuse** stable fly

**mouche commune / domestique** house fly ; housefly

**mouche d'Espagne / de Milan** blister beetle / fly

**mouche de l'étable** stable fly

**mouche du cerf / daim** deer fly

**mouche du chevreuil** deer fly

**mouche noire** black fly

**mouche piqueuse des étables** stable fly

**mouches des chevaux** horseflies

**mousqueton** snap

**mouvement** movement

**mue** shedding

**mule** mule (female ~)

**mulet** mullet

**muletier** muleteer

**muqueuse** mucosa

**mur** wall

**mur de pierres** stone wall

**muraille** wall (of the hoof)

**muscle (à contraction) volontaire** striated muscle

**muscle à contraction involontaire** smooth muscle

**muscle anconé** anconeus muscle

**m. biceps brachial** biceps brachii m.

**m. biceps fémoral** biceps femoris m.

**m. brachial** brachialis m.

**m. cardiaque** cardiac m.

**muscle cutané du tronc** cutaneus trunci muscle

**m. deltoïde** deltoid(eus) m.

**m. extenseur** extensor m.

**m. extenseur antérieur des phalanges** common digital extensor m.

**m. extenseur commun des doigts** common digital extensor m.

**m. extenseur dorsal du doigt** common digital extensor m.

**m. extenseur latéral des phalanges** lateral digital extensor m.

**m. extenseur latéral du doigt** lateral digital extensor m.

**m. fessier superficiel** superficial gluteal m.

**m. fléchisseur** flexor m.

**m. fléchisseur externe / péronéal des phalanges** deep digital flexor m.

**m. fléchisseur interne / tibial / oblique des phalanges** medial head of the deep digital flexor m.

**m. fléchisseur médial du doigt** medial head of the deep digital flexor m.

**m. fléchisseur profond du doigt / des phalanges** deep digital flexor m.

**m. glutéobiceps** biceps femoris m.

**m. grand dorsal** latissimus dorsi m.

**m. grand fessier** superficial gluteal m.

**m. interosseux (III)** suspensory ligament

**muscle lisse** smooth muscle

**muscle long vaste** biceps femoris muscle

**muscle longissimus dorsi** longissimus (dorsi) muscle

**muscle masséter** masseter muscle

**muscle perforant** deep digital flexor muscle

**muscle releveur de la lèvre supérieure** levator muscle of upper lip

**muscle sterno-céphalique** sternocephalicus muscle

**muscle strié** striated muscle

**muscle viscéral** smooth muscle

**museau** muzzle

**muselière** muzzle

**muserolle** noseband

**muserolle croisée** cross-over noseband

**muserolle éclair / combinée** flash noseband

**muserolle en forme de 8** cross-over noseband

**mustang** mustang ; Mustang

**myase / myiase cutanée** cutaneous blowfly myiasis

**myocarde** cardiac muscle

**myoglobinurie** azoturia

**myorelaxant** muscle-relaxant drug

**naissance de la queue** tail head

**narine** nostril

**naseau** nostril

**navet** turnip

**naviculaire (maladie ~)** navicular disease / lameness / bursitis

**nématode** nematode

**néphrite** nephritis

**nerf** nerve

**nerf optique** optic nerve

**nerveux** nervous

**nettoyeur (d'étable, automatique)** barn cleaner (automatic ~)

**neurectomie** neurectomy

**névrectomie** neurectomy

**new-forest** New-Forest (pony)

**nez (dos du ~)** bridge of the nose

**niveau d'entraînement** degree of training

**noeud lymphatique** lymph node

**noir** black

**noir pie** piebald

**nombril** navel

**nourrir** feed

**nuque** poll

**obéissance** obedience

**obstacle** obstacle

**obstacle fixe** solid fence

**obstacle large** spread fence / jump

**obstacle naturel** natural obstacle

**obstacle simple** simple obstacle

**oedème** oedema

**oeil** eye

**oeil (globe de l'~)** eyeball

**oeil carré** hardy / hardie hole

**oeil porte-outils** hardy / hardie hole

**oeil vairon** silver eye

**oeillère** blinker

**oesophage** oesophagus

**oestre** bot fly (horse ~)

**oestrus** heat

**oldenbourg ; oldenburg** Oldenburg (horse)

**olécrane / olécrâne** olecranon

**ombilic** navel

**omoplate** scapula

**ongulés (les ~)** ungulates (the ~)

**orbite (de l'oeil)** eye socket

**oreillard** lop-eared

**oreille** ear

**oreille (interne // moyenne // externe)** ear (internal // middle // external ~)

**orge** barley

**os** bone

**os accessoire du carpe** accessory carpal bone

**os costal** rib (bone)

**os de la couronne** middle phalanx

**os du canon** cannon bone

**os du canon (antérieur)** metacarpal bone (large / third ~)

**os du canon (postérieur)** metatarsal bone (large / third ~)

**os du carpe (les ~)** carpal bones

**os du genou (les ~)** carpal bones

**os du métatarse (les ~)** metatarsal bones

**os du paturon** proximal phalanx

**os du pied** distal phalanx

**os du tarse (les ~)** tarsal bones

**os ethmoïde** ethmoid bone

**os frontal** frontal bone

**os grands sésamoïdes** proximal sesamoid bones

**os hyoïde** hyoid apparatus / bone

**os ilium** ilium

**os incisif** incisive bone

**os intermaxillaire** incisive bone

**os interpariétal** interparietal bone

**os ischium** ischium

**os lacrymal** lacrimal bone

**os métacarpien principal** metacarpal bone (large / third ~)

**os métatarsien principal** metatarsal bone (large / third ~)

**os nasal** nasal bone

**os naviculaire** distal sesamoid bone

**os occipital** occipital bone

**os palatin** palatine bone

**os pariétal** parietal bone

**os petit sésamoïde** distal sesamoid bone

**os pisiforme** accessory carpal bone

**os ptérygoïde** pterygoid bone

**os pubis** pubis (bone)

**os sésamoïde distal** distal sesamoid bone

**os sphénoïde** sphenoid bone

**os sus-carpien** accessory carpal bone

**os temporal** temporal bone

**os zygomatique** zygomatic bone

**ossifier (s'~)** ossify

**ostéite** osteitis

**otite** otitis

**ouvert (du devant // du derrière)** base wide

**ovaire** ovary

**oviducte** uterine tube

**oxer** oxer

**oxer ascendant** ascending oxer

**oxer carré** square oxer

**oxer en ciseaux** Swedish oxer

**oxer suédois** Swedish oxer

**oxyure** pinworm (horse ~)

**pacage** pasture

**paddock** paddock

**paille** straw

**paille hachée** chopped straw

**paître** graze

**palais** palate

**palais mou** soft palate

**palanque(s)** plank(s)

**palefrenier** groom

**palefroi** palfrey

**palomino** palomino

**palonnier** swingle-tree

**panard du pied (cheval ~)** toed-out

**pancréas** pancreas

**pansage** grooming

**pansement** dressing

**panser** groom

**pantalon de cuir** chaps

**pantalons d'équitation** breeches

**parade** halt
parade

**parage (de la corne)** trimming (of the hoof)

**parasite** parasite

**parasite interne** internal parasite

**parasympathique** parasympathetic nervous system

**parcours** course

**parcours d'obstacles** course of obstacles

**parcours de cross** cross-country course

**parcours routier** roads and tracks

**parcours sans fautes** clear (round)

**parenchyme** parenchyma

**parer (un sabot)** pare (a hoof)

**pari** bet

**pari mutuel** pari-mutuel

**parier** bet

**parieur** bettor

**paroi (du sabot)** wall (of the hoof)

**parotide (glande ~)** parotid gland

**partie pétreuse (de l'os temporal)** petrous part (of temporal bone)

**partir** break into

**partir au galop** start at the canter

**partir au pas** start at a walk

**partir au trot** start at a trot

**parturition** foaling
**pas** step
    walk
**pas, les rênes longues** walk on a long rein
**pas allongé** extended walk
**pas de coq** stringhalt
**pas de côté** side step
**pas espagnol** Spanish walk
**pas libre** free walk
**pas moyen / ordinaire** medium walk
**pas rassemblé** collected walk
**paso fino** Paso Fino
**passage** passage
**passage de la gourmette** chin groove
**passage de langue** port
**passer la langue sur l'embouchure** get the
    tongue over the bit
**patte** limb
**pâturage** pasture
**pâturer** graze
**paturon** pastern
**paupières** eyelids
**peau** skin
**pedigree** pedigree
**Pégase** Pegasus
**peigne** comb
**pelage (le ~)** coat
**pelage à la naissance** birth coat
**pelage hivernal** winter coat
**pelage terne** dull coat
**pelham** pelham bit
**peloton** field
**pelvis** pelvis
**pénalité de temps** time penalty
**pénicilline** penicillin
**pénis** penis
**pepsine** popsin
**perce-trou** pritchel (hot work ~)
**perche** rail
**percheron** Percheron
**père** sire
**péricarde** pericardium
**périmètre thoracique** girth's circumference
**périnée** perineum
**périople** periople
**périoste** periosteum
**périostite** periostitis ; periosteitis
**péritoine** peritoneum
**péritonite** peritonitis
**péroné** fibula

**peser** weigh
**peser (après la course)** weigh in
**peste équine africaine** African horse sickness
**petit-fils** grandson
**petite-fille** granddaughter
**peu généreux (cheval ~)** unwilling (horse)
**peur** fear
**phalange** phalanx
**phalange distale** distal phalanx
**phalange intermédiaire** middle phalanx
**phalange proximale** proximal phalanx
**phalange unguéale** distal phalanx
**pharynx** pharynx
**phléole** timothy (grass)
**phosphore** phosphorus
**photophobie** photophobia
**piaffé ; piaffer** piaffé ; piaffer ; piaffe
**piaffer** paw the ground
**piano** step (obstacle)
**pica** pica
**pie** pinto ; pintado
**pie noir** piebald
**pied** foot
**pied bot** club foot
**pied cagneux** toed-in
**pied dérobé** brittle foot / hoof
**pied panard** toed-out
**pied rampin** club foot
**pierre à lécher** salt lick
**pif** cryptorchid
**pigment** pigment
**piliers** pillars
**pince** central incisor
**pince (d'un sabot)** toe (of a hoof)
**pince à sonder** hoof tester(s)
**pince arrache-clous / tire-clous** crease nail
    puller
**pince coupante / à parer** nipper(s) (hoof ~)
**pince exploratrice** hoof tester(s)
**pince(s) à river** clincher(s) / clencher(s) (nail ~)
**pinces** central incisors
**pinchard** blue roan
**pinçard (cheval / pied ~)** club foot
**pinçon** clip
**pinçon en pince** toe clip
**pinto** pinto ; pintado
**piqueur** huntsman
**piqueux** huntsman
**piqûre** quicking
**piroplasmose** babesiasis ; babesiosis

pirouette pirouette

pirouette au galop pirouette at a canter

pirouette renversée reversed pirouette

piste (dans un manège) track (in a riding arena)

piste de course race track ; racetrack

pivot sur les antérieurs turn on the forehand

pivot sur les postérieurs turn on the haunches / quarters / hocks

placer collect

placer (un cheval) d'aplomb make a horse stand correctly

plaie wound

plaie de selle saddle sore

plaies d'été summer sores

plaignant complainant

plainte complaint

plaisance pleasure

plan du parcours plan of the course

planer suspension

plantain plantain

plasma (sanguin) plasma (blood ~)

pleurésie pleuritis ; pleurisy

pleuropneumonie contagieuse du cheval equine contagious pleuropneumonia

plèvre pleura

plexus solaire solar plexus

pli du grasset / flanc flank fold

pli latéral flank fold

pneumonie pneumonia

poids de handicap handicap weight

poil (le ~) ; poils (les ~) coat

poil (un ~) hair (a ~)

poil d'été summer coat

poil d'hiver winter coat

poinçon emporte-pièce pritchel (hot work ~)

point de bonification bonus point

point de départ starting point

point de pénalité penalty point

point de repère marker letter

pointe (d'un clou) point (of a nail)

pointe de l'épaule point of shoulder

pointe de la hanche point of hip

pointe du jarret point of hock

pointes de feu pin firing (scars)

poitrail breast

poitrail de chèvre pigeon breast

poitrine chest

poitrine étroite narrow chest

polo polo

pomme apple

pommeau pommel

poney pony

poney de polo polo pony

poney de selle riding pony

poney welsh Welsh pony

porte-billets ticket rack

porte-étrivière (couteau ~) stirrup bar

porte-tickets ticket rack

porter le nez au vent star-gaze

position de course jockey seat

position de dressage dressage seat

position de saut forward seat

position du cavalier position of the rider

position en avant forward seat

posologie dosage

postérieur hind leg / limb

pou louse (biting ~)

pouce inch

poulain // pouliche (de moins d'un an) foal (colt // filly ~)

poulain // pouliche d'herbe weanling

poulain // pouliche d'un an yearling (colt // filly)

poulain // pouliche de lait milk foal

poulain // pouliche non-sevré(e) milk foal

poulain // pouliche sevré(e) weanling

poulain (mâle entier) colt

pouliche filly (foal)

poulinage foaling

pouliner foal

poulinière broodmare ; brood mare

pouls pulse

poumon lung

pourriture de la fourchette thrush

pousse broken wind

poussière dust

poussif broken winded

poux lice

prêle horsetail

prélèvement levy

première articulation interphalangienne pastern joint

première dentition milk (set of) teeth

première phalange proximal phalanx

prémolaires premolars ; premolar teeth

préposé au chronomètre timekeeper

prépuce sheath

près de terre well let down

présentation à volonté kur

présenter (un cheval) en main show (a horse) in hand

**président du jury** president of the jury

**prime à l'éleveur ; prime d'élevage** breeder's premium

**principe de balzane** white coronet

**prix** price

    prize

**prix (en argent)** prize (cash / money ~)

**Prix des nations** Nations' Cup

**Prix Saint Georges** Prix St. George

**processus épineux** spinous process

**processus extensorius** extensor process

**processus transverse** transverse process

**profondeur de la poitrine** depth of chest

**profondeur des flancs / de l'abdomen** depth of flank

**prognathisme / prognathie (mandibulaire)** prognathism / prognathia (mandibular ~)

**programme** programme

**promenade (équitation de ~)** pleasure

**propriétaire** owner

**propriété** ownership

**prostate** prostate

**protecteur** boot (for horses)

**protège-~** boot (for horses)

**protège-queue** tail wrap

**protéine** protein

**prurit** itching

**pulpe de betteraves** sugar beet pulp

**pulpe dentaire** pulp tooth

**pupille** pupil

**pur-sang ; pur sang** purebred ; pure bred

**pur-sang anglais** Thoroughbred

**pus** pus

**pylore** pylorus

**quadrille** quadrille

**qualification** qualification

**quartier (d'une selle)** flap (of a saddle)

**queue** tail

**queue-de-cheval** horse tail

**queue de rat** rat tail

**queue de renard** brush

**raccourcir les rênes** shorten the reins

**race** breed

**rachis** vertebral column

**rachitisme** rickets

**racine d'une dent** tooth root

**radius** radius

**rage** rabies

**raid** long-distance ride

**raie de mulet** dorsal stripe / list / band

**raifort** horseradish

**rainette** hoof knife

**randonnée** ride (trail ~)

**râpe** rasp

**râper** rasp

**raser (se ~)** brush

**rassemblé** collected

**rassembler (d'un cheval)** collection (of a horse)

**rassembler (un cheval)** collect (a horse)

**rate** spleen

**râtelier (à fourrage)** hay rack

**ration d'entretien** maintenance ration

**ration de base** maintenance ration

**ration de travail** working ration

**ration journalière** daily ration

**ration supplémentaire** supplementary ration

**réception** landing

**récessif** recessive

**recevoir (se ~)** land

**récompenser** reward

**rectangle de dressage** dressage ring / arena

**rectum** rectum

**reculement** breeching

**reculer** back

**reculer** rein-back ; reinback

**rédhibition** annulment

**refus** refusal

**refuser** refuse

**région intermandibulaire** intermandibular region / space

**région métacarpo-phalangienne // métatarso-phalangienne** fetlock

**région présternale** breast

**région sternale** brisket

**registre (général)** stud-book (general ~)

**régularité** regularity

**rein** kidney

**rein(s)** loin(s)

**rejeton** offspring

**remède** medicine

**remorque (à) deux places** two-horse trailer

**remorque (à chevaux)** trailer (horse ~)

**remorque (pour) deux chevaux** two-horse trailer

**rêne** rein

**rêne (de mors) de bride** curb-rein

**rêne allemande** draw rein

**rêne de filet** snaffle-rein

**rêne en guirlande** hanging rein

**rêne extérieure** outside rein

**rêne fixe** side rein

rêne flottante  hanging rein

rêne intérieure  inner rein

rênes  reins

rênes longues (les ~)  long rein (on / at a ~)

rénette ; reinette  hoof knife

renvers  renvers

renverser un obstacle  knock down an obstacle

reprise  dressage test

reproducteur (mâle)  stud horse

reproducteurs (sujets ~)  breeding stock

résistance  resistance

résistance  stamina

retarder sur le mouvement (du cheval)  behind the motion

rétif  stubborn

rétine  retina

retirer  withdraw

rhabdomyolyse d'effort / induite à l'exercice  azoturia

rhinopneumonie (virale du cheval)  rhinopneumonitis (equine viral ~)

rhume  rhinopneumonitis (equine viral ~)

rigide (filet / canon ~)  straight bar bit / snaffle

rivière  water jump (open ~)

riz  rice

robe  coat (colour)

robe brillante / lustrée  glossy coat

robe terne  dull coat

rocher  petrous part (of temporal bone)

rogne-pied  sole knife

rogneuses  nipper(s) (hoof ~)

rompre  break into

rompre au pas  start at a walk

ronde  round

rosette  rosette

rotule  patella

rouan  bay roan

ruade  kick

ruban  rosette

ruban à mesurer  measuring tape

ruer  kick

sabot  hoof

sacrum (os ~)  sacrum

saignée  blood-letting

saillie  service

saillie assistée  hand service

saillie naturelle  natural service

saillir (une jument)  cover (a mare)

sain  sound

saison de monte  service season

salière  supraorbital fossa

salive  saliva

salut  salute

sang  blood

sangle  girth
    girth

sangle de brancards  belly band

sangle sous-ventrière  belly band

sangler  girth

sarcoptide ; sarcoptoïdé  mange mite

sarrasin  buckwheat

saut  jump

saut d'extension  flying jump

saut d'obstacles  jumping

saut de pied ferme  standing jump

saut de puce  in-and-out (obstacle / combination)

saut de volée  flying jump

saut en hauteur  high jump

saut en largeur  spread jump

saut par équipes (compétition de ~)  team jumping (competition)

sauter  jump

sauter juste / net  clear (jump ~)

sauteur  jumper

scapula  scapula

scapulum  scapula

sclérotique  sclera

scrotum  scrotum

seau  pail

sébum  sebum

seigle  rye

seime  sandcrack / sand crack

sel  salt

sélection (pour l'élevage)  breeding selection

sélection en lignée  line breeding ; linebreeding

sélectionner (pour élimination)  cull

sélénium  selenium

selle  droppings
    saddle
    saddle (harness ~)

selle anglaise  English saddle

selle d'amazone  sidesaddle

selle d'obstacle  jumping saddle

selle de chasse  hunting saddle

selle de course  racing saddle

selle de dressage  dressage saddle

selle de polo  polo saddle

selle de saut  jumping saddle

selle français  French Saddle (horse)

**selle western** western saddle
**seller** saddle
**sellerie** saddlery; saddler's shop
**sellerie (de l'écurie)** saddle room
**sellette** saddle (harness ~)
**sellier** saddler
**semence** sperm
**semence congelée** frozen semen
**semi-remorque** gooseneck trailer
**seringue** syringe
**serpentine** serpentine
**serré (du devant // du derrière)** base narrow
**serré de poitrail / poitrine** narrow at the chest
**serré des genoux** knock-kneed
**sérum** serum
**sérum antitétanique** antitetanus serum
**sérum antivenimeux** antivenene ; antivenin
**servir** cover (a mare)
**servir l'animal** kill
**sésamoïdes (os grands ~)** proximal sesamoid bones
**sevrage** weaning
**sevrer** wean
**shagya arabe** Shagya (Arab) horse
**shetland** Shetland (pony) ; Shetlie
**siège (d'une selle)** seat (of a saddle)
**signalement** description
**sillon jugulaire** jugular groove
**sinus concho-frontal** frontal sinus
**sinus frontal** frontal sinus
**sinus maxillaire** maxillary sinus
**six barres (épreuve des ~)** six bars
**smegma (préputial)** smegma
**société d'élevage** breed society
**sodium** sodium
**soeur propre** full sister
**soeur utérine** half-sister
**soin(s) aux / des sabots** care of hooves
**sole** sole
**sommet du calcanéum** calcanean tuber
**son** bran
**sonde** catheter
**sorgho** sorghum
**sortir la langue** hang out the tongue
**souffle** broken wind
**souffleur (étalon ~)** teaser (stallion)
**soulier médical** poultice boot
**souplesse** suppleness
**souris** mouse-dun ; mouse-coloured
**sous-gorge** throatlash ; throatlatch

**sous-lui** standing under
**spa** triple bar(s)
**spéculum** speculum
**sperme** sperm
**sperme congelé** frozen semen
**sport équestre** equestrian sport
**sprinter** sprinter
**squelette** skeleton
**squelettique** skeletal
**stabulation** stabling
**stalle (d'écurie)** stall (standing ~)
**standardbred** Standardbred
**stapes** stirrup (of the ear)
**station de monte** service station
**stationata** post and rail (vertical fence)
**statisticien** chart maker
**steeple ; steeple-chase** steeplechase
**steeple (phase de ~)** steeplechase phase
**stérile** barren
**sternum** sternum
**stratum germinativum** stratum germinativum (epidermidis Malpighii)
**strongle respiratoire** lungworm ; lung worm
**suc gastrique** gastric juice
**sucre** sugar
**sudation** sweating
**sueur** sweat
**sujet à des hémorragies** bleeder
**sulfamide** sulfonamide
**sulky** sulky
**support (d'un obstacle)** stand (of an obstacle)
**sur les épaules** heavy on the forehand
**surenchérir** make a higher bid
**suros** splint
**surveillant d'écurie** stable fatigue
**suspension (temps de ~)** suspension (moment of ~)
**suture** suture
**sympathique** sympathetic nervous system
**synoviale vaginale** synovial sheath
**synovie** synovial fluid
**syphilis du cheval** dourine
**système de chronométrage électronique** automatic timing device
**système digestif** digestive system
**système lymphatique** lymphatic system
**système nerveux autonome / végétatif** autonomic nervous system
**système nerveux central** central nervous system

Français => English

**système nerveux cérébro-spinal** central nervous system

**système nerveux parasympathique** parasympathetic nervous system

**système nerveux sympathique** sympathetic nervous system

**systole** systole

**tabanidés** horseflies

**table** table

**table (d'une enclume)** face (of an anvil)

**table dentaire** dental table

**tablier (de maréchal-ferrant)** apron (shoeing / farrier's ~)

**taenia** tapeworm

**taille (au garrot)** eight (at withers)

**tailler (se ~)** overreach

**tailler (se ~) ; entretailler (s'~)** brush

**tailleur** tailor

**talon** heel

**talus** bank

     talus

**tantième** levy

**taons** horseflies

**tapis de selle** saddle pad

**tapis de selle** saddle blanket

**tare** defect

**tare héréditaire** inborn defect

**tarse** hock

**tatouage** tattooing

**technique d'équitation** riding technique

**teigne** ringworm

**tempe** temple

**tempérament** temperament

**température** temperature

**temps** time

**temps accordé** time allowed

**temps limite** time limit

**tenaille(s) serre-clou** clincher(s) / clencher(s) (nail ~)

**tenailles à arracher** puller (shoe ~)

**tenailles à corne** nipper(s) (hoof ~)

**tendinite** tendinitis

**tendon** tendon

**tendon (du) fléchisseur profond (des phalanges / du doigt)** deep (digital) flexor tendon

**tendon (du) perforant** deep (digital) flexor tendon

**tendon calcanéen commun** common calcanean / calcaneal tendon

**tendon claqué** bowed tendon

**tendon d'Achille** common calcanean / calcaneal tendon

**tendon de l'extenseur antérieur des phalanges / du doigt** common (digital) extensor tendon

**tendon de l'extenseur dorsal du doigt** common (digital) extensor tendon

**tendon extenseur des phalanges** common (digital) extensor tendon

**tendon fléchisseur** flexor tendon

**ténia** tapeworm

     taenia / tenia

**tenir ferme (se ~)** stand square

**tenue des rênes** manner of handling / holding reins

**térébenthine** turpentine

**test de consanguinité** inbreeding test

**test de flexion** flexion test

**test sanguin** blood test

**testicule** testicle ; testis

**tétanos** tetanus

**tête** head

**tête au mur** travers

**tête de maure** dark head

**têtière** headpiece

**têtu** stubborn

**thermocautère** firing iron

**thorax** thorax

**thoroughbred** Thoroughbred

**thrombose** thrombosis

**thymus** thymus

**thyroïde (glande ~)** thyroid (gland)

**tibia** tibia

**tic à l'air** wind-sucking

**tic à l'appui** crib biting

**tic aérophagique (à l'appui)** crib biting

**tic aérophagique (sans appui)** wind-sucking

**tic de l'ours** weaving

**timon** shaft

**tiques** ticks

**tirage au sort** draw

**tire-botte** bootjack

**tire-botte (crochet ~)** boot hook

**tiré par des chevaux** horse-drawn

**tirer (sur la main)** pull

**tisonnier** poker

**tocard** worthless horse

**toile sous-cutanée** subcutis

**toise à potence** measuring stick

**tondeuse** clipper

**tondre** clip

toquard worthless horse

toque cap (hunting / skull / jockey's ~)

torus carpien // tarsien chestnut

toscan Maremma / Maremmana horse

toucher (se ~) overreach
                 brush

toupet forelock

tour de sangle / poitrine girth's circumference

tour du canon cannon's circumference

tournant turn

tourner (sur les antérieurs // postérieurs) turn (on the forehand // haunches)

tourner court turn short / sharply

tourner de pied ferme turn (on the forehand // haunches)

tourner large turn wide

tourner sur les antérieurs turn on the forehand

tourner sur les postérieurs turn on the haunches / quarters / hocks

tournoi tournament

tousser cough

toux cough

trace scent

tracé du parcours line of the course

trachée trachea

trait trace

trait lourd (cheval de ~) heavy draught / draft horse

trakehnen ditch with rail(s)

trakehner Trakehner ; Trakehnen horse

tranche(t) (d'enclume) hardy

tranchet sole knife

tranquillisant tranquillizer

transition transition

transpiration sweat

travail à la main work in hand

travail entre (les) piliers work between the pillars

travail sur / aux longues rênes work in long reins

travail sur deux pistes work on two tracks

travers travers

trèfle clover

tresser plait

tricher cheat

tricherie cheating

trichophytose ringworm

tricoises à déferrer puller (shoe ~)

tricoises à parer nipper(s) (hoof ~)

tricorne tricorne

triple (obstacle ~) triple (combination)

trochlée du fémur femoral trochlea

trois pièces (embouchure à ~) double jointed mouthpiece

troisième paupière nictitating membrane

troisième phalange distal phalanx

trompe auditive auditory tube

trompe d'Eustache auditory tube

trompe de Fallope uterine tube

trompe utérine uterine tube

tronc trunk

tronçonner dock

trophée trophy

trot trot

trot à l'anglaise posting trot

trot allongé extended trot

trot allongé assis extended trot sitting

trot allongé enlevé extended trot rising

trot assis sitting trot

trot de travail working trot

trot en extension extended trot

trot enlevé posting trot

trot moyen medium trot

trot moyen assis medium trot sitting

trot rassemblé collected trot

trot rassemblé assis collected trot sitting

trotter trot

trotter enlevé trot rising

trotteur trotter

trotteur américain Standardbred

trotteur français French trotter

trottiner jig

trou occipital foramen magnum

troupeau d'élevage breeding herd

troupier charger

troussequin cantle

tube digestif digestive tract

tuber coxae coxal tuber

tuber sacrale sacral tuber

tubérosité du calcanéus calcanean tuber

tubérosité ischiatique ischial tuber

tuméfaction swelling

tympan tympanic membrane

type de (la) race breed type

ulcère ulcer

ulcère corrosif de l'os naviculaire navicular disease / lameness / bursitis

ulna ulna

unité animale animal unit

uretère ureter

urètre urethra

urine urine
urticaire urticaria
utérus uterus
uvéite (récidivante) equine recurrent uveitis
vaccin vaccine
vaccination vaccination
vacher cowboy
vagin vagina
vainqueur winner
vaisseau lymphatique lymphatic vessel
valet-de-chiens whipper-in
variole équine horse pox ; horsepox
veine vein
veine axillaire axillary vein
veine céphalique cephalic vein
veine céphalique accessoire accessory cephalic vein
veine faciale facial vein
veine fémorale femoral vein
veine porte portal vein
vendre à l'encan auction
vendre aux enchères auction
vente aux enchères auction (sale)
ventre belly
ventre avalé cow-belly
ventre de levrette herring gut
ventre de vache cow-belly
ventre retroussé herring gut
ventre tombant cow-belly
ver worm
ver plat segmenté tapeworm
ver rond nematode
verge penis
vermicide anthelmintic (drug)
vermifuge anthelmintic (drug)
vermifuger deworm
vert cryptorchid
vert green fodder
vertèbre vertebra
vertèbres caudales / coccygiennes caudal vertebrae
vertèbres cervicales cervical vertebrae
vertèbres lombaires lumbar vertebrae
vertèbres sacrées / sacrales sacral vertebrae
vertèbres thoraciques thoracic vertebrae
vertical (obstacle ~) vertical
vésicatoire blister ; blistering
vésicule blister
vésicule séminale vesicular gland
vessie bladder (urinary ~)

vessigon wind puff / windpuff
vessigon articulaire wind gall / puff (articular ~)
vessigon articulaire tarsien / du jarret bog spavin
vessigon tendineux wind gall / puff (tendinous ~)
vessigon tendineux de la gaine tarsienne thoroughpin
veste / veston d'équitation riding coat
vestibule du vagin vestibule of vagina
vétérinaire veterinarian
vétérinaire veterinary
vétérinaire de chevaux equine veterinarian
viande de cheval horse meat
vice vice
victoire win
vigueur stamina
virage turn
virus de la rage rabies rhabdovirus / virus
vitamine vitamin
vitesse speed
voile du palais soft palate
voix voice
volte volte ; volt
volte (à gauche // droite) volte (to the left // right)
volte au pas volte at the walk
voltige vaulting
volvulus volvulus
vomer vomer
vulve vulva
wurtemberg Württemberg horse
württemberg Württemberg horse
yearling yearling (colt // filly)
yeux eyes
zain whole colour(ed)
zèbre zebra
zéro-pâturage zero-grazing
zigzag counter-change of hand

126

# DEUTSCH

## Index

**Anglo-Normänner Warmblut** French Saddle (horse)

**anhalten** halt

**Anhänger** two-horse trailer

**Anhänger** trailer (horse ~)

**Anhangsbein des Karpus** accessory carpal bone

**Anlehnung** contact with the bit (horse moving into a ~)

**Annäherungswinkel** angle of the approach

**Anöstrus** anestrus ; anoestrus

**anreiten** break into

  break (a horse)

**anreiten im Schritt** start at a walk

**Anreitephase** take off (stride)

**Ansager** announcer (house / track ~)

**anspannen** hitch

**Anspannung des Wagenpferdes** harnessing

**ansteckend** infectious

**ansteckende Blutarmut der Pferde** equine infectious anaemia / anemia

**Ansteckung** infection

**Ansteckungsfestigkeit** immunity

**Anthrax** anthrax

**Antibiotikum** antibiotic

**antiphlogistisch** anti-inflammatory

**antraben** start at a trot

**Anus** anus

**Anzieher** adductor

**Anziehung** adduction

**Anzug** branch (of a bit)

**Apfel** apple

**Apfelschimmel** dapple(d) grey / gray

**Aponeurosis** aponeurose

**Appaloosa** Appaloosa

**Araber** Arab ; Arabian

**arabisches Vollblut** Arab ; Arabian

**Arbeit am langen Zügel** work in long reins

**Arbeit an der Hand** work in hand

**Arbeit auf zwei Hufschlägen** work on two tracks

**Arbeit in den Pilaren** work between the pillars

**Arbeitsgalopp** working canter

**Arbeitsration** working ration

**Arbeitstrab** working trot

**Ardenner** Ardennais ; Ardennes (horse)

**Armhöhle** axilla

**Arterie / Arteria** artery

**Ataxie** ataxia

**Atlantoaxialgelenk** atlanto-axial articulation

**Atlas** atlas

**Atlas-Axis-Gelenk** atlanto-axial articulation

**Atmungssystem** respiratory system

**Ätzmittel** firing

**Auflage** cup

**aufschirren** harness (up)

**Aufsetzkoppen** crib biting

**aufsitzen** get in the saddle

**Aufsteigblock** mounting step

**aufsteigende Oxer** ascending oxer

**aufzäumen** bridle (a horse)

**Aufziehtrense** gag bit

**Aufzüchter** breeder (up)

**Aufzug eines Hufeisens** clip

**Augapfel** eyeball

**Auge** eye

**Augen** eyes

**Augenbogen** superciliary arch

**Augenbrauenwölbung** superciliary arch

**Augengrube** supraorbital fossa

**Augenhöhle** eye socket

**Augenlider** eyelids

**Auktion** auction (sale)

**Ausbildungsgrad** degree of training

**Ausbindezügel** side rein

**Ausbrechen** run-out

**Ausdauer** stamina

**Ausfluß** discharge

**Ausgangspunkt** starting point

**ausgeprägtes Sprunggelenk** well-defined hock

**ausgeprägtes Vorderfußwurzelgelenk** well-defined knee

**Ausgleichsgewicht** handicap weight

**Auslosen** draw

**ausrangieren** cull

**Ausreißung** avulsion

**Ausrüstung** equipment

**Ausschlag(en)** kick

**ausschlagen** kick

**Ausschluß** elimination

**aussichtsreichstes Pferd** favourite / favorite

**Austreiber** pritchel (hot work ~)

**Austrocknung** dehydration

**Auswärtsbewegung** abduction

**Auswärtszieher** abductor

**Auswurf** discharge

**Auszubildender** apprentice

**Außengalopp** canter counter-lead

**außer Konkurrenz** excluded from competition

**äußerer / großer Kaumuskel** masseter muscle

**äußerer Gehörgang** external acoustic / auditory meatus

**äußerer Zügel** outside rein

**automatische Stallreiniger** barn cleaner (automatic ~)

**autonomes Nervensystem** autonomic nervous system

**Axthieb** dip in front of the withers

**Azetabulum** acetabulum

**Azoturie** azoturia

**Babesiose** babesiasis ; babesiosis

**Backe** cheek

**Backenriemen** cheekpiece

**Backenstück** cheekpiece

**Backenzähne (hintere ~)** molars ; molar teeth

**Bahn (die gehärtete ~)** face (of an anvil)

**Bahnpeitsche** lunge(ing) whip

**Bahnpunkt** marker letter

**Ballen** bulb (of a heel)

**Ballotade** ballotade

**Band** ligament

**Bandage** bandage

**Bandmaß** measuring tape

**Bandwurm** tapeworm

**Barrierenspringprüfung** six bars

**basten** put on the pack saddle

**Bastsattel** pack saddle

**Bauch** belly

**Bauch** abdomen

**Bauchfell** peritoneum

**Bauchfellentzündung** peritonitis

**Bauchgurt** girth

**Bauchhöhle** abdominal cavity

**Bauchraum** abdominal cavity

**Bauchspeicheldrüse** pancreas

**Bauchtiefe** depth of flank

**Baum** branch (of a bit)

**Becken** pelvis

**Beckengliedmaße** hind leg / limb

**Beckenpfanne** acetabulum

**Beckenwinkel** pelvis angle

**Begattung** breeding

**beigezäumt** collected

**Bein** limb

**beißen** bite

**Belgisches Kaltblut** Belgian (draft / heavy draught horse)

**belohnen** reward

**Benzimidazol** benzimidazole

**Berber** barb

**bereiten** mount (a horse)

**Berufungsgericht** appeal committee

**Berufungskommission** appeal committee

**Beruhigungsmittel** tranquillizer

**besamen** inseminate

**Beschäler** stallion

**Beschälseuche** dourine

**Beschälstation** service station

**beschlagen (Huf ~)** shoe

**Beschlaghammer** hammer (shoeing / driving / nailing ~)

**Beschlagschmied** horseshoer

**Beschneiden (des Hufes)** trimming (of the hoof)

**Besitz** ownership

**Besitzer(in)** owner

**Besitztum** ownership

**Besitzung** ownership

**Bete** beet

**Beugefläche eines Gelenks** articular cartilage

**Beugemuskel ; Beuger** flexor muscle

**Beugeprobe** flexion test

**Beugesehne** flexor tendon

**Beurteilungsverfahren** scheme of marking

**Bewegung** action

**Bewegung** movement

**Bewertung** judging

**Biertreber** brewer's draff / grains

**Binde** bandage

**Binde** bandage

**Bindehaut** conjunctiva

**Biotin** biotin

**Biotinum** biotin

**Bläschen** blister

**Bläschendrüse** vesicular gland

**Blase** blister

**Blässe** stripe

**bleibende Zähne** permanent teeth

**Bleigewichte** weight cloth

**Blendkappe** blinker

**Blesse** stripe

**Blinddarm** cecum / caecum

**Blinkers** blinker hood

**Blinzhaut** nictitating membrane

**Blümchen** small star

**Blut** blood

**Blutarmut** anaemia

**Blutentnahme** blood-letting

**Blutentziehung** blood-letting

**Bluterguß** haematoma

**Blutgemeinschaft** consanguinity

Blutlinie lineage
Blutplasma plasma (blood ~)
Blutprobe blood test
Blutstrom lineage
Blutuntersuchung blood examination
Blutverlust haemorrhage
Bockhuf club foot
bodeneng base narrow
Bodenrick cavaletti
bodenweit base wide
Bogen bowed tendon
Bogengänge semicircular canals
Bor boron
Bornasche Krankheit Borna disease
Bosal bosal
Botulismus botulism
Boulonnais Boulonnais (horse)
boulonnaiser Kaltblut Boulonnais (horse)
Box box (stall)
Brabanter Belgian (draft / heavy draught horse)
Brandeisen branding iron
Brandfuchs liver chestnut
Brandmarken branding (hot ~)
Brandzeichen branding (hot ~ mark)
Braun bay
braun bay
Braune bay
Brauner bay
Breeches breeches
breite Blesse broad stripe
Breiumschlag poultice
Bremsen horseflies
Brennapparat firing
Brenneisen branding iron
Brennmittel firing
Brennstift firing iron
Brieftasche (kleine ~) ticket rack
Bröckelhuf ; bröckeliger Huf brittle foot / hoof
Bronchiole bronchiole
Bronchiolus bronchiole
Bronchitis bronchitis
Bronchus bronchus
Brucellose brucellosis
Brunst heat
Brunstlosigkeit anestrus ; anoestrus
Brust chest
Brustbein sternum
Brustbein-Rippen-Gelenke sternocostal articulations
Brustblatt breast collar

Brustbreite width of chest
brusteng narrow at the chest
Brustfell pleura
Brustfellentzündung pleuritis ; pleurisy
Brusthöhle thoracic cavity
Brustkasten ; Brustkorb thorax
Brustkiefermuskel sternocephalicus muscle
Brustseuche der Pferde equine contagious pleuropneumonia
Brusttiefe depth of chest
Brustumfang girth's circumference
brustweit wide at the chest
Brustwirbel thoracic vertebrae
Buchweizen buckwheat
Bügeleinlage stirrup pad / tread
Bügeltritt bottom of a stirrup
Bugspitze point of shoulder
Bullfinch bull-finch / bullfinch
Buschhürde hedge
Caballo de Paso (Peruano) Peruvian paso / ambler
Calcaneus calcaneus
Camionnage-Pferd dray horse
Carpitis carpitis
Carree-Oxer square oxer
Cavaletti cavaletti
Cervix cervix of uterus
Chambon chambons
Chaps chaps
Charakter character
Charollais-Pferd Charolais
Chef d'Equipe Chef d'équipe
Chlor chlorine
Chromosom chromosome
chronische obstruktive Bronchiolitis asthma
Clydesdale Clydesdale (horse)
Connemarapony Connemara (pony)
Cowboy cowboy
Crioller Criollo
Criollo Criollo
Damenpferd lady's mount
Damensattel sidesaddle
Damm perineum
Dampf broken wind
dämpfig broken winded
Dämpfigkeit broken wind
Darm intestine
Darmbein ilium
Darmverschlingung volvulus
Dasselfliege bot fly (horse ~)

**Dauergebiß** permanent (set of) teeth
**Dauerritt** long-distance ride
**Dauerzähne** permanent teeth
**Deckakt** service
**Decke** blanket (horse ~)
**decken** cover (a mare)
**Decksaison** service season
**Deckstation** service station
**Deltamuskel** deltoid(eus) muscle
**derb** short-coupled
**Dermatitis** dermatitis
**Deutschtraben** sitting trot
**diagonale Beinpaar** diagonal pair
**diagonale Hilfe** diagonal aid
**Diaphragma** diaphragm
**Diarrhö(e)** diarrhoea
**Dickdarm** large intestine
**Disqualifikation** disqualification
**Distanz** distance
**Distanz-Ritt / Distanzritt** long-distance ride
**Donpferd / Don-Pferd** Don (horse)
**Doping** doping
**Dopingmittel** drug
**doppelgliedrige Trense** double jointed mouthpiece
**Dorn** billet (of a buckle)
**Dornfortsatz** spinous process
**Dosierung** dosage
**dreifache Kombination** triple (combination)
**Dreimaster** tricorne
**Dreispitz** tricorne
**Dressur** dressage (classical ~)
**Dressuraufgabe** dressage test
**Dressurgerte** dressage whip
**Dressurgrad** schooling level
**Dressurpeitsche** dressage whip
**Dressurpferd** dressage horse
**Dressurprüfung** dressage competition
**Dressurprüfung** dressage test
**Dressurreiter** dressage rider
**Dressursattel** dressage saddle
**Dressursitz** dressage seat
**Dressurviereck** dressage ring / arena
**drittes Augenlid** nictitating membrane
**drittes Zehengelenk** coffin joint
**Drosselrinne** jugular groove
**Druckwirkung des Beckens** action of the seat
**Druse** strangles
**Dunkelfuchs** dark chestnut
**Dunkelfuchs** liver chestnut

**Dünndarm** small intestine
**durch den Zirkel wechseln** change of hand in / through the circle
**durchbrennen** bolt
**Durchfall** diarrhoea
**Durchgang** round
**durchgehen** bolt
**Durchlässigkeit** handiness of the horse
**Durchtreiber** pritchel (hot work ~)
**Durchziehtrense** gag bit
**Ebonit** vulcanite
**Ecke** corner
**Eckzahn ; Eckschneidezahn** corner incisor
**Ecuyer** riding master
**Ehrenpreis** prize
**Eichel** glans penis
**Eierstock** ovary
**Eierstockzyste** ovarian cyst
**eifrig** on the bit (horse ~)
**Eigentum** ownership
**Eileiter** uterine tube
**Eimer** pail
**Einergespann** one-horse draught
**einfacher Galoppwechsel** simple change of lead / leg (through the trot)
**einfaches Hindernis** simple obstacle
**einfahren** break (a horse)
**einfahren** school a horse
**einfarbig** whole colour(ed)
**einflechten** plait
**Einführungssonde** catheter
**Einhauen** self-injury
**Einreibemittel** liniment
**Einreibung** embrocation
**einreiten** school a horse
**Einsatz** entry fee
**einseitige Hilfe** lateral aid
**Einspänner** one-horse draught
**einteiliges Mundstück** straight bar bit / snaffle
**Einwärtszieher** adductor
**Eisen** iron
**Eisen abnehmen** unshoe
**Eiter** pus
**Eiweißstoff** albumin
**Ekzem** eczema
**elektrische Zeitmeßanlage** automatic timing device
**Elektrolyte** electrolytes
**Ellbogen** elbow
**Ellbogengelenk** elbow joint
**Ellbogenhöcker** olecranon

Deutsch => English

Ellbogenhöckermuskel anconeus muscle

Elle ulna

Ellenbogen elbow

Ellenbogengelenk elbow joint

Embryonalhülle amnion

Endokard endocardium

Endoparasit internal parasite

Engagement entry

Engagement (der Hinterhand) engagement (of the hindquarters)

englische Reithalfter / Halfter mit Pulleriemen / Sperriemen flash noseband

englisches Vollblut Thoroughbred

Enkel grandson

Enkelin granddaughter

Entwicklungslehre genetic

entwöhnen wean

entwurmen deworm

Entzündung inflammation

Entzündung chafing

entzündungshemmend anti-inflammatory

Enzephalomyelitis der Pferde (seuchenhafte ~) encephalomyelitis (equine viral ~)

Epidermis epidermis

Epiglottis epiglottis

Epistaxis epistaxis

Epithel epithelium

Equiden equines (the ~)

Equipenchef Chef d'équipe

Erbfehler inborn defect

Erblichkeit heredity

Erbsbein accessory carpal bone

Erbsenbein accessory carpal bone

Erhaltungsration maintenance ration

Ersatzpferd second horse

Ersatzzähne permanent teeth

erschrecken shy

erschrocken frightened

erster Halswirbel atlas

Esel donkey

Esel schreien (wie ein ~) bray

Eselfüllen / Eselfohlen donkey foal

Eselhengst donkey stallion

Eselin jenny-ass ; jenny

Eselstute jenny-ass ; jenny

Eustachische Röhre auditory tube

Euter udder (the ~)

Exmoorpony Exmoor

Exterieur external conformation

Fahrer driver

Fahrer jockey

Fahrpeitsche driving whip

Fahrturnier horse show

Falbe buckskin

falsche Rippen asternal ribs

falscher Galopp canter on / at the wrong lead

falscher Sitz incorrect seat

Fangzähne canine teeth

Farbe coat (colour)

Farbstoff pigment

Fascie fascia

Favorit favourite / favorite

Fehler defect
        fault

fehlerloser Ritt clear (round)

Feiertagskrankheit azoturia

Feile file (finishing ~)

Feld field

Feldsteinmauer stone wall

Feldstiefel riding boot (laced ~)

Fellpony Fell (pony)

Felsenteil petrous part (of temporal bone)

Femur femur

Fersenbein calcaneus

Fersenhöcker calcanean tuber

Fersensehnenstrang common calcanean / calcaneal tendon

Fessel pastern
        ankle

Fesselbehang fetlock (tuft)

Fesselbein proximal phalanx

Fesselgelenk fetlock joint

Fesselgelenkgalle wind puff / windpuff

Fesselgelenkgegend fetlock

Fesselhaare fetlock (tuft)

Fesselkopf fetlock

festes Hindernis solid fence

Feuerhaken poker

Fieber fever

Filz felt

Fjordpony ; Fjordpferd Fjord pony

flachen Gang shuffling gait

Flachrennen flat race

Flanke flank

Flankentiefe depth of flank

Flankierbaum swinging rail

Fleischkrone coronary band

Fliegen-Schimmel ; Fliegenschimmel flea-bitten grey

Fliegendecke fly sheet (scrim ~)

**fliegender Galoppwechsel / Wechsel** flying change of lead / leg

**fliegender Sprung** flying jump

**Flucht** flight

**Flügelbein** pterygoid bone

**Flußeisenstahl** mild steel

**Flußstahl** mild steel

**fohlen** foal

**Fohlen (Hengst... // Stut...)** foal (colt // filly ~)

**Fohlenataxie** foal ataxia

**Fohlenstute** broodmare ; brood mare

**Fohlenzähne** milk teeth

**Folgsamkeit** docility

**Formaldehyd** formalin

**Formbeurteilung** judgment of (external) conformation

**Formbewertung** judgment of (external) conformation

**französischer Traber** French trotter

**Französisches Reitpferd** French Saddle (horse)

**freier Arbeitstrab ausgesessen** medium trot sitting

**freier Schritt** free walk

**Fremdzucht** outbreeding

**Fruchthülle** amnion

**Fuchs** chestnut

**fuchsfarbig** chestnut

**Fuchsjagd** fox-hunting

**Fuchslunte** brush

**fuchteln** paddle

**Führstrick** lead rope

**Furioso-Northstar** Furioso ; Furioso-North Star (horse)

**Fuß** foot

**Fuß fliegend wechseln** change (of lead) in the air

**fußen** land

**Fußgelenk** ankle

**Fußknöchel** ankle

**Fußwurzelknochen** tarsal bones

**Futter** fodder

**Futterkrippe** feed tub

**füttern** feed

**Futterrübe** turnip

**Futterverwertung** feed (conversion) efficiency

**Galle (weiche ~)** wind puff / windpuff

**Galopp / Fuß wechseln** change of leg

**Galopp (kurzer ~)** canter

**Galopp reiten ; galoppieren** gallop

**Galopptraversale** half-pass in canter

**Galoppwechsel** change of lead / leg

**Gamasche** open-front boot

**Ganasche** ventral border of mandible

**Gangart ; Gang** gait

**Gangarten** gaits

**Ganglion** ganglion

**ganzfarbig** whole colour(ed)

**Gaster** stomach

**Gastritis** gastritis

**Gaumen** palate

**Gaumenbein** palatine bone

**Gaze** gauze

**Gebärmutter** uterus

**Gebärmutterhals** cervix of uterus

**Gebärmutterhorn** uterine horn

**Gebiss / Gebiß** bit

mouth(piece)

**Gebiss gestellt** on the bit (horse ~)

**Gebiss sein** on the bit (horse ~)

**Gebot** bid

**Gebrauchsschritt** medium walk

**gebrochenes (Mundstück)** jointed

**Geburt** foaling

**Gefäßeinschnitt** intermandibular region / space

**geflochtene Mähne** plaited mane

**Gegengerade** back stretch ; backstretch

**Gegenseite** back stretch ; backstretch

**Gehirn** brain

**Gehorsam** docility

obedience

**gehorsam** docile

**Gekröse** mesentery ; mesenterium

**Geländepferd** cross-country horse

**Geländeprüfung** endurance test / phase (speed and ~)

**Geländeritt** cross country riding

**Gelbkörper** yellow body

**Gelbsucht** jaundice

**Geldpreis** prize (cash / money ~)

**Geldstrafe** fine

**Gelehrigkeit** docility

**Gelenk** joint

**Gelenkgalle (weiche ~)** wind gall / puff (articular ~)

**Gelenkkapsel** joint capsule

**Gelenkknorpel** articular cartilage

**Gelenkpfanne des Hüftgelenks** acetabulum

**Gelenkschmiere** synovial fluid

**gemeinsamer Zehenstrecker** common digital extensor muscle

**Gen** gene

**Genealogie** genealogy

Genetik genetic
Genick poll
Genickstück headpiece
Genickwölbung bend at the poll
Genpaar allele
gequetschtes Getreide rolled grains
gerittenes Pferd well-schooled (horse)
Gerste barley
Geschirr tack ; tackle
Geschirrmacher harness-maker
geschlossen short-coupled
geschmeidiger Sitz good and easy seat
Geschmeidigkeit suppleness
Geschröte scrotum
Geschwür ulcer
gesenkter Rücken saddle-back
Gesicht face
Gesichtsblutader facial vein
Gespann harnessed team
Gespannführer driver
gestellt sein bay (to be / stand at ~)
gestreckt camped (out)
Gestüt stud farm
Gestütsbrand branding (hot ~ mark)
Gestütsbuch stud-book ; stud book
gesund sound
Gesundheit soundness
geteilt jointed
Gewichtseinwirkung action of the seat
Gewichtshilfe action of the seat
Gewinnanteil levy
gewölbter Rücken arch-back
gezähmtes Pferd on the bit (horse ~)
Gidran Gidran
glänzendes Haarkleid / Fell glossy coat
glanzloses Haarkleid / Fell dull coat
glatter Muskel smooth muscle
Gleichbeine proximal sesamoid bones
gleichmäßiges stehen auf allen vier Füßen
    stand square
Gleichmäßigkeit regularity
Glied limb
Gliedheranführung adduction
Gliedmaßen limbs (the ~)
Gliedmaßenfehler limb faults
Glocke bell
        bell boot
Glycerin glycerin
Gold-Fuchs / Goldfuchs golden chestnut
Goldaugenbremse deer fly

Goldbrauner golden bay
Graben open ditch
        ditch
Grand Prix de Dressage Grand Prix de
    Dressage
Grand Prix der Nationen Nations' Cup
Gras grass
Grasbauch cow-belly
grasen graze
grau grey
Grausamkeit cruelty
greifen (sich ~) overreach
Griff clip
Griffelbein ergot
Grimmdarm colon
große Bauchgurt girth
Große Olympische Dressurprüfung Grand
    Prix de Dressage
großer Leberegel fluke (common liver ~)
großer Preis der Nationen Nations' Cup
großer Rollhügel greater trochanter (of the
    femur)
großer Rückenmuskel latissimus dorsi muscle
großer Umdreher greater trochanter (of the
    femur)
Großvater grandsire
Grundration maintenance ration
Grünfutter green fodder
Gruß salute
Gummiglocke bell boot
Gummistriegel rubber curry comb
Gurt girth
gurten ; Gurte anziehen girth
Gurtriemen girth
Gurtumfang girth's circumference
güsste (Stute) barren
güsste Stute empty mare
güst barren
gut sitzender Reiter good seat (rider with a ~)
guter Sitz good seat
Gutschrift bonus point
Gymkhana gymkhana
Haar hair (a ~)
Haarbalgdrüsen sebaceous glands
Haardecke coat
Haardrüsengrübchen hair follicle
Haarfollikel hair follicle
Haargefäß capillary (vessel)
Haarkleid coat
Haarkleid bei der Geburt birth coat
Haarling louse (biting ~)

Haarwechsel shedding
Haarwirbel whorl
Hack hack
Hackamore / Hackemore hackamore
Hacke point of hock
Hackney Hackney (horse)
Häcksel chopped straw
        chaff
Hafer oats
Hahnentritt stringhalt
Hakenstute barren
Hakenzahn canine (tooth)
Hakenzähne canine teeth
halb weiß gestiefelt (Bein) white to
  half-cannon
Halbblut half-bred
Halbblüter half-bred
Halbbruder half-brother
halbe Parade half-halt
halbe Pirouette half-pirouette
halbe Volte half-volt ; half volte
Halber-Arrêt half-halt
halbgestiefelt weiß white to half-cannon
Halbschwester half-sister
halbwildes Pferd semiwild horse
Hals neck
Halswirbel cervical vertebrae
Halten halt
Haltung des Reiters position of the rider
Hämatom haematoma
Hämaturie haematuria
Hammer hammer (of the ear)
Hämorrhagie haemorrhage
Hand hand
Hand (auf der rechten // linken ~) lead (on /
  at the right // left ~)
Hand vorführen (ein Pferd an der ~) show (a
  horse) in hand
Hand wechseln change rein
Handicap handicap
Handschuh glove
Handwechsel change of rein
Handwurzelgelenkentzündung carpitis
Hängeband suspensory ligament
Hängebauch cow-belly
Hanke-herein haunches-in
Hannoveraner Hanover horse; Hanoverian
  (horse)
Harmlosigkeit safety margin
Harnblase bladder (urinary ~)
Harnblutung haematuria

Harnleiter ureter
Harnröhre urethra
hartes Maul hard mouth
Hartfutter grains
Hartgummi vulcanite
Hasenhacke curb
Hauklinge sole knife
Haupt head
Hauptast der Luftröhre bronchus
Hauptgestüt national stud
Hauptteil trunk
Hausesel donkey
Haut skin
Hautentzündung dermatitis
Hautjucken itching
Hautkrankheit dermatosis
Hautmyiasis cutaneous blowfly myiasis
Hautödem anasarca
Hautwassersucht anasarca
Heber der Oberlippe levator muscle of upper
  lip
Hechtgebiss prognathism / prognathia
  (mandibular ~)
Hechtkopf dished (face)
Heilung healing
Hell-Fuchs / Hellfuchs light chestnut
Hellbraune light bay
Hengst stallion
Hengstdepot stud farm
Hengstfohlen colt
heranstellen (die Hinterhand ~) engage (the
  haunches)
Herde herd
Herdentrieb herding instinct
Herz heart
Herzbeutel pericardium
Herzmuskel cardiac muscle
Hetzpeitsche hunting whip
Heu hay
Heubauch cow-belly
Heubündel hay bale
Heunetz hay bag / net
Heuraufe hay rack
Hilfe aid
Hilfen aids
Hilfszielrichter assistant judge
Hilfszügel reins
hinauftreiben (den Preis ~) make a higher bid
Hindernis obstacle
Hindernis anreiten (ein ~) approach an
  obstacle

Deutsch => English

**Hindernis überwinden (ein ~)** clear an obstacle

**Hindernis umwerfen (ein ~)** knock down an obstacle

**Hindernisrennen** race over jumps

**Hindernisrichter** obstacle judge

**hinken** limp

**hinten faßbeinig** bandy-legged (in the hindlimb)

**hinter dem Zügel** behind the bit

**hinter der Bewegung sitzen** behind the motion

**hinter der Hand** behind the bit

**Hinterbacke** buttock

**Hinterbein** hind leg / limb

**Hinterbeine** hind-legs

**Hintergeschirr** breeching

**Hinterglied(maße)** hind leg / limb

**Hinterhand** rear end

**Hinterhand beherrschen** control the hindquarters

**Hinterhauptbein** occipital bone

**Hinterhauptloch** foramen magnum

**Hinterknie** stifle

**Hinterschienbein** metatarsal bone (large / third ~)

**Hinterteil** rear end

**Hinterzwiesel** cantle

**Hippologie** hippology

**Hirschhals** ewe neck

**hoch (weiß) gestiefelt (Bein)** white to above knee // hock

**hochgestiefelt weiß** white to above knee // hock

**Hochspringen** high jump

**Höchstzeit** time limit

**Hochweitsprung** spread jump

**Hoden** testicle ; testis

**Hodensack** scrotum

**hohe Schule** haute école

**hohe Stiefel** riding boot

**Höhenmaß** height measurement

**hoher Nase gehen (mit ~)** star-gaze

**hoher Widerrist** high withers

**hohle Wand** hollow wall

**Holsteiner** Holsteiner; Holstein (horse)

**horizontale Kruppe** flat croup

**Horn** horn

**Horn** horn (of an anvil)

**Hornhaut des Auges** cornea

**Hornplatte** wall (of the hoof)

**Hornspalt(e)** sandcrack / sand crack

**Hornwand** wall (of the hoof)

**Huf** hoof

**Huf auskratzen** pick out a foot

**Huf ausräumen** pick out a foot

**Huf richten** pare (a hoof)

**Hufabszeß** abscess (in a hoof)

**Hufballen** bulb (of a heel)

**Hufbein** distal phalanx

**Hufbeinkappe** extensor process

**Hufbeschlag** horseshoeing

**Hufbeschlaghammer** hammer (shoeing / driving / nailing ~)

**Hufbeschlagschmied** horseshoer

**Hufbeschlagschürze** apron (shoeing / farrier's ~)

**Hufbeschlagzange** nipper(s) (hoof ~)

**Hufbeschneidzange** nipper(s) (hoof ~)

**Hufeisen** horseshoe

**Hufeisen abnehmen** unshoe

**Hufeisenabnehmzange** puller (shoe ~)

**Huffett** hoof grease

**Hufgelenk** coffin joint

**Hufgelenkschale** low ringbone

**Hufgeschwür** abscess (in a hoof)

**Hufknorpel** fibrocartilage of the third phalanx

**Hufknorpelfistel** quittor (of horses)

**Hufknorpelverknöcherung** side bone ; sidebone

**Hufkratzer** hoof pick

**Hufmesser** hoof knife

**Hufnagel** nail (horseshoe ~)

**Hufnietzange** clincher(s) / clencher(s) (nail ~)

**Hufpflege** care of hooves

**Hufraspel** rasp

**Hufrehe (akute ~)** laminitis (acute ~)

**Hufrehe (chronische ~)** founder

**Hufschlag** beat (hoof...)

**Hufschlag** track (in a riding arena)

**Hufschlagfiguren** school figures

**Hufschmied** horseshoer

**Hufschmiede** farriery

**Hufschuh** barrier boot

**Hüftbreite** width of hips

**Hüfte** hip

**Hüftgelenk** hip joint

**Hüfthöcker** point of hip

**Hüfthöcker** coxal tuber

**Huftiere** ungulates (the ~)

**Hüftpfanne** acetabulum

**Hüftweite** width of hips

**Hufuntersuchungszange** hoof tester(s)

**Hufwand** wall (of the hoof)

Humerus humerus
Hund hound
Hundsmann huntsman
Hungergrube hollow of the flank
Huntsman huntsman
Hürde hedge
Hürdenrennen hurdle(s) race
Husten cough
husten cough
Hypophyse hypophysis
i-ahen bray
Ileum ileum
im Damensitz reiten ride side-saddle
Impfstoff vaccine
Impfung vaccination
in die Enge getrieben sein bay (to be / stand at ~)
in großem Bogen wenden turn wide
in-out Kombination in-and-out (obstacle / combination)
Index indicator
Industriepferd dray horse
Infektion infection
infektiöse Anämie der Pferde / Einhufer equine infectious anaemia / anemia
infektiöse Arteritis / Arteriitis des Pferdes equine viral arteritis
infektiöse Meningoenzephalitis der Pferde Borna disease
Innengalopp canter / gallop at / on the true lead
innere Fuß inside leg
innerer Armmuskel brachialis muscle
innerer Zügel inner rein
insektenvernichtend insecticide
Insektenvernichtungsmittel insecticide
intermittierendes Hinken intermittent limping
Internationale Reiterliche Vereinigung International Equestrian Federation
Internationaler Reitverband International Equestrian Federation
Inzestzucht incestuous breeding
Inzucht inbreeding
Inzuchttest inbreeding test
Iris iris
irische Bank Irish bank
irischer Hunter Irish hunter
Isabelle chestnut
Jagdgalopp gallop
Jagdherr master of the hunt
Jagdhose beige breeches
Jagdmartingal running martingale
Jagdpferd hunter (field ~)

Jagdrennen steeplechase
Jagdsattel hunting saddle
Jagdspringen jumping phase / test
Jährling yearling (colt // filly)
Jochbein zygomatic bone
Jochbeinbogen zygomatic arch
Jockey / Jockei jockey
Jockeystiefel jockey boot
Jod iodine
Jungfuchsjagd cubbing ; cub-hunting
Junghengst colt
Kaff chaff
Kakerlakenauge silver eye
kalbsbeinig calf-knee / calf knee
Kalbsknie calf-knee / calf knee
Kaltblut coldblood ; cold-blooded (horse)
Kaltblüter coldblood ; cold-blooded (horse)
kaltblütige Schlag coldblood ; cold-blooded (horse)
Kaltbrand freeze branding
Kalzium calcium
Kamm comb
Kampfrichter steward
Kandare curb bit
Kandare mit Walzen roller bit
Kandarenmundstück curb bit
Kandarenzaum double bridle
Kaninus canine teeth
Kanter canter
kantern canter
Kantharide blister beetle / fly
Kapillare capillary (vessel)
Kappe clip
Kappzaum cavesson (lungeing / longeing / breaking ~)
Kapriole capriole
Karabinerhaken snap
Kardätsche brush
Kardia cardia
Karotte carrot
Karpalballen chestnut
Karpalgelenk(e) carpal joint(s)
Karpalknochen carpal bones
Karpfengebiss brachygnathia ; brachygnathism
Karpfenrücken arch-back
Karzinom carcinoma
Kastanie chestnut
Kastration castration
kastrieren geld
Käufer buyer

Kavallerie cavalry
Kavalleriepferd cavalry horse
Kehldeckel epiglottis
Kehle throat
Kehlkopf larynx
Kehlkopfentzündung laryngitis
Kehlkopfpfeifen laryngeal hemiplegia / paralysis
Kehlriemen throatlash ; throatlatch
Kehrtvolte half-volt ; half volte
Keilbein sphenoid bone
Keratin keratin
Kette chain
Kiefer jaw
Kieferhöhle (Ober...) maxillary sinus
Kindspech meconium
Kinn chin (swelling)
Kinnbacken jaw
Kinngrube chin groove
Kinnkette curb chain
Kinnkettengrube chin groove
Kinnkettenhaken hooks
Kirschbrauner cherry bay
Kissen panel (saddle ~)
Klage complaint
Kläger(in) complainant
Klauenbein distal phalanx
Klee clover
kleine Bauchgurt belly band
kleiner Stern small star
Kleinhirn cerebellum
Kleinpferd pony
Knie stifle
Knieaktion knee action
Kniebeule carpal hygroma
knieeng knock-kneed
Kniefalte flank fold
Kniegelenk stifle joint
Kniekappe knee cap (boot)
Kniepausche knee roll
Kniescheibe patella
Kniescheibenrolle femoral trochlea
Knieschwamm carpal hygroma
knieweit knee-wide
Kniewulst knee roll
knirschen (mit den Zähnen ~) grind the teeth
Knöchel ankle
Knochen bone
Knochenbruch bone fracture
Knochenentzündung osteitis

Knochenhaut periosteum
Knochenhautentzündung periostitis ; periosteitis
Knochenmark bone marrow
Knorpel cartilage
Kohlensäure carbon dioxide
Kolik colic
Kolon colon
Kolostralmilch colostrum
Kolostrum colostrum
Kombination combination (of obstacles)
kombinierte Reithalfter flash noseband
kongenital congenital
konkaver Kopf dished (face)
kontagiöse equine Metritis contagious equine metritis
Kontakt contact
Konter-Wechsel counter-change of hand
Kontergalopp canter counter-lead
Kontrolle des Schwungs impulsion control
Kopf head
Kopf schlagen (mit dem ~) bob the head
Kopflänge length of the head
Kopflausei louse egg
Kopfräude sarcoptic mange
Kopfstück hood
Kopfstück headpiece
Koppen wind-sucking
Korium dermis
Kornea cornea
Körperbau conformation
Körperlänge body length
korrekt hinstellen (ein Pferd ~) make a horse stand correctly
Köte fetlock
Kötenbehang fetlock (tuft)
Kötengelenk fetlock joint
Kötenhaare fetlock (tuft)
Kötenschopf fetlock (tuft)
Kotflügel mud guard
Krallenbein distal phalanx
Krankenschuch poultice boot
Krankheit disease
Krebs carcinoma
Kreuzbein sacrum
Kreuzbeinhöhe height of rump
Kreuzdarmbeingelenk sacroiliac joint
Kreuzgalle bog spavin
Kreuzgalopp disunited canter
Kreuzhöcker sacral tuber

**Kreuzung(zucht)** cross-breeding ; crossbreeding

**Kreuzverschlag** azoturia

**Kreuzwirbel** sacral vertebrae

**Kriebelmücke** black fly

**Kriegspferd** war horse

**Krippe** feed tub

**Krippensetzen** crib biting

**Kronbein** middle phalanx

**Krone** coronet

**Krongelenk** pastern joint

**Krongelenkschale** high ringbone

**Krontritt** injury to the coronet (overreach / self ~)

**Kropf** goitre

**Krummdarm** ileum

**Kruppe** croup

**Kruppe-heraus ; Kruppe-zur-Wand** renvers

**Kryptorchide** cryptorchid

**Kryptorchismus** cryptorchidism ; cryptorchism

**Kübel** pail

**Kuhbauch** cow-belly

**Kumt ; Kummt ; Kummet** collar

**Kumtbügel** hame

**Kunst** art

**Künstlerschleife** stock tie

**künstliche Besamung** artificial insemination

**künstliche Hilfe** artificial aid

**Kupfer** copper

**kupieren** dock

**Kür** kur

**Kurbengalle** thoroughpin

**Kurve** turn

**kurz wenden** turn short / sharply

**kurze Fessel** short pastern

**kurzen Galopp gehen (in ~)** canter

**kurzer Widerrist** camel withers

**Kurzkehrtwendung** half-pirouette

**Kutsche** coach

**Kutscher** coachman

**Lade** bar (of the mouth)

**lahm** lame

**lahmen ; lahm gehen** limp

**Lahmheit** lameness

**Landauer** landau

**landen** land

**Landeseite (bei Hindernis)** landing side (of an obstacle)

**Landgestüt** national stud

**Landung** landing

**lang gefesselt** long pastern

**lange Fessel** long pastern

**lange Reithose** Jodhpurs ; jodhpurs ; Jodhpur breeches

**lange Zügel** long rein

**langen Zügel (am ~)** long rein (on / at a ~)

**langer Rückenmuskel** longissimus (dorsi) muscle

**langer Schritt** free walk

**Larve** larva

**Larynx** larynx

**Lasso** lasso

**Laterne** white face

**Laus** louse (biting ~)

**Läuse** lice

**Leber** liver

**Leckstein** salt lick

**Lederhaut** dermis

**Leerdarm** jejunum

**leere Stute** empty mare

**Lehrling** apprentice

**leichter Trab** posting trot

**leichtes Wagenpferd** light draught horse

**leichtes Zugpferd** light draught horse

**Leichtigkeit** lightness

**leichttraben** post (to the trot)

**leichttraben** trot rising

**Leinöl** linseed oil

**Leinsamen** linseed

**leistungsbereit** willing (horse)

**Leistungsbeurteilung** production assessment

**Leistungsbewertung** production assessment

**Lende** loin(s)

**Lendenpartie** loin(s)

**Lendenwirbel** lumbar vertebrae

**Lerberegelbefall** fluke (common liver ~)

**Levade** levade

**Lichtempfindlichkeit** photophobia

**Lichtfuchs** light chestnut

**Lidbindehautentzündung** conjunctivitis

**Linienführung des Parcours** line of the course

**Linienzucht** line breeding ; linebreeding

**Liniment(um)** liniment

**linkes Vorderbein** left foreleg

**Linksgalopp** canter (on the) left (lead)

**Linse** lens

**Lipizzaner** Lipizzaner

**Lippen** lips (of the mouth)

**Loch** hardy / hardie hole

**Longe** longeing line

**longieren** lunge / longe

lose Wand hollow wall
Losen draw
loser Zügel hanging rein
losgürten ungird
Luftröhre trachea
Luftschlucken aerophagia
Luftschnappen aerophagia
Lunge lung
Lungen Alveolen pulmonary alveolus
Lungenemphysem emphysema (pulmonary ~)
Lungenentzündung pneumonia
Lungenwurm lungworm ; lung worm
Lusitano Lusitanian horse
Luzerne alfalfa
Luzerne-Pellets alfalfa pellets / cubes
Lymphangitis lymphangitis
Lymphe lymph
Lymphgefäß lymphatic vessel
Lymphknoten lymph node
Lymphsystem lymphatic system
Mächtigkeitsspringprüfung puissance jumping
Magen stomach
Magenbremse bot fly (horse ~)
Mageneingang cardia
Magenferment pepsin
Magenfliege bot fly (horse ~)
Magenkatarrh gastritis
Magenpförtner pylorus
Magensaft gastric juice
magerer Widerrist bony withers
Mähne mane
Mähne verziehen thin the mane
Mähnenkamm crest
Mais corn
männliches Glied penis
Mannschaftsspringen team jumping (competition)
Maremmenpferd Maremma / Maremmana horse
Markierung der Reitbahn / des Parcours marking of the course
Martingal martingale
Mastdarm rectum
Mauer wall
Mauke scratches
Maul mouth
Maulesel hinny
Maulesel (männlicher ~) hinny (horse ~)
Mauleselin hinny (female ~)
Maulhöhle buccal cavity

Maulkorb muzzle
Maultier (männliches ~) mullet
Maultier (weibliches ~) mule (female ~)
Maultierführer muleteer
Maultiertreiber muleteer
Maulwinkel corner of the lips
Mausfalbe mouse-dun ; mouse-coloured
Mausgrau mouse-dun ; mouse-coloured
mausgrau mouse-dun ; mouse-coloured
Maxilla upper jaw
Medikament medicine
Meerrettich horseradish
Meile mile
Melasse molasses
Melone bowler (hat)
Merkmal character
merzen cull
Mesenterium mesentery ; mesenterium
Meßband measuring tape
Meßstock measuring stick
Metakarpus / Metacarpus metacarpus
Metatarsalien metatarsal bones
Metatarsus metatarsus
Meter metre / meter
Meute hounds (the ~)
mexikanische Reithalfter cross-over noseband
Milchgebiß milk (set of) teeth
Milchmangel galactia
Milchzähne milk teeth
Milz spleen
Milzbrand anthrax
Mindestzeit time allowed
Mischling ; Mischblut crossbred (animal)
Missouri Foxtrotter Fox trotter (Missouri ~)
Mist manure
Mittelgalopp medium canter
Mittelhand barrel (of the horse)
Mittelhand barrel (of the horse)
Mittelleib barrel (of the horse)
Mittelschritt medium walk
Mittelstück barrel (of the horse)
Mitteltrab medium trot
Mittelzahn central incisor
Moder mildew
mogeln cheat
Mohrenkopf dark head
Mohrrübe carrot
Mondblindheit equine recurrent uveitis
Morgan Horse Morgan

Mund mouth
Mundhöhle buccal cavity
Muskelbinde fascia
muskelrelaxierende Medikament muscle-relaxant drug
Mustang mustang ; Mustang
Muster sample
Mutter dam
mütterliche Linie female line
Mutterstute broodmare ; brood mare
Muttertier dam
Myokard cardiac muscle
Nabel navel
nach Belieben free choice
Nachhand rear end
Nachkomme offspring
Nachkommenprüfung progeny test(ing)
Nachkommenschaft descendants (the ~)
Nacken poll
Nackenband nuchal ligament
Nackenriemen headpiece
Nageltritt nail prick / tread
Nagelziehzange crease nail puller
Nagelzwang quicking
Naht suture
Nasenbein nasal bone
Nasenbluter bleeder
Nasenriemen noseband
Nasenrücken bridge of the nose
Nasenschoner shadow roll ; shadow blind
Nasenspitze muzzle
Natrium sodium
Natur-Mauer stone wall
Naturhindernis natural obstacle
natürliche Hilfe natural aid
Natursprung natural service
Nebenniere adrenal gland
Nennungsgeld entry fee
Nephritis nephritis
Nerv nerve
Nervenblockade nerve-blocking
Nervenknoten ganglion
nervös nervous
Nesselausschlag urticaria
Netzhaut retina
Neurektomie neurectomy
New Forest Pony New-Forest (pony)
nichttragend barren
Nickhaut nictitating membrane
Niere kidney

Niere(n) loin(s)
Nierenentzündung nephritis
Nierenpartie loin(s)
Nierenschlagader renal artery
Nierenverschlag / Nierenschlag azoturia
Nietzange clincher(s) / clencher(s) (nail ~)
Nisse louse egg
Nüster nostril
Oberarm arm (upper / true ~)
Oberarmknochen humerus
oberflächlicher Kruppenmuskel superficial gluteal muscle
Oberhaut epidermis
Oberkiefer upper jaw
Oberlippe upper lip
Oberschenkel thigh
Oberschenkelbein femur
Oberschenkelblutader femoral vein
Obmann president of the jury
Ochsenknie knock-knees
Ödem oedema
ohne (jegliche) Abzeichen whole colour(ed)
ohne Sattel reiten ride bareback
Ohr ear
Ohr (inneres // mittel // äußeres ~) ear (internal // middle // external ~)
Ohrenentzündung otitis
Ohrspeicheldrüse parotid gland
Ohrtrompete auditory tube
Oldenburger Oldenburg (horse)
Olekranon olecranon
Olivenkopftrense egg-butt / eggbutt snaffle
Olympia-Dressurprüfung Grand Prix de Dressage
olympische Spiele Olympic Games
Ortscheit swingle-tree
Ostitis osteitis
Otitis otitis
Ovidukt uterine tube
Oxer oxer
paaren mate (horses)
Paarung breeding
Packpferd pack horse ; packhorse
Paddock paddock
Palomino palomino
Pankreas pancreas
Parade halt
        parade
Paradepferd palfrey
Parasit parasite

parasympathisches Nervensystem parasympathetic nervous system

Parcours course

Parcourschef course designer

Parcoursskizze plan of the course

Parenchym parenchyma

Parenchyma parenchyma

Parotis parotid gland

Paso Fino Paso Fino

Passage passage

passiver Schenkel inactive leg

Paß amble

Paß gehen (den ~) amble

Paßgang / Passgang amble

Paßgänger / Passgänger ambler

Patella patella

Paukenhöhle tympanic cavity

Pegasus Pegasus

Peitsche whip

Peitschenhieb whiplash

Pelham ; Pelhamgebiß ; Pelhamkandare pelham bit

Penicillin penicillin

Penis penis

Pepsin pepsin

Percheron Percheron

Perikard pericardium

Perineum perineum

periodische Augenentzündung equine recurrent uveitis

Periost periosteum

Peritonäum peritoneum

Peritoneum peritoneum

Peritonitis peritonitis

perverser Appetit pica

Pfeifen laryngeal hemiplegia / paralysis

Pferd horse

Pferd euthanasieren destroy a horse

Pferd in der Gewalt haben control of the horse

Pferd schlachten destroy a horse

Pferd töten (ein ~) destroy a horse

Pferdeäpfel droppings

Pferdebox box (stall)

Pferdebremse ; Pferdemagenbremse bot fly (horse ~)

Pferdedecke trappings (horse's ~)

Pferdefleisch horse meat

Pferdehändler horse dealer / trader

Pferdekenner expert

Pferdekrankheit(en) disease(s) (horse / equine ~)

Pferdekunde hippology

Pferdelänge length

Pferdemann horse person

Pferden gezogen (von ~) horse-drawn

Pferdepest African horse sickness

Pferdepfleger groom

Pferdepocken horse pox ; horsepox

Pferderennbahn race track ; racetrack

Pferdeschwanz horse tail

Pferdestammbuch stud-book ; stud book

Pferdestärke horsepower

Pferdetierarzt equine veterinarian

Pferdetransportwagen trailer (horse ~)

Pferdezucht horse-breeding

Pflege grooming

Pfortader portal vein

Pfriemenschwanz des Pferdes pinworm (horse ~)

Pharynx pharynx

Phosphorverbindung phosphorus

Piaffe piaffé ; piaffer ; piaffe

Piephacke capped hock

Pigment pigment

Pikör whipper-in

Pilaren pillars

Piroplasmose des Pferdes babesiasis ; babesiosis

Pirouette pirouette

Pirouette im Galopp pirouette at a canter

Planke(n) plank(s)

Pleura pleura

Polo(spiel) polo

Polohelm polo helmet

Polopferd polo pony

Polosattel polo saddle

Polostiefel polo boot

Polsterung panel (saddle ~)

Pony pony

Porzellan-Schimmel porcelain white

Präputium sheath

Preis prize
price

Prellung bruise

Probe sample

Probestück sample

Probieren trial

Probierhengst teaser (stallion)

Programm programme

Promenadenpferd hack

Promenadenreiten pleasure

**Protein** protein
**Prüfen** trial
**Prüfung mit Stechen** competition with jump-off
**Pruritus** itching
**pullen** pull
**Puls** pulse
**Punktbrennen** pin firing (scars)
**Pupille** pupil
**Putzen** grooming
**putzen** groom
**Pylorus** pylorus
**Quaddelausschlag** urticaria
**Qualifikation** qualification
**Querfeldeinstrecke** cross-country course
**Querfortsatz** transverse process
**quergestreift(er) Muskel** striated muscle
**Quetschung** bruise
**Rachen** pharynx
**Rachitis** rickets
**Rammskopf** roman nose
**Rapp-Schecke** piebald
**Rapp-Schecke** piebald
**Rappe** black
**Rappschimmel** blue roan
**raspeln** rasp
**Rasse** breed
**Rassetyp** breed type
**Rattenschweif** rat tail
**Räude** mange (horse ~)
**Räudemilbe** mange mite
**Rauhfutter / Raufutter** roughage
**Rechtsgalopp** canter (on the) right (lead)
**Regenbogenhaut** iris
**rehbraun** fawn bay
**Rehbrauner** fawn bay
**Reibfläche** dental table
**Reis** rice
**Reit... ; Relter...** equestrian
**Reitbahn** indoor arena
**reiten** mount (a horse)
**Reiten** horseback riding
**reiten (auf der rechten // linken Hand ~)** riding to the right // left
**reiten im Damensattel** ride side-saddle
**reiten ohne Sattel** ride bareback
**reiten zu Hirschhunden** stag-hunting
**Reiter** rider
**Reiter-Quadrille** quadrille
**Reiter von Vielseitigkeitsprüfungen** event rider

**Reiterei** horseback riding
cavalry
**Reiterin** lady rider
**Reitgerte** crop
**Reithalle** indoor arena
**Reithose** breeches
**Reithosenschneider** breeches-maker
**Reitkandare** curb bit
**Reitkappe** cap (hunting / skull / jockey's ~)
**Reitkunst** art of equestrian riding
**Reitlehrer** riding instructor
**Reitmeister** riding master
**Reitpeitsche** crop
**Reitpeitsche schlagen (mit der ~)** whip
**Reitpferd** saddle horse
**Reitpony** riding pony
**Reitrock** riding coat
**Reitschule** riding school
**Reitsport** equestrian sport
**Reitstiefel** riding boot
**Reittechnik** riding technique
**Reitturnier** horse show
**Reitturnier** horse show
**Rektum** rectum
**Rennbahn** steeplechase phase
**Rennbahn** race track ; racetrack
**Rennbahngalopp** racing gallop
**Renngalopp** racing gallop
**Renngericht** appeal committee
**Rennjacke** jacket
**Rennpferd** race horse ; racehorse
**Rennreiter** jockey
**Rennsattel** racing saddle
**Rennsitz** jockey seat
**Rennsport** races (the ~)
**Rennstiefel** jockey boot
**Renntrense** egg-butt / eggbutt snaffle
**Rennwette** pari-mutuel
**Renvers** renvers
**Retina** retina
**rezessiv** recessive
**Rhinopneumonie des Pferdes** rhinopneumonitis (equine viral ~)
**Richter** judge
**Richterhäuschen** judges' box
**richtiger Galopp** canter / gallop at / on the true lead
**Richtungsänderung ; Richtungswechsel** change of direction
**Richtverfahren** scheme of marking

**Richtverfahren (nach Fehlerpunkten)** penalty table

**Riemer** harness-maker

**Ringbein** ringbone ; ring bone ; ring-bone

**Ringe** rings (of a bit)

**Ringelflechte** ringworm

**Ringmartingal** running martingale

**Rinnmesser** hoof knife

**Rippe** rib

**Rippen** ribs

**Rippenbein** rib (bone)

**Rippenbogen** costal arch

**Rippenfellentzündung** pleuritis ; pleurisy

**Rippenknorpel** costal cartilage

**Rittertum** chivalry

**rittlings aufsitzen** ride astride

**Rizinusöl** castor oil

**Roggen** rye

**Röhrbein** cannon bone

**Röhrbeinumfang** cannon's circumference

**Röhre** cannon

**Rohren** laryngeal hemiplegia / paralysis

**Rohrschwingel** tall fescue (grass)

**Rollengebiß** roller bit

**Röntgenuntersuchung** X-ray examination

**Rosenschimmel** albino

**Roßhaar** horsehair (a ~)

**Rotschimmel** bay roan

**Rotz ; Rotzkrankheit** glanders (equine ~)

**Rübe** beet

**Rübennaßschnitzel** sugar beet pulp

**rückbiegig** calf-knee / calf knee

**Rücken** back

**Rückenmark** spinal cord

**Rückgrat** spine

**Rückwärtsrichten** rein-back ; reinback

**ruhig** quiet

**Ruhr** diarrhoea

**Rumpf** trunk

**Rumpfhautmuskel** cutaneus trunci muscle

**Rundwurm** nematode

**Rute** penis

**säbelbeinig** sickle-hocked

**Salz** salt

**Salzleckstein** salt lick

**Samenblase** vesicular gland

**Samenleiter** deferent duct

**Sattel** saddle

**Sattelanhänger** gooseneck trailer

**Sattelbaum** tree (of a saddle)

**Sattelblatt** flap (of a saddle)

**Satteldecke** saddle pad

**Satteldecke** saddle blanket

**Satteldruck** saddle sore

**Sattelgurt** girth

**Sattelgurtüberzug** girth cover

**Sattelhorn** horn (of a saddle)

**Sattelkammer** saddle room

**Sattelkissen** panel (saddle ~)

**Sattelkranz** cantle

**Sattellage** saddle site

**satteln** saddle

**Sattelpferd** saddle horse

**Sattelrücken** saddle-back

**Sattler** saddler

**Sattlerei** saddlery; saddler's shop

**sauber springen** clear (jump ~)

**Säugen** suckling

**Saugfohlen** milk foal

**Saumband** periople

**Saumpferd** pack horse ; packhorse

**Saumsattel** pack saddle

**Schabracke** saddle pad

**Schachtelhalm** horsetail

**Schädel** skull

**Schädling** pest (insect)

**Schafhaut** amnion

**Schale** ringbone ; ring bone ; ring-bone

**Scham** vulva

**Schambein** pubis (bone)

**scharf wenden** turn short / sharply

**scharren** paw the ground

**scharzgesichtig** black-faced

**Schaum** foam

**Scheck** pinto ; pintado

**Schecke** pinto ; pintado

**scheckig** pinto ; pintado

**Scheidenvorhof** vestibule of vagina

**Scheitelbein** parietal bone

**Schenkel** branch (of a shoe)

**Schenkelhilfen** aid of the legs

**Schenkelweichen** leg-yielding

**Schere** shaft

**scheren** clip

**Scherenoxer** Swedish oxer

**Scherenriemen** breeching strap

**Schermaschine** clipper

**Scherriemen** lipstrap

**Scheu** fear

**scheuen ; scheu werden** shy

**Scheuklappe** blinker
**Scheuleder** blinker
**Schiedsgericht** appeal committee
**schiefer Zehenbeuger** medial head of the deep digital flexor muscle
**Schilddrüse** thyroid (gland)
**Schilddrüsenwucherung** goitre
**Schimmel** mildew
      white foaled
      grey
**Schlachthaus** slaughterhouse
**Schlachthof** slaughterhouse
**Schlachtpferd** slaughter horse
**Schlachtroß** war horse
**Schläfe** temple
**Schläfenbein** temporal bone
**Schlag** kick
**Schlagader** artery
**schlagen** kick
**Schlangengiftserum** antivenene ; antivenin
**Schlangenlinie** serpentine
**Schlappohren (Pferd mit ~)** lop-eared
**Schlauch** sheath
**Schlaufzügel** draw rein
**schlechtes Pferd** worthless horse
**Schleife** rosette
**Schleimbeutel** synovial bursa
**Schleimhaut** mucosa
**Schlempe** brewer's draff / grains
**schleppende Bewegung** shuffling gait
**Schleppjagd** drag-hunting
**Schlundkopf** pharynx
**schmale Brust** narrow chest
**Schmerzausschaltung** analgesic
**Schmerzausschaltung am Nerv** nerve-blocking
**schmerzstillendes Mittel** analgesic
**Schmied** blacksmith
**Schmiede** farriery
**schmieden** forge
**Schnalle** buckle
**Schnallendorn** billet (of a buckle)
**Schnecke** cochlea
**Schneckenklee** alfalfa
**Schneider** tailor
**Schneidezähne** incisors
**Schnelligkeit** speed
**Schopf** forelock
**schräge Fessel** sloping pastern / foot
**schräge Hecke** brush and rails

**schräge Schulter** sloping shoulder
**Schraubstollen** calk (screw-in ~)
**Schritt** walk
**Schritt am langen Zügel** walk on a long rein
**Schritt gehen** walk
**Schritt reiten** ride at the walk
**Schrittvolte** volte at the walk
**Schubrine** forelock
**schummeln** cheat
**schwarz** black
**Schwarz-Schecke** piebald
**schwarze Harnwinde** azoturia
**Schwengel** swingle-tree
**Sehloch** pupil
**Sehnenhaut** aponeurose
**Seitenblatt (des Sattels)** flap (of a saddle)
**seitwärtige Biegung im Genick** bend at the poll
**Senkrücken** saddle-back
**sich verzweifelt zur Wehr setzen** bay (to be / stand at ~)
**Skelettmuskel** striated muscle
**Skrotum** scrotum
**Spazierenreiten** pleasure
**Sporn** ergot
**Spreu** chaff
**springen** cover (a mare)
**Springglocke** bell boot
**Springkappe** cap (hunting / skull / jockey's ~)
**Sprung** service
**Sprung anreiten (einen ~)** approach an obstacle
**Sprungbeinhöcker** point of hock
**Sprunggelenksgalle** thoroughpin
**Sprungglocke** bell boot
**Spur** track (in a riding arena)
**Stallbaum** swinging rail
**Stamm** trunk
**stampfen** paw the ground
**Stangenzaum** double bridle
**starkes Karpalgelenk** well-defined knee
**starres Hindernis** solid fence
**Stechbremsen** horseflies
**Steiggebiss** gag bit
**steiler Huf** club foot
**Steinmauer** stone wall
**Stelzhuf** club foot
**Sternum** sternum
**Stichwunde** nail prick / tread
**Stirnschopf** forelock
**Stockmaß** measuring stick

Streckfortsatz extensor process

streichen kick

Strichblesse stripe

Stuhlgang droppings

stumpfes Haarkleid / Fell dull coat

Sturzkappe cap (hunting / skull / jockey's ~)

Stutbuch stud-book ; stud book

Synovia synovial fluid

Synovialbeutel synovial bursa

Talgdrüsen sebaceous glands

Tantieme levy

Testikel ; Testis testicle ; testis

Thorax thorax

Thyreoidea thyroid (gland)

Tierpiroplasmose durch Babesia babesiasis ; babesiosis

Tragpferd pack horse ; packhorse

Tragsattel pack saddle

Trockentreber brewer's draff / grains

Truppen (berittene ~) cavalry

Überbiß brachygnathia ; brachygnathism

Übertragung auf die Beine leg-yielding

Ulna ulna

Umlauf round

unfruchtbar barren

Untergesicht bridge of the nose

Unterhautödem anasarca

unträchtige Stute empty mare

Uterus uterus

Uterushorn uterine horn

vegetatives Nervensystem autonomic nervous system

verkehrter Hals ewe neck

verkürzter Unterkiefer brachygnathia ; brachygnathism

Vernageln quicking

verteuern make a higher bid

Verwandtschaftszucht inbreeding

Vesikulardrüse vesicular gland

Vitamin H biotin

Vorderfußwurzelgelenk(e) carpal joint(s)

Vorderfußwurzelknochen carpal bones

Vorhaut sheath

vorne faßbeinig knee-wide

vorstehender Unterkiefer prognathism / prognathia (mandibular ~)

Vulva vulva

waagerechte Kruppe flat croup

Wange cheek

Wasserhaut amnion

wässerige Schwellung oedema

weibliche Linie female line

weiche Spat ; Weichteilspat bog spavin

Weitsprung spread jump

Westernpad saddle blanket

willig willing (horse)

Willigkeit docility

X-beinig knock-kneed

Zahnlücke bar (of the mouth)

Zäkum / Zaekum cecum / caecum

zäumen bridle (a horse)

Zerebellum cerebellum

Zervix cervix of uterus

Zick-Zack / Zickzack Traversale counter-change of hand

Zuchtbetrieb stud farm

Zuchthengst stallion

Zuchtstute broodmare ; brood mare

Zuckfuß stringhalt

Zügelringe rings (of a bit)

Zugtrense gag bit

zum Äußersten getrieben sein bay (to be / stand at ~)

zureiten break (a horse)

Zurücksetzen des Gespanns rein-back ; reinback

zweites Kopfgelenk atlanto-axial articulation

zweites Zehengelenk pastern joint

Zwerchfell diaphragm

zwischen Hand und Schenkel on the aids

Zyklusstillstand anestrus ; anoestrus

# ESPAÑOL

## Index

**anglo-árabe** Anglo-Arab(ian) (horse)

**ángulo de la espalda** shoulder angle

**ángulo de la pelvis** pelvis angle

**ángulo del aproche** angle of the approach

**anillos** rings (of a bit)

**animal de carga** pack animal

**ano** anus

**antebrazo** forearm

**antemano** forehand

**anteojera** blinker

**antibiótico** antibiotic

**antihelmíntico** anthelmintic (drug)

**antiinflamatorio** anti-inflammatory

**ántrax** anthrax

**anunciador** announcer (house / track ~)

**apacentar** pasture

**aparato digestivo** digestive system

**aparato respiratorio** respiratory system

**apareamiento** breeding

**aparear** mate (horses)

**aparejar** harness (up)

**aparejar (un caballo)** break (a horse)

**apeadero** mounting step

**aplomo(s)** stand(s)

**apófisis espinosa** spinous process

**apófisis transversa** transverse process

**aponeurosis** aponeurose

**apostante** bettor

**apostar** bet

**apoyar** half-pass

**apoyar en el freno** lean (heavily) on the hand / bit

**apoyo** half-pass

**apoyo al galope** half-pass in canter

**apoyo de la boca** contact with the bit (horse moving into a ~)

**appaloosa** Appaloosa

**apreciación de la producción** production assessment

**aprendiz** apprentice

**apretado** short-coupled

**apretado de delante** narrow at the chest

**apretador de clavos** clincher(s) / clencher(s) (nail ~)

**aproximarse un obstáculo** approach an obstacle

**apuesta** bet

**apuestas mutuas** pari-mutuel

**apunte** entry

**árabe** Arab ; Arabian

**árabe shagya** Shagya (Arab) horse

**arador de (la) sarna** mange mite

**arción** stirrup leather / strap

**arco costal** costal arch

**arco superciliar** superciliary arch

**ardenés ; ardenas** Ardennais ; Ardennes (horse)

**arena cubierta** indoor arena

**arenilla** abscess (in a hoof)

**argollas** rings (of a bit)

**arnés** tack ; tackle

**arpeo ; arpeado** stringhalt

**arrastrar la lengua** hang out the tongue

**arreo** tack ; tackle

**arrollar un obstáculo** knock down an obstacle

**arroz** rice

**arte** art

**arte ecuestre** art of equestrian riding

**arteria** artery

**arteria renal** renal artery

**arteria vertebral** vertebral artery

**arteritis viral equina** equine viral arteritis

**articulación** joint

**articulación(/ones) del carpo** carpal joint(s)

**articulación atlantoaxial** atlanto-axial articulation

**articulación coxofemoral / del anca** hip joint

**articulación cubital / del codo** elbow joint

**articulación de la babilla** stifle joint

**articulación de la cuarta** pastern joint

**articulación de la espalda / del hombro** shoulder joint

**articulación femoro-tibia-rotuliana** stifle joint

**articulación interfalangiana distal** coffin joint

**articulación metacarpofalangiana // metatarsofalangiana** fetlock joint

**articulación sacroilíaca** sacroiliac joint

**articulaciones esternocostales** sternocostal articulations

**arueses** harnessed team

**ascáride** ascarid

**ascendencia** ancestry

**aseo** grooming

**aserrín** shavings

**asiento** seat (of a rider) seat (of a saddle)

**asiento correcto** good seat

**asiento de adiestramiento** dressage seat

**asiento de carrera** jockey seat

**asiento elástico / flexible** good and easy seat

**asiento falso** incorrect seat

**asiento para caballería** mule chair

asiento para correr jockey seat
asiento para saltar forward seat
asma asthma
asmático broken winded
asna jenny-ass ; jenny
asno donkey
asno joven donkey foal
asociación de ganaderos / criadores
    breeder's association
astrágalo talus
asustado frightened
asustarse shy
ataharre breeching
atalaje harnessing
ataxia ataxia
        foal ataxia
atizador poker
atlas atlas
avena oats
avulsión avulsion
axila axilla
axis axis
ayuda aid
ayuda artificial artificial aid
ayuda de peso del cuerpo action of the seat
ayuda de piernas aid of the legs
ayuda diagonal diagonal aid
ayuda lateral lateral aid
ayuda natural natural aid
ayudas aids
azoturia azoturia
azúcar sugar
baba ; babaza foam
babesiosis babesiasis ; babesiosis
babilla stifle
bagazo de cervecería brewer's draff / grains
bajador (martingala de ~) standing martingale
balotada ballotade
banda coronaria coronary band
banqueta bank
banqueta irlandesa Irish bank
barba chin groove
barba ; barbilla chin (swelling)
barbada curb chain
baremo de nota scheme of marking
baremo de penalizaciones penalty table
barra rail
      bar (of the mouth)
barra de estribo stirrup bar
barra triple triple bar(s)

barrera gate
barrera fija post and rail (vertical fence)
barriga belly
barriga de pescado / anguilla herring gut
barriga de vaca cow-belly
barriguera (cincha ~) belly band
baticola crupper dock
batida beat (hoof...)
batida (de llamada) take off (stride)
batilla pommel
bayo bay
bayo cereza cherry bay
bayo dorado golden bay
bayo leonado fawn bay
bayo obscuro / oscuro brown
bayo pálido light bay
bazo spleen
benzimidazole benzimidazole
beréber barb
bicorne bicorne
bien sentado (jinete ~) good seat (rider with a ~)
bigornia anvil (portable ~)
billetero ticket rack
biotina biotin
bípedo diagonal diagonal pair
bípedo lateral lateral pair
blanco white
blanco (desde el nacimiento) white foaled
blanco porcelana porcelain white
blistera blister ; blistering
bloque de sal salt lick
bloqueo nervioso nerve-blocking
boca mouth
boca cerrada full mouth
boca de loro brachygnathia ; brachygnathism
boca dura hard mouth
boca sensitiva soft mouth
bocado curb bit
bocio goitre
bolitas de alfalfa alfalfa pellets / cubes
bolsa scrotum
bolsa sinovial synovial bursa
bombín bowler (hat)
Borna Borna disease
boro boron
borrén delantero pommel
borrén trasero cantle
bota boot (for horses)
bota campera / de campo riding boot (laced ~)
bota de embarque / transporte shipping boot

**bota de goma cubrecasco** bell boot

**bota de medicación** poultice boot

**bota frente abierto** open-front boot

**bota para jockey** jockey boot

**bota para montar** riding boot

**bota para polo** polo boot

**botar un obstáculo** knock down an obstacle

**botas** boots

**botero** bootmaker

**botín** Jodhpur boot

**botín** paddock boot

**botulismo** botulism

**box** box (stall)

**bozal** bosal
        muzzle

**brabanzón** Belgian (draft / heavy draught horse)

**bracear** paddle

**bracicorto** over at / in the knees

**brazo** arm (upper / true ~)

**brazuelo** forearm

**brida** bridle

**brida completa; brida doble** double bridle

**brida de filete** snaffle (bridle)

**bridón** snaffle (bridle)

**bridón** bridoon

**bridón ovalado** egg-butt / eggbutt snaffle

**bronquio** bronchus

**bronquiolo** bronchiole

**bronquitis** bronchitis

**bronquitis obstructiva crónica** asthma

**brucelosis** brucellosis

**buche** donkey foal

**bucle** buckle

**buena acción** good action

**bull-finch** bull-finch / bullfinch

**bullones** Boulonnais (horse)

**burdégana** hinny (female ~)

**burdégano** hinny (horse ~)

**burra** jenny-ass ; jenny

**burro** donkey stallion

**bursitis del codo** capped elbow

**bursitis del corvejón** capped hock

**cabalgar** mount (a horse)

**caballada** herd

**caballería** cavalry

**caballería** chivalry

**caballeriza** barn

**caballerizo** riding master

**caballerizo** groom

**caballete** cavaletti

**caballista** rider

**caballo** horse

**caballo aguililla** Peruvian paso / ambler

**caballo bien hecho / domado / riendado** well-schooled (horse)

**caballo campero** cross-country horse

**caballo castrado / capón** gelding

**caballo de ambladura** ambler

**caballo de batalla** hobby-horse

**caballo de carga / albarda** pack horse ; packhorse

**caballo de carrera malo** worthless horse

**caballo de carrera(s)** race horse ; racehorse

**caballo de carro / coche** cart-horse

**caballo de caza / cacería** hunter (field ~)

**caballo de concurso completo** event horse

**caballo de damas** lady's mount

**caballo de doma clásica** dressage horse

**caballo de ejército** cavalry horse

**caballo de frisa** cheval de frise

**caballo de guerra** war horse

**caballo de Holstein** Holsteiner; Holstein (horse)

**caballo de labor** plough horse

**caballo de larga distancia** stayer

**caballo de los fiordos** Fjord pony

**caballo de paseo** hack

**caballo de polo** polo pony

**caballo de prueba completa / militar** event horse

**caballo de raza de temperamento frío** coldblood ; cold-blooded (horse)

**caballo de salto** jumper

**caballo de sangre (caliente)** warmblood ; warm-blooded horse

**caballo de silla** saddle horse

**caballo de silla americano** American Saddlebred

**caballo de tiro** cart-horse

**caballo de tiro** draught horse

**caballo de tiro belga** Belgian (draft / heavy draught horse)

**caballo de tiro industrial** dray horse

**caballo de tiro ligero** light draught horse

**caballo de tiro pesado** heavy draught / draft horse

**caballo de vapor** horsepower

**caballo desbocado** bolting horse ; bolter

**caballo difícil** unruly horse

**caballo enano** miniature horse

**caballo enseñado** well-schooled (horse)

**caballo entero** stallion

caballo linfático coldblood ; cold-blooded (horse)

caballo para sacrificio slaughter horse

caballo pesado heavy horse

caballo salvaje wild horse

caballo sangrante bleeder

caballo semi-salvaje semiwild horse

caballo trote-zorro de Misuri Fox trotter (Missouri ~)

caballo trotón francés French trotter

cabecear bob the head

cabecilla pommel

cabestro halter

cabeza head

cabeza acarnerada roman nose

cabeza afuera travers

cabeza al muro travers

cabeza de moro dark head

cabezón (de trabajo a cuerda) cavesson (lungeing / longeing / breaking ~)

cabriola capriole

cacho horn (of a saddle)

cadena chain

cadenilla / cadena (para la brida) curb chain

cagajón / cagajones droppings

caída fall
      landing

caja del tímpano tympanic cavity

calcáneo calcaneus

calcio calcium

calentador teaser (stallion)

calificación qualification

calmo quiet

calores heat

calostro colostrum

calzado white marking on a limb / leg

calzado alto white to above knee // hock

cama branch (of a bit)
      litter

cambiar de mano change rein

cambiar de pie change of leg

cambiar de pie en el aire change (of lead) in the air

cambio de aire change of gait / pace

cambio de dirección change of direction

cambio de galope con pasos intermedios simple change of lead / leg (through the trot)

cambio de galope simple simple change of lead / leg (through the trot)

cambio de mano change of rein

cambio de pie change of lead / leg

cambio de pie / galope en el aire flying change of lead / leg

cambio de rienda dentro del círculo change of hand in / through the circle

cambio simple de pie simple change of lead / leg (through the trot)

caminar la cancha / el curso walk (over) the course

caminos y pistas roads and tracks

camisa blanket (horse ~)

campana bell

campana de hule bell boot

canal vertebral vertebral canal

canal yugular jugular groove

canino canine (tooth)

caninos (dientes ~) canine teeth

cantárida blister beetle / fly

cantileja cantle

caña cannon

caña (hueso) cannon bone

caña anterior forecannon

cañera de viaje shipping boot

capa coat (colour)
      coat

capacidad de transformación de alimentos feed (conversion) efficiency

capadura castration

capar geld

caparazón trappings (horse's ~)

capilar (vaso ~) capillary (vessel)

cápsula articular joint capsule

cápsula suprarrenal adrenal gland

capucha hood

cara face

cara cóncava dished (face)

caracol cochlea

carácter character

carcinoma carcinoma

cardias cardia

careto white face

carinegro black-faced

carne de caballo horse meat

carpitis carpitis

carpo knee

carrera de los trotones trot race

carrera de obstáculos race over jumps

carrera de salto hurdle(s) race

carrera de trote / trotadores trot race

carrera lisa / plana flat race

carreras (las ~) races (the ~)

carrillera cheekpiece

**carrillo** cheek
**cartílago** cartilage
**cartílago articular** articular cartilage
**cartílago de la escápula** scapula(r) cartilage
**cartílago del hueso del casco** fibrocartilage of the third phalanx
**cartílagos de las costillas** costal cartilage
**cascabillo** chaff
**casco** hoof
**casco** polo helmet
**casco protector** cap (hunting / skull / jockey's ~)
**casco quebradizo** brittle foot / hoof
**caseta del jurado** judges' box
**castración** castration
**castrar** geld
**catéter** catheter
**cauterio** firing
**cavidad abdominal** abdominal cavity
**cavidad bucal** buccal cavity
**cavidad occipital** foramen magnum
**cavidad torácica** thoracic cavity
**caza de arrastre** drag-hunting
**caza de cachorro / zorrillo** cubbing ; cub-hunting
**caza de ciervo** stag-hunting
**caza de zorros** fox-hunting
**cebada** barley
**cebra** zebra
**celo** heat
**celo silencioso** silent heat
**cemento** cement (of a tooth)
**centeno** rye
**centro de gravedad** centre of gravity
**cepillo de agua** water brush
**cepillo de cuerpo** brush
**cerca de la tierra** well let down
**cerdas** tail hairs
**cerebelo** cerebellum
**cerneja** fetlock (tuft)
**cerrado de abajo** base narrow
**cerrado de atrás** base narrow
**cerrado de brazos / adelante** base narrow
**cerrado de rodillas** knock-kneed
**cesión a la pierna** leg-yielding
**cestodos** cestodes
**chalina** stock tie
**chambón** chambons
**chaparreras** apron (shoeing / farrier's ~)
**chaparreras** chaps
**chaqueta de montar** riding coat

**charollais** Charolais
**chasquido (de la lengua)** click (of the tongue)
**chistera** top-hat
**ciego (intestino ~)** cecum / caecum
**cierre** snap
**cincha** girth
**cinchar** girth
**cinta métrica** measuring tape
**círculo** circle
**circunferencia de la caña** cannon's circumference
**circunferencia del pecho** girth's circumference
**cisticercosis muscular** cysticercosis
**claudicación** lameness
**clavo (de herrar)** nail (horseshoe ~)
**clavor** hammer (shoeing / driving / nailing ~)
**clavos** nail prick / tread
**cloro** chlorine
**clydesdale** Clydesdale (horse)
**cobre** copper
**cocear** kick
**coche** coach
**cochero** coachman
**codillera** capped elbow
**codo** elbow
**codo hacia adentro** turned-in elbow
**codo hacia afuera** turned-out elbow
**coeficiente de parentesco** coefficient of relationship
**cojear** limp
**cojera** lameness
**cojera intermitente** intermittent limping
**cojinete digital / plantar** digital cushion
**cojo** lame
**cojo en la pierna izquierda // derecha delantera** lame, left // right fore
**cola** tail
**cola cortada** docked tail(ed) ; docked
**cola de caballo** horse tail
**cola de caballo** horsetail
**cola de rata** rat tail
**cola de zorro** brush
**colchoneta de un estribo** stirrup pad / tread
**colección** collection (of a horse)
**cólico** colic
**collar** collar
**collera ; collerón** collar
**colocación de la montura** saddle site
**colocar (un caballo) bien parado** make a horse stand correctly

152

colocar el caballo en la rienda collect
colon colon
colores jacket
colostro colostrum
columna vertebral vertebral column
comanditario sponsor
combinación (de obstáculos) combination (of obstacles)
combinación doble double (obstacle)
combinación triple triple (combination)
combo sledge hammer
comedero feed tub
comedero hay rack
comerciante de caballos horse dealer / trader
comisario steward
comisura de los labios corner of the lips
comité de apelación appeal committee
compacto short-coupled
compartimiento stall (standing ~)
comprador buyer
concurso completo horse trial
concurso de doma clásica dressage competition
concurso de equitación horse show
concurso de saltos horse show
concurso de saltos de obstáculos jumping competition
concurso hípico horse show
concurso hípico horse show
concurso hípico horse show
conducta behaviour
conducto auditivo externo external acoustic / auditory meatus
conducto deferente deferent duct
conductor jockey
conductor (de carruaje) driver
conductos semicirculares semicircular canals
confianza confidence
conformación conformation
congénito congenital
conjuntiva conjunctiva
conjuntivitis conjunctivitis
connemara Connemara (pony)
consanguinidad consanguinity
contacto contact
contra galope canter counter-lead
contracambio de mano counter-change of hand
control de la impulsión impulsion control
control del caballo control of the horse

contusión bruise
contusión de la suela / de piedra bruise (of the sole)
Copa de las Naciones Nations' Cup
copete forelock
corazón heart
corbata stock tie
corcel charger
cordón stripe
cordón corrido broad stripe
cordoncillo stripe (narrow ~)
córnea cornea
corona (del casco) coronet
corona blanca white coronet
correa de retranca breeching strap
correa labial lipstrap
corrida bullfight
corta de cuartilla short pastern
cortar las riendas shorten the reins
corto service
corto de resuello broken winded
corva ; corvaza curb
corvejón hock
corvejón(/ones) acodado(s) sickle hock(s)
corvejón bien definido well-defined hock
corvo over at / in the knees
costado de la batida take-off side (of an obstacle)
costado de la recepción landing side (of an obstacle)
costilla rib
costillar brisket
costillas ribs
costillas asternales asternal ribs
costillas esternales sternal ribs
coz kick
cráneo skull
crema para el casco hoof grease
cresta (del cuello) crest
cría breeding
cría caballar horse-breeding
cría en líneas line breeding ; linebreeding
criadero (rancho de ~) stud farm
criador breeder (up)
crin horsehair (a ~)
crin ; crinera mane
crinera trenzada plaited mane
criollo Criollo
criptorquidia cryptorchidism ; cryptorchism
criptórquido cryptorchid
cristalino lens

153 Español => English

cromosoma chromosome
cronometrador timekeeper
cronómetro (de detención) automático
automatic timing device
croquis de recorrido plan of the course
crueldad cruelty
cruz withers
cruz alta high withers
cruz corta camel withers
cruz delgada bony withers
cruzado half-bred
cruzamiento (método de crianza por ~)
cross-breeding ; crossbreeding
cruzamiento abierto outbreeding
cruzamiento entre líneas line crossing
cryptorchidio cryptorchid
cryptorchidismo cryptorchidism ; cryptorchism
cuadra barn
cuadrarse stand square
cuadrilla quadrille
cuadrilongo (de doma) dressage ring / arena
cuartilla pastern
cuartilla angulada sloping pastern / foot
cuartilla corta short pastern
cuartilla erguida knuckling (over)
cuartilla larga long pastern
cuarto sandcrack / sand crack
cuarto de monturas saddle room
cuartos traseros rear end
cubeta de comida feed tub
cubículo box (stall)
cubierta de la cincha girth cover
cúbito ulna
cubo pail
cubos de alfalfa alfalfa pellets / cubes
cubrición service
cubrir cover (a mare)
cuchilla (inglesa) hoof knife
cuchillo herrero hoof knife
cuello neck
cuello de ciervo ewe neck
cuello de cisne arched neck
cuello grueso / de toro bull neck
cuello hundido ewe neck
cuello invertido ewe neck
cuello uterino cervix of uterus
cuenca del ojo eyeball
cuerda lead rope
cuerda (larga) longeing line
cuerno horn (of a saddle)

cuerno horn
cuerno (del yunque) horn (of an anvil)
cuerno uterino uterine horn
cuerpo length
cuerpo lúteo yellow body
cuidado de los cascos trimming (of the hoof)
cuidado(s) de los cascos care of hooves
culpable offending
cura dressing
curación healing
curva turn
curva ; curvatura flexion
curva en el tendón tendon bow
dar coces kick
dar de beber water
dar la salida give the signal to start
dar servicio cover (a mare)
darle cuerda lunge / longe
dedo toe (of a hoof)
defecto defect
defecto hereditario / innato inborn defect
defectos de los miembros limb faults
defensa resistance
dehesa pasture
delante de la mano above the bit
delegado técnico technical delegate
demanda complaint
demandante complainant
dentadura completa full mouth
dentición dentition
dentro y fuera (obstáculo) in-and-out
(obstacle / combination)
deporte ecuestre equestrian sport
depósito de padrillos / sementales stud farm
depósito de yeguas broodmare station
derecho de inscripción entry fee
dermatitis ; dermitis dermatitis
dermatitis aguda del casco laminitis (acute ~)
dermatitis crónica del casco founder
dermatitis estival summer sores
dermatosis dermatosis
dermis dermis
derribar (el / al jinete) throw the rider
derribar un obstáculo knock down an obstacle
desalbardar put off the pack saddle
desaparejar unharness
desatento inattentive
desbocarse bolt
descabalgar dismount
descabestrar take off the halter

**descalificación** disqualification

**descendencia** descendants (the ~)

**descendente femenino** female descendant

**descinchar** ungird

**descolar** dock

**desembridar** unbridle

**desempate** jump off / jump-off

**desensillar** unsaddle

**desfile** parade

**desherrar** unshoe

**deshidratación** dehydration

**desmontar** dismount

**desobediencia** disobedience

**despapar** star-gaze

**desparasitar** deworm

**destetar** wean

**destete** weaning

**detrás de la mano** behind the bit

**diafragma** diaphragm

**diarrea** diarrhoea

**diente** tooth

**diente de lobo** wolf tooth

**dientes de leche** milk teeth

**dientes permanentes** permanent teeth

**diseñador (del curso)** course designer

**distancia** distance

**distensión de un tendón** tendon bow

**distensión sinovial** wind puff / windpuff

**distoma hepático** fluke (common liver ~)

**doble articulación (embocadura con ~)** double jointed mouthpiece

**doble hermana** full sister

**doble hermano** full brother

**doble valla con seto** oxer

**dócil** docile

**docilidad** docility

**doma clásica** dressage (classical ~)

**domar** school a horse

**domar (un caballo)** break (a horse)

**dominar el posterior** control the hindquarters

**don** Don (horse)

**dorso de carpa** arch-back

**dorso ensillado** saddle-back

**dos pistas (en / de ~)** two tracks (on ~)

**droga** drug

**drogado** doping

**duela del hígado** fluke (common liver ~)

**dueño** owner

**duodeno** duodenum

**durina** dourine

**ebonita** vulcanite

**echada** length

**ecografía** ultrasound scanning

**ecuestre** equestrian

**eczema** eczema

**edema** oedema

**efecto de las riendas** effect of reins

**electrólitos** electrolytes

**elevador del labio superior** levator muscle of upper lip

**eliminación** elimination

**eliminar** cull

**émascular** geld

**embalarse** bolt

**embocadura** mouth(piece)

**embridar** bridle (a horse)

**embrocación** embrocation

**eminencia piramidal** extensor process

**empinar** rear

**emplasto** poultice

**emplear las ancas** engage (the haunches)

**en la mano / rienda (caballo ~)** on the bit (horse ~)

**enalbardar** put on the pack saddle

**encabritamiento** rearing

**encabritarse** rear

**encapotado** over-bent

**encéfalo** brain

**encefalomielitis equina** encephalomyelitis (equine viral ~)

**encuadrarlo entre pantorrilla y rienda** keep the horse on the aids

**endeblez** weakness

**endocardio** endocardium

**endogamia** inbreeding

**endoparásito** internal parasite

**endurecimiento de los cartílagos de las patas** side bone ; sidebone

**enfermedad** disease

**enfermedad (del) navicular** navicular disease / lameness / bursitis

**enfermedad equina africana** African horse sickness

**enfermedad(es) del ganado caballar** disease(s) (horse / equine ~)

**enfermedad pulmonar obstructiva crónica** asthma

**enfisema** emphysema (pulmonary ~)

**enfoque** angle of the approach

**enganchar** hitch

**enganche** harnessed team

**enganche de seis caballos** six horse hitch

ensillar saddle
entrada entry
entrar / emplear el posterior engage (the haunches)
entre las manos y las piernas on the aids
entrenador trainer
entrenamiento training
entrenar train (a horse)
entresacar la crin thin the mane
envardura azoturia
epidermis epidermis
epiglotis epiglottis
epistaxis epistaxis
epitelio epithelium
epizootia epizooty
época de cubrición / monta service season
équidos equines (the ~)
equinos equines (the ~)
equipo equipment
equiseto horsetail
equitación horseback riding
equitación a mano derecha // izquierda riding to the right // left
equitación de exterior cross country riding
ergot ergot
error de recorrido error in the course
escapada run-out
escaparse bolt
escápula scapula
esclerótica sclera
escofina rasp
escofinar rasp
escroto scrotum
escuela de equitación riding school
esmalte enamel (of a tooth)
esmegma smegma
esófago oesophagus
espalda back
espalda shoulder
espalda adentro shoulder-in
espalda corvada arch-back
espalda hueca / hundida saddle-back
espalda inclinada sloping shoulder
espantarse shy
esparaván spavin
esparaván falso bog spavin
esparaván oculto occult spavin
esparaván óseo bone spavin
espéculo speculum
espejuelo chestnut

esperma sperm
esperma congelado frozen semen
espina de la escápula spine of the scapula
espina dorsal ; espinazo spine
espolear spur
esponja sponge
espuela spur
esquelético skeletal
esqueleto skeleton
esquilador clipper
esquilar clip
estabulación stabling
estación de monta / cubrición service station
estadista chart maker
estadístico chart maker
esternón sternum
estero de atrás back stretch ; backstretch
estevado bandy-legged (in the hindlimb)
estevado toed-in
estiércol manure
estómago stomach
estrato germinativo stratum germinativum (epidermidis Malpighii)
estrella ; estrellado star
estrellita small star
estribera stirrup leather / strap
estribo stirrup (of the ear)
　　　　stirrup
estro heat
　　　　bot fly (horse ~)
eutanasiar un caballo destroy a horse
evacuador transportador de estiércol barn cleaner (automatic ~)
examen (del) veterinario veterinary examination
exmoor Exmoor
exóstosis exostosis
experto expert
exterior external conformation
extremidad limb
falange phalanx
falda flap (of a saddle)
faldón (lateral) flap (of a saddle)
faldón de pesas weight cloth
falsa barbada lipstrap
falso faldón sweat flap (of a saddle)
falta fault
falta por / de tiempo time penalty
fance ventral border of mandible
faringe pharynx
fascia fascia

156

**fasciola hepática** fluke (common liver ~)

**fase de (concurso de) salto** jumping phase / test

**fase de steeple chase** steeplechase phase

**fase de velocidad y resistencia** endurance test / phase (speed and ~)

**fauces** intermandibular region / space

**favorito** favourite / favorite

**Federación Ecuestre Internacional** International Equestrian Federation

**fell poney** Fell (pony)

**fémur** femur

**ferrador** horseshoer

**festuca arundinacea** tall fescue (grass)

**festuca pratensis** meadow fescue

**fiador** throatlash ; throatlatch

**fibrocartílago lateral** side bone ; sidebone

**fiebre** fever

**fieltro** felt

**figura de ocho** figure (of) eight

**figuras escuelas** school figures

**filete** snaffle bit

**filete ovalado** egg-butt / eggbutt snaffle

**filiación** description

**filo cigomático** zygomatic arch

**final** finish

**fístula de la cruz** fistulous withers

**fisura del casco** sandcrack / sand crack

**flanco** flank

**fleo** timothy (grass)

**flexibilidad** suppleness

**flexión** flexion

**flexión en la nuca** bend at the poll

**fluido sinovial** synovial fluid

**folículo piloso** hair follicle

**forgador** blacksmith

**forja** farriery

**forjar** forge

**formol** formalin

**forraje** fodder

**forraje grosero** roughage

**forraje verde** green fodder

**fosa supraorbitaria** supraorbital fossa

**fósforo** phosphorus

**foso** ditch

**foso abierto** open ditch

**foso con barrera** ditch with rail(s)

**foso de agua** water jump (open ~)

**fotofobia** photophobia

**fractura** bone fracture

**fragua** farriery

**franquear un obstáculo** clear an obstacle

**freno** bit

**freno con rodadura** roller bit

**freno de palanca / curva** curb bit

**freno de palanca corta** kimblewick bit

**freno para dos riendas** pelham bit

**frente** forehead

**frontalera** browband

**fuego** firing

**fuera de concurso** excluded from competition

**fuera de la carrera** excluded from competition

**fuete** crop

**fuete de adiestramiento / dressage** dressage whip

**fuete de caza** hunting whip

**fuete de tiro** driving whip

**fullería** cheating

**fundas** weight cloth

**furioso** Furioso ; Furioso-North Star (horse)

**fusta (de montar)** crop

**fusta de dressage** dressage whip

**fustazo** stroke of the whip

**fuste** tree (of a saddle)

**fustigar** whip

**gabarro cartilaginoso** quittor (of horses)

**galápago** canker

**galopar** gallop

**galopar (corto)** canter

**galope** gallop

**galope (corto)** canter

**galope (en) falso** canter counter-lead

**galope a la derecha** canter (on the) right (lead)

**galope a la izquierda** canter (on the) left (lead)

**galope cruzado** disunited canter

**galope de carrera** racing gallop

**galope de trabajo** working canter

**galope desunido** disunited canter

**galope en firme** canter / gallop at / on the true lead

**galope en trocado** canter counter-lead

**galope falso** canter on / at the wrong lead

**galope largo** extended canter

**galope largo elevado** extended canter, half-seat

**galope medio** medium canter

**galope reunido** collected canter / gallop

**gamarra** martingale

**ganador** winner

**gancho para botas** boot hook

**ganchos** hooks

**ganglio** ganglion

**ganglio linfático** lymph node

**garañón** donkey stallion

**garañón** stallion

**garganta** throat

**garganta** intermandibular region / space

**garra** ergot

**garrapatas** ticks

**garrón** hock

**gas carbónico** carbon dioxide

**gasa** gauze

**gastritis** gastritis

**gastrophilus ; gastrófilo** bot fly (horse ~)

**gen(e)** gene

**genealogía** genealogy

**genético** genetic

**genitor** sire

**gestación** gestation

**gidranés** Gidran

**glande** glans penis

**glándula lacrimal** lacrimal gland

**glándula pituitaria** hypophysis

**glándula salivar** salivary gland

**glándula tiroidea** thyroid (gland)

**glándulas sebáceas** sebaceous glands

**glándulas sudoríparas** sweat glands

**glicerina** glycerin

**globo ocular / del ojo** eyeball

**golpe de hacha** dip in front of the withers

**gorra (de montar)** cap (hunting / skull / jockey's ~)

**grado de doma** schooling level

**grado de entrenamiento** degree of training

**gran metatarsiano** metatarsal bone (large / third ~)

**Gran Premio Olímpico de Doma** Grand Prix de Dressage

**granos** grains

**granos laminados / aplastados** rolled grains

**grasa para cascos** hoof grease

**gravamen** levy

**grieta en el casco** sandcrack / sand crack

**grietas** injury to the coronet (overreach / self ~)

**gripe (caballar / equina)** influenza (equine ~)

**grupa** croup

**grupa a fuera** renvers

**grupa adentro** haunches-in

**grupa al muro** renvers

**grupa caída** sloping croup

**grupa de ganso / pollo** goose rump

**grupa plana** flat croup

**grupo de los caballos en la carrera (el ~)** field

**guadarnés** saddlery; saddler's shop

**guante** glove

**guardabarros** mud guard

**guardia en la caballeriza** stable fatigue

**guarnicionería** saddlery; saddler's shop

**guarnicionero** saddler

**guarnicionero** harness-maker

**gurma** strangles

**gymkhana** gymkhana

**habito** habit

**hackney** Hackney (horse)

**handicap** handicap

**hannoveriano** Hanover horse; Hanoverian (horse)

**hebijón** billet (of a buckle)

**hebilla** buckle

**heces** droppings

**hematoma** haematoma

**hematuria** haematuria

**hembra** female

**hemiplejía laríngea** laryngeal hemiplegia / paralysis

**hemorragia** haemorrhage

**hemorragia pulmonar inducida por esfuerzo** epistaxis

**heno** hay

**herencia** heredity

**herida** wound
      injury

**herida de la silla** saddle sore

**herida podal por pinchazo** nail prick / tread

**hermanastra** half-sister

**hermanastro** half-brother

**herrador** horseshoer

**herradura (de caballo)** horseshoe

**herradura de aluminio** aluminium shoe / plate

**herradura de barra** bar shoe

**herraje** horseshoe
      horseshoeing

**herrar** shoe

**herrería** farriery

**herrero** horseshoer
      blacksmith

**hierba** grass

**hierro** iron
      branding (hot ~ mark)

**hierro de marcar** branding iron

**hígado** liver

**higroma carpiano** carpal hygroma

**higroma del codo** capped elbow

**higroma del corvejón** capped hock

hija daughter
hijo son
hinchazón swelling
hinchazón tarsal thoroughpin
hipódromo race track ; racetrack
hipófisis hypophysis
hipología hippology
hipomóvil horse-drawn
hocico muzzle
hoja falsa sweat flap (of a saddle)
hoja lateral flap (of a saddle)
hombre del caballo horse person
hombro shoulder
hombro angulado sloping shoulder
hombro derecho upright shoulder
hongo (sombrero ~) bowler (hat)
horcate hame
horma de bota tree (boot ~)
hormiguillo hollow wall
huasca larga lunge(ing) whip
huélfago broken wind
huella scent
hueso bone
hueso cigomático zygomatic bone
hueso corona middle phalanx
hueso costal rib (bone)
hueso cuartilla / cuarta proximal phalanx
hueso del pie / casco distal phalanx
hueso esfenoides sphenoid bone
hueso etmoides ethmoid bone
hueso frontal frontal bone
hueso hioides hyoid apparatus / bone
hueso incisivo incisive bone
hueso interparietal interparietal bone
hueso lacrimal lacrimal bone
hueso nasal nasal bone
hueso navicular distal sesamoid bone
hueso occipital occipital bone
hueso palatino palatine bone
hueso parietal parietal bone
hueso petroso del temporal petrous part (of temporal bone)
hueso pisiforme accessory carpal bone
hueso podal distal phalanx
hueso premaxilar incisive bone
hueso pterigoides pterygoid bone
hueso pubis pubis (bone)
hueso temporal temporal bone
huesos carpianos carpal bones
huesos del carpo carpal bones

huesos metatarsianos metatarsal bones
huesos tarsianos tarsal bones
huida flight
huir bolt
húmero humerus
hunter irlandés Irish hunter
ictericia jaundice
igualar la crin thin the mane
ijada ; ijar flank
íleon ileum
ilion ilium
impulsión impulsion
incisivo (central) central incisor
incisivo del borde corner incisor
incisivos incisors
incitador teaser (stallion)
independencia de las ayudas independence of the aids
índice indicator
infección infection
infeccioso infectious
infecunda barren
inflamación inflammation
influenza (equina) influenza (equine ~)
infosura founder
inmovilidad immobility
inmunidad immunity
innocuidad safety margin
inscripción entry
insecticida insecticide
insecto dañino pest (insect)
inseminación artificial artificial insemination
inseminar inseminate
instinto instinct
instinto gregario herding instinct
instructor de equitación riding instructor
intestino intestine
intestino delgado small intestine
intestino grueso large intestine
ir al paso walk
iris iris
irritación chafing
isabela ; perla isabela buckskin
isquion ischium
izquierdo (caballo ~) toed-out
jaca pony
jaca de silla riding pony
jaeces harnessed team
jaez tack ; tackle
jalar (a mano) pull

159

**jalonamiento del recorrido** marking of the course

**jáquima** hackamore

**jarrete** hock

**jauría** hounds (the ~)

**jefe de equipo** Chef d'équipe

**jeringuilla ; jeringa** syringe

**jinete** rider

**jinete de circo** circus rider

**jinete de concurso completo** event rider

**jinete de doma** dressage rider

**jinete de prueba completa / militar** event rider

**jinete de salto** show jumper (rider)

**jockey** jockey

**jodhpurs** Jodhpurs ; jodhpurs ; Jodhpur breeches

**joroba del lomo** point of hip

**Juegos Olímpicos** Olympic Games

**juez** judge

**juez auxiliar** assistant judge

**juez de obstáculos** obstacle judge

**juez de salida** starting judge

**jugo gástrico** gastric juice

**juicio** judging

**juzgamiento por conformación** judgment of (external) conformation

**labio inferior** lower lip

**labio superior** upper lip

**labios** lips (of the mouth)

**lactancia** suckling

**lado de partida** take-off side (of an obstacle)

**lado de recepción** landing side (of an obstacle)

**ladrería** cysticercosis

**lamedura** salt lick

**laminitis** laminitis (acute ~)

**landó** landau

**lanzada** levade

**lanzamiento** take off impulsion

**larga de cuartilla** long pastern

**largo de lo estribo** bottom of a stirrup

**laringe** larynx

**laringitis** laryngitis

**larva** larva

**lastimados de verano** summer sores

**latigazo** whiplash

**látigo** whip

**látigo de caza** hunting whip

**látigo de coche** driving whip

**látigo de picadero** lunge(ing) whip

**látigo largo** lunge(ing) whip

**latiguillo** girth strap

**lazo** lasso

**legra (cuchillo de ~)** hoof knife

**lengua** tongue

**leopardo** leopard

**levantar (al trote** post (to the trot)

**libertad de la lengua** port

**libro genealógico** stud-book (general ~)

**libro genealógico / registro** stud-book ; stud book

**liendre** louse egg

**ligamento** ligament

**ligamento de la nuca** nuchal ligament

**ligamento suspensorio** suspensory ligament

**ligereza** lightness

**lima** rasp
    file (finishing ~)

**limar** rasp

**limpiar** groom

**limpiar un casco** pick out a foot

**limpieza** grooming

**linaza** linseed

**línea blanca** white line (of the hoof)

**línea de final** finish(ing) line

**línea de llegada** finish(ing) line

**línea de procedencia** lineage

**línea de salida** starting line

**línea de sangre** lineage

**línea femenina / materna** female line

**línea masculina / paterna** male line

**linfa** lymph

**linfangitis** lymphangitis

**linimento** liniment

**lipizano** Lipizzaner

**líquido sinovial** synovial fluid

**lista** stripe

**litera** litter

**liverpool** liverpool

**llantén** plantain

**llegada** landing

**llegada** finish

**llegar** land

**locutor** announcer (house / track ~)

**lombriz** worm

**lombriz del pulmón** lungworm ; lung worm

**lombriz solitaria** tapeworm

**lomo blando** weak back

**lomo(s)** loin(s)

**longitud corporal** body length

**longitud de la cabeza** length of the head

**lucero** broad stripe
**lucero** star
**lugar de batida** take-off side (of an obstacle)
**lugar de contacto** landing side (of an obstacle)
**lusitano** Lusitanian horse
**machete** sole knife
**macho de fragua** sledge hammer
**macho romo** hinny (horse ~)
**machorra** barren
**madre** broodmare ; brood mare
**madre (yegua ~)** dam
**maestro de equitación** riding master
**maestro de la caza** master of the hunt
**maestro de los perros** huntsman
**maíz** corn
**mal de cruz** fistulous withers
**mal del coito** dourine
**manada** herd
**mancha blanca** white marking on a limb / leg
**manco** lame
**mandíbula** mandible
**maneas** breeding hopples / hobbles
**manejabilidad del caballo** handiness of the horse
**manejo de las riendas** manner of handling / holding reins
**manga** round
**mano** hand
**mano (a ~ derecha // izquierda)** lead (on / at the right // left ~)
**mano izquierda** left foreleg
**manos (acción de ~)** hands (action of the ~)
**manos (del caballo)** forelegs
**manta (para caballos)** blanket (horse ~)
**manta para enfriar** cooler (horse ~)
**manta para proteger de moscas** fly sheet (scrim ~)
**manta sudadera** saddle blanket
**mantilla ; manta** saddle pad
**mantilla de peso / plomo** weight cloth
**manzana** apple
**máquina de rasurar** clipper
**marca** marking
**marca (a hierro) candente** branding (hot ~ mark)
**marca de / a fuego** branding (hot ~ mark)
**marcación a fuego** branding (hot ~)
**marcación en frío** freeze branding
**marcha** gait
**marchar al paso** walk
**marchar de andadura** amble

**maremmano** Maremma / Maremmana horse
**marfil** dentine
**marrón** brown
**martillo** hammer (of the ear)
**martillo de dos manos** sledge hammer
**martillo de herrador** hammer (shoeing / driving / nailing ~)
**martingala** martingale
**martingala de anillas / anillos** running martingale
**mascarilla** blinker hood
**maslo** dock
**masticar la embocadura** champ (the bit)
**mastín** hound
**matadero** slaughterhouse
**matadura** saddle sore
**matar** kill
**matriz** uterus
**maxilar (superior)** upper jaw
**mechón** forelock
**meconio** meconium
**media gamarra** false martingale
**media hermana** half-sister
**media parada** half-halt
**media pirueta** half-pirouette
**media sangre** half-bred
**media sangre irlandés** Irish hunter
**media vuelta** half-volt ; half volte
**medicamento ; medicina** medicine
**medicina veterinaria** veterinary medicine
**medidas de alzada** height measurement
**medio calzado blanco** white to half-cannon
**medio hermano** half-brother
**médula espinal** spinal cord
**médula ósea** bone marrow
**mejilla** cheek
**mejillera** cheekpiece
**mejora de caballos** horse improvement
**melaza** molasses
**melena** mane
**membrana nictitante** nictitating membrane
**menear la cola** switch the tail
**mentón** chin (swelling)
**menudillo** fetlock
**mesa** table
**mesenterio** mesentery ; mesenterium
**mestengo** mustang ; Mustang
**mesteño** mustang ; Mustang
**mestizo** half-bred
**metacarpo** metacarpus

161                                    Español => English

**metatarso** metatarsus

**metritis contagiosa equina** contagious equine metritis

**metro** measuring stick
    metre / meter

**miasis del gusano barrenado** cutaneous blowfly myiasis

**miedo** fear

**miembro anterior** forelimb ; foreleg

**miembro posterior** hind leg / limb

**miembros** limbs (the ~)

**milla** mile

**miocardio** cardiac muscle

**mioclonia de las patas traseras** stringhalt

**mioglobinuria** azoturia

**miorelajante** muscle-relaxant drug

**moho** mildew

**molares** molars ; molar teeth

**monta** service

**monta a mano** hand service

**monta natural** natural service

**montar** cover (a mare)

**montar (a caballo)** mount (a horse)

**montar a horcajadas** ride astride

**montar a la amazona** ride side-saddle

**montar a mujeriegas** ride side-saddle

**montar a pelo** ride bareback

**montar al paso** ride at the walk

**montura** saddle

**montura de amazona** sidesaddle

**montura vaquera** western saddle

**monturía** saddlery; saddler's shop

**morder** bite

**morgan** Morgan

**morro** muzzle

**mosca** house fly ; housefly

**mosca de ciervo** deer fly

**mosca de establo** stable fly

**mosca negra** black fly

**moscas de caballo** horseflies

**movimiento** movement

**mozo de caballos** groom

**mozo de cuadra** stable boy / man

**mozo de perros** whipper-in

**mucosa** mucosa

**muda** shedding

**muermo** glanders (equine ~)

**muestra** sample

**mula** mule (female ~)

**mula (roma)** hinny (female ~)

**mulero** muleteer

**muletero** muleteer

**mulo** mullet
    hinny

**mulo (romo)** hinny (horse ~)

**multa** fine

**muro** wall

**muro de piedra** stone wall

**músculo ancóneo** anconeus muscle

**músculo bíceps del brazo** biceps brachii muscle

**músculo bíceps femoral** biceps femoris muscle

**músculo braquial** brachialis muscle

**músculo cardiaco** cardiac muscle

**músculo cutáneo abdominal** cutaneus trunci muscle

**músculo deltoides** deltoid(eus) muscle

**músculo esternofalico** sternocephalicus muscle

**músculo estriado** striated muscle

**músculo extensor** extensor muscle

**músculo extensor común digital / de las falanges** common digital extensor muscle

**músculo extensor digital lateral** lateral digital extensor muscle

**músculo flexor** flexor muscle

**músculo flexor digital profundo** deep digital flexor muscle

**músculo flexor oblicuo de las falanges** medial head of the deep digital flexor muscle

**músculo glúteo superficial** superficial gluteal muscle

**músculo gran dorsal** latissimus dorsi muscle

**músculo involuntario** smooth muscle

**músculo largo dorsal** longissimus (dorsi) muscle

**músculo liso** smooth muscle

**músculo longissimus dorsi** longissimus (dorsi) muscle

**músculo masetero** masseter muscle

**músculo voluntario** striated muscle

**muserola** noseband

**muserola de ocho** cross-over noseband

**muserola doble** flash noseband

**muslo** thigh

**mustango ; mustang** mustang ; Mustang

**nabo** turnip

**nacimiento de la cola** tail head

**nalga** buttock

**nariz** nostril

**nariz acarnerada / romana** roman nose

**nefritis** nephritis

negro black
nematodo nematode
nervio nerve
nervio óptico optic nerve
nervioso nervous
neumonía pneumonia
neurectomía neurectomy
new forestal New-Forest (pony)
nieta granddaughter
nieto grandson
nuca poll
nuquera headpiece
nutrir feed
obediencia obedience
obstáculo obstacle
obstáculo doble double (obstacle)
obstáculo escalonado / en escalera step (obstacle)
obstáculo fijo solid fence
obstáculo natural natural obstacle
obstáculo simple simple obstacle
obstáculo triple triple (combination)
obstáculo vertical vertical
ocho (de cifra) figure (of) eight
oído ear
oído (interno // medio // externo) ear (internal // middle // external ~)
ojiblanco silver eye
ojo eye
ojo (para los suplementos) hardy / hardie hole
ojos eyes
oldenburg ; oldenburgo Oldenburg (horse)
olécranon olecranon
olfato scent
ollar nostril
ombligo navel
omóplato scapula
órbita del ojo eye socket
oreja ear
oreja péndula / gacha / caída lop-eared
orina urine
osificarse ossify
osteítis osteitis
otitis otitis
ovario ovary
oviducto uterine tube
oxer oxer
oxer cuadrado square oxer
oxer de barras desiguales ascending oxer
oxer sueco Swedish oxer

oxiuro pinworm (horse ~)
paca de heno hay bale
pacer graze
paddock paddock
padre sire
padrillo stallion
paja straw
paja picada / cortada chopped straw
paladar palate
palafrén palfrey
palafrenero groom
palas central incisors
palomino palomino
páncreas pancreas
pantalón de caza beige breeches
pantalón de montar breeches
pantalonero breeches-maker
papera / papo (del caballo) strangles
parada halt
      halt
parada de cubrición service station
parada de sementales del Estado national stud
parar ; pararse halt
parásito parasite
pared wall
pared del casco wall (of the hoof)
parénquima parenchyma
parición foaling
parir foal
parótida parotid gland
párpado interno nictitating membrane
párpados eyelids
partida start
partir break into
parto (de la yegua) foaling
parturición foaling
paseo ride (trail ~)
paseo a caballo pleasure
pasmudo saddle sore
paso step
      walk
paso castellano Spanish walk
paso con riendas largas walk on a long rein
paso de costado side step
paso de gallo stringhalt
paso español Spanish walk
paso extendido extended walk
paso fino Paso Fino
paso franco free walk

163                              Español => English

paso largo extended walk
paso libre free walk
paso medio / ordinario medium walk
paso peruano (caballo de ~) Peruvian paso /
  ambler
paso reunido collected walk
passage; pasaje passage
pastar pasture
pastar graze
pasto pasture
pastoreo en reclusión zero-grazing
pasturaje pasture
pata limb
pata(s) de sable sickle hock(s)
patas traseras hind-legs
patear kick
patizambo knock-knees
pechera breast collar / plate
pecho chest
pecho (parte delantera del ~) breast
pecho angosto narrow chest
pecho de pichón pigeon breast
pedigrí ; pedigree pedigree
Pegaso Pegasus
peine ; peineta comb
pelaje coat (colour)
      coat
pelaje de nacimiento birth coat
pelero saddle pad
pelham pelham bit
pelo hair (a ~)
pelo brillante glossy coat
pelo de rata mouse-dun ; mouse-coloured
pelo de verano summer coat
pelo del invierno winter coat
pelo(s) coat
pelo sombrío dull coat
pelvis pelvis
penalidad de tiempo time penalty
pene penis
penicilina penicillin
pepsina pepsin
percherón Percheron
pericardio pericardium
perilla pommel
perímetro de la caña cannon's circumference
perímetro torácico girth's circumference
perineo perineum
perioples periople
periostio periosteum

periostitis periostitis ; periosteitis
peritoneo peritoneum
peritonitis peritonitis
peroné fibula
perrada ; perrería hounds (the ~)
perrera kennel
perro de caza hound
persona a caballo horse person
pesar weigh
      weigh in
pescuezo crest
pesebre hay rack
peso de handicap handicap weight
pestaña clip
pestaña / agarradera de punta toe clip
peste equina africana African horse sickness
petral breast collar
petral (pecho-~) breast collar / plate
piafar paw the ground
piafe ; piaffer piaffé ; piaffer ; piaffe
pica pica
picadero riding school
picadero indoor arena
picazo pinto ; pintado
pie foot
pie de paloma toed-in
pie zopo club foot
piedra de sal salt lick
piel skin
pienso fodder
pierna gaskin
pierna limb
pierna activa active leg
pierna de adentro inside leg
pierna interior / interna inside leg
pierna pasiva inactive leg
pierna posterior / trasera hind leg / limb
pieza para mejilla cheekpiece
pigmento pigment
pilares pillars
píloro pylorus
pinchazo quicking
pintado ; pinto pinto ; pintado
pinza central incisor
pinza de casco toe (of a hoof)
pinza de casco hoof tester(s)
pinza de palpación / testar hoof tester(s)
pinzas central incisors
pinzas para sacar los clavos de la clavera
      crease nail puller

**pío** pinto ; pintado

**pío negro** piebald

**piojo** louse (biting ~)

**piojos** lice

**piquete para el casco** hoof pick

**piroplasmosis** babesiasis ; babesiosis

**pirueta (sobre el tercio posterior)** pirouette

**pirueta a galope** pirouette at a canter

**pirueta directa** pirouette

**pirueta inversa** reversed pirouette

**pirueta sobre el tercio anterior** reversed pirouette

**pisar el recorrido** walk (over) the course

**pista** track (in a riding arena)
   scent

**pista cubierta** indoor arena

**pista de doma** dressage ring / arena

**planicie del ijar** hollow of the flank

**plano** face (of an anvil)

**plano del recorrido ; plano por el curso** plan of the course

**plantado adelante // de atrás** camped (out)

**plantaina** plantain

**plasma** plasma (blood ~)

**pleura** pleura

**pleuresía** pleuritis ; pleurisy

**pleuroneumonía contagiosa de los equinos** equine contagious pleuropneumonia

**plexo solar** solar plexus

**pliegue de la babilla** flank fold

**podredumbre de la ranilla** thrush

**pollero** pelham bit

**polo** polo

**polvo** dust

**poner la lengua sobre el freno** get the tongue over the bit

**póney** pony

**póney de polo** polo pony

**póney de Shetland** Shetland (pony) ; Shetlie

**póney galés / galense** Welsh pony

**poni / pony** pony

**portalón** port

**portante** amble

**posición de salto** forward seat

**posición del jinete** position of the rider

**posología** dosage

**poste** stand (of an obstacle)

**potrilla ; potranca ; potra** filly (foal)

**potrillo // potrilla** foal (colt // filly ~)

**potrillo // potrilla de un año** yearling (colt // filly)

**potrillo // potrilla lactante** milk foal

**potrillo destetado // potrilla destetada** weanling

**potro // potra de un año** yearling (colt // filly)

**potro (con arzón)** pommel horse

**potro destetado // potra destetada** weanling

**potro macho / entero** colt

**precio** price

**premiar** reward

**premio** prize

**premio (de honor)** prize

**premio (en dinero)** prize (cash / money ~)

**premio al criador** breeder's premium

**premio San Jorge** Prix St. George

**premolares** premolars ; premolar teeth

**prepucio** sheath

**presa** quarry

**presentar (un caballo) a la mano** show (a horse) in hand

**presidente del jurado** president of the jury

**primera articulación interfalangiana** pastern joint

**primera dentición** milk (set of) teeth

**primera falange** proximal phalanx

**primera vértebra cervical** atlas

**procreación en consanguinidad** inbreeding

**procreación incestuosa** incestuous breeding

**producto de cruza** crossbred (animal)

**profesor de equitación** riding instructor

**profundidad de los flancos / del abdomen** depth of flank

**profundidad del pecho** depth of chest

**progenitor (padre)** stud horse

**prognatismo (de la mandíbula)** prognathism / prognathia (mandibular ~)

**programa** programme

**prole** offspring

**promazin** acepromazin

**propiedad** ownership

**propietario** owner

**próstata** prostate

**protector** boot (for horses)

**proteína** protein

**prueba** trial

**prueba completa / militar** horse trial

**prueba con desempate** competition with jump-off

**prueba contra el reloj** scurry jumping (with time factor)

**prueba de (la) descendencia** progeny test(ing)

prueba de adiestramiento para principiantes basic dressage test

prueba de consanguinidad inbreeding test

prueba de doma (clásica) dressage test

prueba de fondo endurance test / phase (speed and ~)

prueba de la flexión flexion test

prueba de potencia puissance jumping

prueba de saltos en pista jumping phase / test

prueba de tres días three-day event

prurito itching

puente arch

puente de la nariz bridge of the nose

puerta gate

puesta en mano bringing in hand

puja bid

pujar make a higher bid

pulgada ; pulgarada inch

pulmón lung

pulmonía pneumonia

pulpa de betarragas sugar beet pulp

pulpa de remolacha(s) sugar beet pulp

pulpa dental pulp tooth

pulso pulse

punta point (of a nail)

punta de pie toe (of a hoof)

punta del anca point of hip

punta del corvejón point of hock

punta del hombro point of shoulder

punta del talón bulb (of a heel)

puntas de fuego pin firing (scars)

puntilla point (of a nail)

punto de bonificación bonus point

punto de partida starting point

punto de penalidad penalty point

punto de picar / saltar take off point

pupila pupil

pura sangre purebred ; pure bred

pura sangre inglés Thoroughbred

pus pus

queratina keratin

quieto quiet

quijada jaw

quijera cheekpiece

quiste cyst

quiste ovárico ovarian cyst

quitar las lombrices deworm

rábano blanco horseradish

rabia rabies

rabo tail

rabón docked tail(ed) ; docked

ración de conservación / mantenimiento / sostenimiento maintenance ration

ración diaria daily ration

ración para trabajo working ration

ración suplementaria / extra supplementary ration

radio radius

radiografía X-ray examination

raid long-distance ride

raíz tooth root

rajadura de arena sandcrack / sand crack

rama branch (of a shoe)

ramplón (de herradura) calk ; caulk ; calkin ; caulkin

ranilla frog

raquitismo rickets

rasguños scratches

raspa rasp

raspador para secar sweat scraper

raspaduras scratches

raspar rasp

rasqueta currycomb
metal curry comb

rasquetear curry

rastro scent

rasurar clip

ratonero mouse-dun ; mouse-coloured

raya de mulo dorsal stripe / list / band

raza breed
sandcrack / sand crack

reacio stubborn

rebajar un casco pare (a hoof)

rebuznar bray

recelador ; recela teaser (stallion)

recesivo recessive

rechinar las dientes grind the teeth

reconocimiento veterinario veterinary examination

recorrido course

recorrido a campo través cross-country course

recorrido de obstáculos course of obstacles

recorrido sin faltas clear (round)

recortar un casco pare (a hoof)

recta (embocadura ~) straight bar bit / snaffle

recto rectum

reculada rein-back ; reinback

recular back

red para heno hay bag / net

redaño mesentery ; mesenterium

redhibición annulment
registro de raza stud-book (general ~)
regularidad regularity
rehusar refuse
rehúse refusal
relinchar neigh
relincho neigh
remache atornillado calk (screw-in ~)
remate auction (sale)
remedio medicine
remetimiento (del tercio posterior)
  engagement (of the hindquarters)
remitido adelante // de atrás standing under
remo limb
remo delantero forelimb ; foreleg
remo trasero hind leg / limb
remolacha beet
remolino whorl
remolque (para transporte de caballos)
  trailer (horse ~)
rengo lame
renguear limp
renguera lameness
representa a su raza true to type
reprise dressage test
reprise libre kur
reproductores (animales ~) breeding stock
resabiado stubborn
resistencia resistance
resistencia stamina
retina retina
retirar withdraw
retranca breeching
retroceder back
reunido collected
reunión collection (of a horse)
reunir collect (a horse)
reunir el posterior engage (the haunches)
revulsivo (agente ~) blister ; blistering
ría water jump (open ~)
rienda rein
rienda de adentro inner rein
rienda de afuera outside rein
rienda de atar side rein
rienda de filete snaffle-rein
rienda de plancha draw rein
rienda del bocado curb-rein
rienda exterior outside rein
rienda interna inner rein
rienda larga long rein

rienda suelta hanging rein
riendas reins
riendas reins
riendas (ayuda de ~) hands (action of the ~)
riendas largas (con ~) long rein (on / at a ~)
rincón corner
rinoneumonitis equina viral rhinopneumonitis
  (equine viral ~)
riñón kidney
riñón(/ones) loin(s)
roano bay roan
rodilla knee
rodilla bien definida well-defined knee
rodilla de carnero calf-knee / calf knee
rodilla hueca calf-knee / calf knee
rodillera knee cap (boot)
rollo knee roll
rollo de sombra shadow roll ; shadow blind
romper al galope start at the canter
romper al paso start at a walk
romper al trote start at a trot
roncador laryngeal hemiplegia / paralysis
ronzal halter
roña mange (horse ~)
roñeta sole knife
roseta rosette
rótula patella
rozar brush
sacabocados pritchel (hot work ~)
sacabotas bootjack
sacar la lengua hang out the tongue
sacar una herradura unshoe
saco de montar riding coat
sacro (hueso ~) sacrum
sal salt
salegar salt lick
salida start
saliva saliva
saltar cover (a mare)
saltar jump
saltar limpio clear (jump ~)
salto jump
salto a pie firme standing jump
salto ancho spread fence / jump
salto de agua water jump (open ~)
salto de altura high jump
salto de anchura spread jump
salto de obstáculos jumping
salto de potencia puissance jumping
salto por equipos team jumping (competition)

salto volando flying jump

salud soundness

saludo salute

salvado bran

sanando healing

sangre blood

sangría blood-letting

sano sound

sarna mange (horse ~)

sarna sarcóptica sarcoptic mange

sastre tailor

sebo sebum

secreción discharge

segunda articulación interfalangiana coffin joint

segunda dentición permanent (set of) teeth

segunda falange middle phalanx

segundo caballo second horse

seis barras six bars

selección breeding selection

seleccionador y criador breeder

selenio selenium

semen sperm

semen congelado frozen semen

semental (caballo ~) stallion

semi parada half-halt

seno frontal frontal sinus

seno maxilar maxillary sinus

sentarse delante del movimiento sit too far forward

sentarse detrás del movimiento behind the motion

señal (de referencia) marker letter

serpentina serpentine

sesamoideo distal distal sesamoid bone

sesamoideos proximales proximal sesamoid bones

seto hedge

sien temple

silla (de montar) saddle

silla de cacería / cazamiento hunting saddle

silla de carrera racing saddle

silla de doma dressage saddle

silla de polo polo saddle

silla de salto jumping saddle

silla francesa French Saddle (horse)

silla inglesa English saddle

sillero saddler

sillín saddle (harness ~)

sin voluntad unwilling (horse)

sinovia synovial fluid

sistema linfático lymphatic system

sistema nervioso cerebroespinal / central central nervous system

sistema nervioso parasimpático parasympathetic nervous system

sistema nervioso simpático sympathetic nervous system

sistema nervioso vegetativo / autónomo autonomic nervous system

sístole systole

sobre la brida / el freno above the bit

sobre las manos heavy on the forehand

sobrecaña splint

sobrehueso (en la caña) splint

sobrehueso de la corona low ringbone

sobrehueso de la cuartilla high ringbone

sobrepasar overreach

sobrepie // sobremano ringbone ; ring bone ; ring-bone

sobrepujar make a higher bid

sociedad de cría breed society

sodio sodium

soltar las riendas lengthen the reins

soltura suppleness

sombrero de copa top-hat

sombrero de dos picos bicorne

sombrero de tres picos tricorne

soporte cup

sorgo sorghum

sorteo draw

steeple chase steeplechase

subasta auction (sale)

subir a la silla get in the saddle

subir y bajar la cabeza bob the head

subirse a la parra get on one's high horse

sudación sweating

sudadero saddle pad

sudor sweat

suela sole

suero serum

suero antitetánico antitetanus serum

suero antivenenoso antivenene ; antivenin

sulfamida sulfonamide

sulky sulky

superficie moledora dental table

suspensión suspension

suspensión (tiempo de ~) suspension (moment of ~)

sutura suture

taba talus

tábanos ; tabarros horseflies

**tabla** face (of an anvil)

**tabla de separación en las cuadras** swinging rail

**tabla dentaria** dental table

**tablas (barrera / valla de ~)** plank(s)

**taenia** tapeworm

**tajadera** hardy

**talabartería** saddlery; saddler's shop

**talabartero** saddler
                 harness-maker

**taladro ; taladrador** pritchel (hot work ~)

**talón** heel

**talón de pollo** capped hock

**talud** bank

**tapa (del casco)** wall (of the hoof)

**tara** defect

**tarso** hock

**tarsotibial** talus

**tatuaje** tattooing

**técnica de montar** riding technique

**tejido celular subcutáneo** subcutis

**temperamento** temperament

**temperatura** temperature

**tenaza de corte** nipper(s) (hoof ~)

**tenaza de descalzar** puller (shoe ~)

**tenaza de remachar** clincher(s) / clencher(s) (nail ~)

**tendinitis** tendinitis

**tendón** tendon

**tendón arqueado** bowed tendon

**tendón de Aquiles** common calcanean / calcaneal tendon

**tendón extensor digital** common (digital) extensor tendon

**tendón flexor** flexor tendon

**tendón flexor digital profundo** deep (digital) flexor tendon

**tendón flexor profundo (de las falanges)** deep (digital) flexor tendon

**tenia** taenia / tenia

**tenia** tapeworm

**tercer metacarpiano** metacarpal bone (large / third ~)

**tercer párpado** nictitating membrane

**tercera falange** distal phalanx

**tercera metatarsiano** metatarsal bone (large / third ~)

**tercio anterior** forehand

**tercio medio** barrel (of the horse)

**tercio posterior / trasero** rear end

**terco** stubborn

**termocauterio** firing iron

**terpentina** turpentine

**test sanguíneo** blood test

**testera** headpiece

**testículo** testicle ; testis

**testuz** bridge of the nose

**tétanos ; tétano** tetanus

**tibia** tibia

**tiempo** time

**tiempo concedido** time allowed

**tiempo límite / máximo** time limit

**tierra (a la ~)** bay (to be / stand at ~)

**tijerilla** running martingale

**timbre** bell

**timo** thymus

**tímpano** tympanic membrane

**tiña** ringworm

**tipo racial** breed type

**tira al tipo / a la raza** true to type

**tirabotas** boot hook

**tirado por caballos** horse-drawn

**tirante** trace

**tirar el jinete** throw the rider

**tiro** wind-sucking
                 harnessed team

**tiro de apoyo** crib biting

**tiro de un caballo** one-horse draught

**tiroides** thyroid (gland)

**tobillo** ankle

**tomar el galope** start at the canter

**tomar el paso** start at a walk

**tomar el trote** start at a trot

**tórax** thorax

**tordillo mosqueado** flea-bitten grey

**tordo** blue roan
                 grey

**tordo / tordillo rodado** dapple(d) grey / gray

**tordo obscuro** dark grey

**torneo** tournament

**torso** trunk

**tos** cough

**toscano** Maremma / Maremmana horse

**toser** cough

**trabajar a la cuerda** lunge / longe

**trabajo a la mano** work in hand

**trabajo de dos pistas** work on two tracks

**trabajo en los pilares** work between the pillars

**trabajo en riendas largas** work in long reins

**trabas** breeding hopples / hobbles

**trakehner** Trakehner ; Trakehnen horse

**trampa** cheating

trampear cheat
tranca swinging rail
tranquera swinging rail
tranquilizante tranquillizer
transición transition
tráquea trachea
trasquilar clip
trazado de recorrido line of the course
trébol clover
trementina turpentine
trenzar plait
tricornio tricorne
trigo wheat
trigo sarraceno buckwheat
triples de barras triple bar(s)
trismo tetanus
trochanter mayor greater trochanter (of the femur)
tróclea femoral femoral trochlea
trofeo trophy
trombosis thrombosis
trompa de Eustaquio auditory tube
troncar dock
tronco trunk
tronco (de dos) caballos horse team, two abreast
tropezar stumble
trotador trotter
trotador americano Standardbred
trotador francés French trotter
trotar trot
trote trot
trote a la inglesa posting trot
trote de trabajo working trot
trote extenso extended trot
trote largo extended trot
trote largo a la inglesa extended trot rising
trote largo levantado extended trot rising
trote largo sentado extended trot sitting
trote levantado trot rising
trote levantado posting trot
trote medio / ordinario medium trot
trote ordinario sentado medium trot sitting
trote reunido collected trot
trote reunido sentado collected trot sitting
trote sentado sitting trot
trotinar jig
truncar (la cola) dock
tuberosidad calcánea calcanean tuber
tuberosidad coxal coxal tuber

tuberosidad isquiática ischial tuber
tuberosidad sacra sacral tuber
tubo auditivo auditory tube
tubo digestivo digestive tract
tupé forelock
ubre udder (the ~)
úlcera ulcer
ulceraciones de verano summer sores
ungulados ungulates (the ~)
unidad animal / ganadera animal unit
uréter ureter
uretra urethra
urticaria urticaria
útero uterus
uveítis equine recurrent uveitis
vacuna vaccine
vacunación vaccination
vagina vagina
vaina sheath
vaina sinovial synovial sheath
valla con barras brush and rails
vaquerillo jockey
vaquero cowboy
varal shaft
vaso linfático lymphatic vessel
vejiga articular blanda wind gall / puff (articular ~)
vejiga de la orina bladder (urinary ~)
vejiga tendinosa blanda wind gall / puff (tendinous ~)
vejigatorio blister ; blistering
velo del paladar soft palate
velocidad speed
velocista sprinter
vena vein
vena axilar axillary vein
vena cefálica cephalic vein
vena cefálica accesoria accessory cephalic vein
vena facial facial vein
vena femoral femoral vein
vena porta portal vein
vencedor winner
venda bandage
venda para la cola tail wrap
vendaje bandage
vender en pública subasta auction
verme worm
vermífugo anthelmintic (drug)
vértebra vertebra
vértebras cervicales cervical vertebrae

**vértebras coccígeas** caudal vertebrae
**vértebras de la cola** caudal vertebrae
**vértebras lumbares** lumbar vertebrae
**vértebras sacras** sacral vertebrae
**vértebras torácicas** thoracic vertebrae
**vertical** vertical
**vertical sobre zanja** ditch with rail(s)
**vesicatorio** blister ; blistering
**vesícula seminal** vesicular gland
**vestíbulo vaginal** vestibule of vagina
**veterinario** veterinary
**veterinario** veterinarian
**veterinario especialista en caballos** equine veterinarian
**vicio** vice
**victoria** win
**vientre** belly
**viruela equina** horse pox ; horsepox
**virus de la rabia** rabies rhabdovirus / virus
**vitamina** vitamin
**volquete** swing-tree
**voltear (al jinete)** throw the rider
**volteo ; voltereta** vaulting
**voluntario** willing (horse)
**volver ancho** turn wide
**volver corto** turn short / sharply
**vólvulo intestinal** volvulus
**vómer** vomer
**voz** voice
**vuelta** volte ; volt
**vuelta (a la izquierda // derecha)** volte (to the left // right)
**vuelta (sobre el anterior // posterior)** turn (on the forehand // haunches)
**vuelta al paso** volte at the walk
**vuelta sobre el anterior** turn on the forehand
**vuelta sobre el posterior / la grupa** turn on the haunches / quarters / hocks
**vulva** vulva
**wurtembergués** Württemberg horse
**yearling** yearling (colt // filly)
**yegua** mare
**yegua con su potro ; yegua con rastra** lactating mare
**yegua de cría** broodmare ; brood mare
**yegua de vientre** broodmare ; brood mare
**yegua en gestación** mare in foal
**yegua lactante** lactating mare
**yegua llena** mare in foal
**yegua madre** broodmare ; brood mare

**yegua madre con potro lactante** lactating mare
**yegua original** tap root / taproot mare
**yegua preñada** mare in foal
**yegua vacía** empty mare
**yeguada** stud farm
         mare keeping
**yeguada de cría** breeding herd
**yerba** grass
**yeyuno** jejunum
**yodo** iodine
**yunque** anvil (of the ear)
         anvil
**yunque de espiga / cola** anvil (portable ~)
**zafarse** run out
**zahína** sorghum
**zahones** chaps
**zaino** whole colour(ed)
**zambarco** belly band
**zanahoria** carrot
**zanja** ditch
**zanja abierta** open ditch
**zanja seca** dry ditch
**zapatero** shoemaker
**zapatero (a la medida)** bootmaker
**zapatilla** boot (for horses)
**zapatilla para casco** barrier boot
**zig-zag** counter-change of hand
**zigzagueo** weaving

Español => English

www.ingramcontent.com/pod-product-compliance
Lightning Source LLC
Chambersburg PA
CBHW021233090426
42740CB00006B/509